ROCKIN' THE KREMLIN

ROCKIN' THE KREMLIN

MY INCREDIBLE TRUE STORY OF GANGSTERS, OLIGARCHS, AND POP STARS IN PUTIN'S RUSSIA

DAVID JUNK
WITH FRED BRONSON

ROWMAN & LITTLEFIELD
Lanham • Boulder • New York • London

Published by Rowman & Littlefield
An imprint of The Rowman & Littlefield Publishing Group, Inc.
4501 Forbes Boulevard, Suite 200, Lanham, Maryland 20706
www.rowman.com

86-90 Paul Street, London EC2A 4NE

British Library Cataloguing in Publication Information Available

Library of Congress Cataloging-in-Publication Data

Names: Junk, David, 1965- author. | Bronson, Fred, author.
Title: Rockin' the Kremlin : My Incredible True Story of Gangsters, Oligarchs, and
    Pop Stars in Putin's Russia / David Junk, with Fred Bronson.
Other titles: Rocking the Kremlin
Description: Lanham : Rowman & Littlefield, 2024. | Includes
    bibliographical references and index.
Identifiers: LCCN 2023058514 (print) | LCCN 2023058515 (ebook) | ISBN
    9781538178751 (cloth) | ISBN 9781538178768 (epub)
Subjects: LCSH: Junk, David, 1965- | Sound recording executives and
    producers—United States—Biography. | Music trade—Russia
    (Federation)—History. | Popular music—Russia
    (Federation)—1991–2000—History and criticism. | Popular music—Russia
    (Federation)—2001–2010—History and criticism. | LCGFT:
    Autobiographies.
Classification: LCC ML429.J88 A3 2024 (print) | LCC ML429.J88 (ebook) |
    DDC 781.64092 [B]—dc23/eng/20240110
LC record available at https://lccn.loc.gov/2023058514
LC ebook record available at https://lccn.loc.gov/2023058515

∞™ The paper used in this publication meets the minimum requirements of
American National Standard for Information Sciences—Permanence of Paper
for Printed Library Materials, ANSI/NISO Z39.48-1992.

CONTENTS

CONTENTS

CONTENTS

PART 8: UKRAINE AND RUSSIA

FOREWORD

Misha Kozerev

This is a fascinating book about a fascinating time. It's a story about conquering the "wild East" —the wild post-Soviet East to be precise. David Junk possessed all the qualities—bravery, spirit of adventure, and madness—that allowed him to successfully conquer this territory on the edge of the twenty-first century.

I met David when he started to manage Universal Music Russia. We clicked instantly. He was The Record Guy; I was The Radio Guy (I programmed two of the major national music radio stations). We shared a passion for music and had the same sense of humor, as well as hunger for discovering new stars. David was the bridge between the Western music universe and Russian fans who were deprived of this music during the Soviet era and who had an insatiable desire for pop, rock, and rap ever since the Berlin Wall came down. David Junk had a lot to offer.

It all started with Eminem-mania when David intuitively sensed that, at the time of major social changes when every teenager had to associate with something essential, Slim Shady would be a better choice than S Club 7 or Sophie Ellis-Bextor. He was right.

Each story in this book contains sharp and funny details of a star's behavior in an uncharted territory—like Enrique Iglesias, who agreed to record a duo with Russian singer Alsou and play a show in Moscow only if David promised that he would become bigger than his father in Russia. Like Mariah Carey, who arrived in Moscow with nine trailers full of props and lighting and an entourage larger than a U.S. president's. Like East German rockers Rammstein, who filled Luzhniki Stadium with open pyrotechnics without getting proper permission from the state fire inspection and how this was resolved.

One important thing that I must add: I have never met anyone who believed in Russian music more than David. From the moment we met, he shared his dream to create a major international star from Russia. Many record executives, producers, and promoters tried. David succeeded. Ever since his success, whenever I travel around the world and ask, "Do you know any music from Russia?" The answer is always "t.A.T.u."!

This story is a crown jewel of *Rockin' the Kremlin*. Two teenage girls provoking the world with an innocent kiss would be put on trial and jailed in Russia today (promoting homosexuality is a crime nowadays). But when we were entering the music world, those were different times. We had a lot to say and a lot to offer. David Junk believed in t.A.T.u. and made everything possible for them to become a world phenomenon. He was the one to support them, from their statement that it is okay to kiss each other without feeling ashamed to their controversial appearance on *The Tonight Show with Jay Leno*. I bet that David had more gray hair at the completion of the t.A.T.u. story than at the beginning of their triumphant rise to stardom! But it is clear that he does not regret a single bit of that story.

David's heart is still in Russia and in Ukraine—he developed the music industry in both countries. His heart aches watching Putin destroy everything he achieved. This is a book about a brief period of time when we all had high hopes and firm belief in making a better world. David Junk was a believer who succeeded. And he was a fighter.

In one of the chapters, he describes how he took part in a police raid in the forest outside of Moscow when they traced an illegal factory and tried to stop it from printing pirated CDs. A special police division against piracy along with two ex-Interpol agents were standing by to storm the facility.

One of the ex-agents asked David: "I have not seen an American record executive on a police raid before. How the hell did you end up here?"

"I am here to make sure Mariah Carey gets her royalties!" replied David Junk—an adventurer, music fan, and now, an author of a fascinating book.

ACKNOWLEDGMENTS

I dedicate this book in loving memory to my mother, Lynda Junk, who encouraged and pleaded with me for many years to write it. I finally did it, Mom. I also dedicate it to my father, David; my sister, Jill; my wife, Natalia; and our two sons, Max and Nick. Natalia has been my rock throughout this adventure and my closest confidante. I wouldn't have written it without her support.

I want to thank colleagues from the music business: Adam White, Lee Ellen Newman, Andrey Dakhovskyy, Dmytro Prykordonnyy, Chris Abel-Smith, Jay Berman, and Neil Turkewitz, thanks for the colorful stories for this book. Thank you to our expert researcher and fact-checker, Brian Carroll. I want to thank everyone at Rowman & Littlefield, including our production editor, Jessica Thwaite, and especially our acquisition editor, Michael Tan. Thank you for believing in me, Michael; you've been there from the beginning, improving the book with your intelligent suggestions. Thank you to Ronny Schiff for introducing me to Michael and for preparing our very detailed index. I want to thank Simon Napier-Bell for inspiring me to write. And a special thanks to my friend and cowriter, the multitalented Fred Bronson. Thank you, Fred, for hearing my story and helping me craft it into words.

I want to acknowledge my Russian music industry colleagues, especially my Universal Music and Gibson Guitars staffs. I won't list your names for fear of retribution by the Kremlin, but please know that I recognize we took this journey together. I also want to acknowledge colleagues in the

Ukrainian music industry, especially those on the frontlines who are fighting heroically for their country.

And finally, I'd like to dedicate this book to the brave Russian artists protesting the illegal Russian invasion of Ukraine. Some of you I worked with, many of you I don't know personally, but all of you bravely put your life on the line by speaking and singing the truth. When this war is over, you will be recognized as the true bearers of light in this period of great darkness in Russia.

INTRODUCTION

I've often been accused of being a spy for the CIA. To this day, many people in Russia and America believe that I was undercover for America's foreign intelligence organization. I wasn't a spy, but I have done more to change the perspective of Russian youth than many of their agents by introducing hip hop and Western pop music into the former Soviet Union.

That could have been a CIA project or part of a United States Agency for International Development (USAID) program, but it wasn't. The American pop-cultural invasion of Russia after the collapse of the Soviet Union was one of the most significant achievements by the West in the post–Cold War period, a sounding defeat of communism by free market principles and business know-how.

When the Berlin Wall came down and the Soviet Union collapsed, I left my family farm in Ohio and became one of the first young and idealistic Americans to move to Russia for work and living in the early 1990s. I was inspired by freedom breaking out across Eastern Europe and determined to make a difference. It was a new world of opportunities, and I felt a calling to build bridges between former superpower enemies. Some Americans found their path in Russia working in finance and consulting; others, in technology and oil extraction.

My first job in Russia landed me in the murky world of diamonds. It was a misstep with some frightening consequences. But I didn't give up on my dreams. It was then that fate led me to my next venture—bringing Western pop music to Russia. I became the first American to run a record label in the former Soviet Union when I was appointed the CEO of Universal Music Russia, the world's largest record company. I got the position because I was willing to work in a country in chaos after the fall of the USSR. Due to gangster capitalism, Moscow was one of the most dangerous places to live in the 1990s. It was the "Wild, Wild East." But this was a dream job since I had the opportunity to promote iconic artists such as U2, Bon Jovi, Sting, and Elton John. This work helped me build those bridges between the West and Russia, as I built a team of young and talented Russians and trained them in business practices that were so common in America but unknown in their country. Later I did the same thing for the countries of Eastern Europe when I was promoted to oversee the entire region, including Ukraine.

However, my path was not without obstacles. Before my arrival, there was no proper music industry in the USSR. As was typical of Communist central planning, a single government agency called Melodiya controlled all music that was listened to legally, but bootleggers tried to circumvent the government censors with smuggled Beatles and Rolling Stones albums. Capitalistic concepts such as marketing and sales were considered subversive activities that could get you arrested, effectively silencing the potential for musical expression. The Russian Mafia controlled many aspects of the music industry, and I had to directly confront organized crime groups whose factories produced pirated music from Universal's artists. In the face of danger, I confronted these nefarious forces, determined to build a legitimate music industry within the depths of this post-communist nation.

As I soon learned, developing local talent could be dangerous. I often dealt with wealthy and powerful oligarchs, some with deep ties to the Kremlin, because they wanted their children to become the next pop star sensation. My biggest discovery, t.A.T.u., became the top-selling Russian music act of all time. But their pioneering embrace of the LGBTQ community in a country that historically criminalized homosexuality put us in direct confrontation with the Kremlin and the Russian Orthodox Church.

There were golden days when we would host some of the most prominent pop artists in the world on their first visit to Russia, creating unforgettable—and sometimes humorous—memories. But there were also terrible dark days involving acts of terrorism that reminded me of the difficult path I had chosen. Eventually, the situation got so bad that I found myself grappling with an agonizing decision: Do I continue to follow my dreams, or do I prioritize the safety of myself and my family by leaving the country?

After Universal, I was associated with another iconic American brand when I opened a Gibson Guitars showroom in Moscow. By this time Russia had transformed into an even darker place with the rise of Vladimir Putin, and the Kremlin had chosen a new enemy. Propaganda blinded cherished colleagues, causing a painful and heartbreaking rift.

The unprovoked Russian invasion of Ukraine in 2014 and again in 2022 changed everything. The bridges between Russia and the West that people like me had built over the last thirty years have been destroyed. The record company I founded in Moscow, Universal Music, is closed, and all of the other Western record labels have left Russia too.

Despite the departure of these Western companies, the Russian music industry has persevered, and some of its bravest artists are speaking against the invasion of Ukraine even under the threat of censorship and possible time in prison. The hip hop community, the country's most popular genre of music now, provides the loudest voices against the war. By introducing American hip hop and other forms of pop to Russia—among many other endeavors during my time at Universal Russia—I played a role in leading an American pop-cultural invasion of Russia that planted seeds of change in young Russians. This is the story of how it all happened.

—David Junk

To give you the full story of how I came to be David Junk's coauthor on *Rockin' the Kremlin*, I will have to take you back to my teenage years, when I worked in an independent record store that subscribed to Billboard. I faithfully read every issue, and when I was sixteen, I noticed a small story about the winner of the Eurovision Song Contest. I had never heard of Eurovision, but I became fascinated with it. The first time I went to London, the no. 1 song in the UK was "Waterloo," which had just won the contest for ABBA a couple of weeks earlier. My interest increased.

I continued to pay attention to the Pan-European competition but never was able to watch it until I lived in London in 1983 and was invited to a friend's home for dinner and a viewing. The show was even better than I thought it was going to be.

I returned to the United States in January 1984, and it was impossible in those days to watch the contest while on American soil. Finally, in 1993, I realized I could ask a friend in the United Kingdom to video record the broadcast for me. I had a friend who worked at a music-publishing company that had a PAL player that would allow us to watch tapes from the United Kingdom, and we both viewed the show in his office. I did the same thing in 1994, and while watching the video, I thought to myself, "Wait a minute, I'm a journalist, I could cover Eurovision in person!" I made up my mind that I would travel to Dublin in 1995 for this annual event, which had been going strong since 1956.

I didn't know at the time that I would be working in *Billboard*'s London bureau for the first half of 1995, which would make it easy to hop over to Ireland. I was working on Billboard's new British publication, *Music Monitor*, and my editor, Adam White, agreed to my request to travel to Dublin to cover the contest in person.

I continued to go to Eurovision for twelve more contests. Whoever wins becomes the host country the following year. In 1999 I was in Israel, and Sweden won, which meant I'd be traveling to Stockholm in 2000. It was one of the best Eurovision experiences ever. My friend Nicki French was representing the United Kingdom. My favorite Eurovision artist of all time, Alex Panayi from Cyprus, was back after competing in 1995. And I interacted with the Olsen Brothers from Denmark, who went on to claim victory with "Fly on the Wings of Love."

The runner-up in 2000 was a teenaged girl from Russia, Alsou. She was the first Russian artist signed to Universal Music Russia. That international music company had opened an office in Moscow, and an American fellow was the CEO. His name was David Junk.

David was traveling with Alsou's British manager, Simon Napier-Bell, who was famous for managing Wham! and for writing the English lyrics to an Italian song that became "You Don't Have to Say You Love Me" by Dusty Springfield.

I really enjoyed David's and Simon's company, and I stayed friends with David for a few years. By 2015 we'd lost touch, as those things happen.

Then, in 2022, Billboard asked me to write an in-depth story about Ukraine and Russia in Eurovision—their histories, their rivalry, and their politics.

I interviewed several people and realized that I needed to talk to David, who represented Russia at Eurovision in 2000. I sent a message to his years-old email address, hoping it was still an active account. He responded almost immediately, and he gave me some great quotes, which made my story better.

He invited me to meet him for dinner soon after, and over some fine food, he told me he wanted to write a book about his time in Russia. He told me about some of his adventures, involving oligarchs, piracy, and murders but also of his mission to build a bridge between the United States and Russia and working with artists like Mariah Carey, Sting, and Shaggy, all of whom had traveled to Moscow to perform live.

I asked David if he had a book publisher, and he did not. I told him I was working with an editor at a publishing company I had not worked with before and that I would be happy to introduce him. He eagerly said, "Yes, please." When I talked to my editor, Michael Tan, about David's idea, Michael gave me an enthusiastic yes. I told David the good news, and he surprised me with his response: "Would you write it with me?" And that's the secret origin of *Rockin' the Kremlin*. It would have existed without me, but thanks to my passion for the Eurovision Song Contest, I had the good fortune to collaborate with David, bringing the amazing story of his life to bookshelves everywhere. The story has twists and turns, highs and lows, and danger around many corners. It's an adventure the likes of which few people have experienced. It's all waiting for you—just turn the page.

—Fred Bronson

PART 1

MY STRANGE PATH TO RUSSIA

1

COLD WAR KID

I'm the last person in the world you would expect to live in Russia—I grew up fearing the Russians. In middle school I represented my 4-H club at a ladies' Rotary club luncheon in London, Ohio. I stood up in front of all of those women who were enjoying their cordon bleu in the most prestigious restaurant in Madison County, the Red Brick Tavern, an inn made famous when President Lincoln lodged in it one night on his way from Illinois to Washington, DC, after winning the presidency in 1860. My mother, who accompanied me to the luncheon as my special guest, was so proud I had been chosen to address the ladies. I had their complete attention. It was the 1970s, and I wanted to impress upon them the reality of a nuclear attack. We'd had drills in school to prepare us for this scenario. We had fallout shelters. We were given pamphlets about what to do in the event of World War III.

And so I delivered my short but important speech to this ladies' luncheon: "There is no surviving a nuclear war. Soviet missiles will wipe out this area before we even have a chance, so my best advice to you is to go to a shelter, put your head between your legs, and kiss your sweet ass goodbye."

As I walked back to the table where my mother was sitting, I could see everyone staring at me. My mother was a redhead, but her face was redder than her hair. We left, and in the car heading home, she screamed at me, "How could you embarrass me like this?"

I tried to explain to her that I wasn't trying to shock anyone. I was sincerely worried about the Russians and felt it was important to warn everyone. It didn't matter. I was grounded for a week. But I was a hero among my friends, who heard about my speech and thought I was brave and cool.

I grew up on a farm in central Ohio, with my family living between two US Air Force bases, Rickenbacker in Columbus and Wright Patterson in Dayton. The latter is the largest Air Force base in the country and a strategically important one for worldwide logistics. Even as a child, I was aware that Wright Patterson was a first-strike target for the Soviet Union if there were ever a nuclear war. In the event of a nuclear war, which seemed inevitable at the time, we were told that Russian intercontinental ballistic missiles (ICBMs) would turn America into an ash heap and our missiles would do the same to them. This became a military concept we would live with known as mutually assured destruction, or MAD. For my hometown, this was a very real possibility.

It wasn't just the threat of nuclear war that caused me to fear the Russians. When I was seven years old, I watched the 1972 Olympics that were being held in Munich. It was a traumatic experience because of the terrorist attack on the Israeli delegation. But I also remember that the Soviet basketball team beat the American team for the first time ever. They'd cheated. It was the biggest scandal to ever hit the Olympics. It was the Soviet Union's pro basketball players against our collegiate team, and the referee had made some terrible calls that gave the Soviets another path to an unfair win.

I was born in 1965 in some of the richest farm country in the Midwest. In ancient days, the glaciers had moved south and created the Great Lakes and filled the land with nutrients, creating fertile soil. Three generations before I was born, my ancestors owned many acres of farmland in Madison County. After the Great Depression, the size of our farm had shrunk to five hundred acres. We grew corn, soybeans, and wheat. We baled hay for horses in the summer and made straw bedding for our cows. We had pigs and chickens and my grandfather's horse-racing operation, his favorite hobby. It was a very active farm and was busy 365 days a year. At the age of ten, I already had a number of responsibilities on our working farm. I would come home from school and feed the cows and horses and then do my homework. As I grew older, I operated heavy machinery. I was driving trucks filled with tons of grain when I was fourteen, before I was even allowed to drive a car.

Farmers were exempt from child labor laws despite the many dangers of farm work.

My father was a hard-working man, but I always felt that he wanted to escape the farm and live a more cosmopolitan life. He tried and moved to Redondo Beach in California before he married my mother. But his dream to live in the Golden State didn't last, and he returned home to help my grandfather manage our family farm and raise a family. He was a great role model who taught me a valuable work ethic. I was also influenced by his father. My grandfather was a John Wayne–type who played on a traveling, semipro football team and who would occasionally wrestle for money.

My grandmother was elegant and glamorous—qualities that served me well years later, when I became a part of the music business. My mother was a real star in high school, throwing parties in the family basement, where she and her many friends played their Frankie Avalon and Shirelles 45s. My grandfather tried to be strict with her; he was the treasurer for the local Methodist Church and a businessman with a stellar reputation, and he probably didn't like his basement being used as a teen social club. My grandmother did her best but my mom as a teenager was a handful. Like many young people growing up in the 1950s, my mother felt that watching artists perform on Dick Clark's *American Bandstand* was one of the high-lights of her teenage life. She was obsessed with music and would insist my father take her to the Coconut Lounge in Springfield, Ohio, to see bands like Frankie Valli and the 4 Seasons.

I learned social skills from my mother, and I loved to listen to her records by Bobby Darin, the Ronettes, and the Shangri-Las. It was my introduction to music.

Our family also included my younger sister, Jill. She was a cheerleader and loved to ride horses. She was (and is to this day) a wonderful human being and an ideal sibling. She never left the farm; I'm the one who moved away, seeking a different life.

In high school I loved history, literature, and government—but not sci-ence or math. I wasn't athletic, but I was a popular kid. By 1982, the start of my senior year in high school, all that mattered to me was having fun with friends. I didn't go to high school football games on Friday nights but attended concerts in nearby Columbus, Ohio, when I could. I saw up and coming artists of that time, like Def Leppard and John Cougar (years before he added his last name Mellencamp). If a really big band like Van Halen was touring, I'd go with friends to Cincinnati, where the concert venues were larger. I was also interested in anything international. I had a globe in my bedroom and would spin it endlessly. My finger would touch down on some random spot, and I would think, "Madagascar. I'm going there someday." I felt like I didn't belong on the farm, that I was meant to see the world. It's not that I hated my life. I empathized with the biblical story about the prodigal son who leaves home and then one day comes back. I always knew I wanted a career that would take me far, far away.

We didn't really have neighbors, as our farm was so large no one lived close by, so I spent a lot of time listening to the radio and was happy when a new classic rock station, Q-FM, started broadcasting from Columbus. That's where I discovered Led Zeppelin and Cheap Trick. I listened to mainstream pop like the Bangles and the Go-Go's on WNCI 97.9. To buy 45s and long play records (LPs), I had to go to the Buzzard's Nest, a record store in Columbus. The first album I ever bought was Pink Floyd's *Dark Side of the Moon*. My first poster was of another band I loved, Queen.

With my eyes set on a global prize, I enrolled at Wittenberg, a prestigious liberal arts college in nearby Springfield, Ohio. The tuition was way beyond my means, but thanks to a local woman, Ruth Allison, who'd set up a scholarship fund for farm kids in her will, I was able to afford the high cost of an education. Wittenberg had one of the leading departments on Chinese language and religion. I was focused on the Russians as our enemy, but I thought the Chinese were our future business partners, so I wanted to learn the language. I even spent the summer of 1987 in Hong Kong and Taiwan, teaching English to young kids and business people. It was also a first step in distancing myself from the farm. I was a valuable commodity because, while many Europeans were in China teaching English, the Chinese preferred their students to learn American English over British English.

I started thinking about Russia differently when I met the man who'd persuaded President Ronald Reagan to end the grain embargo, Secretary of Agriculture John Block. Block was a hero to farmers for having done this. I interned in his office for a semester in college and learned about his optimistic view of Russia. The most powerful man I had ever met was telling me that Americans must get along with Russia. It was smart for business and necessary for survival. He was showing me a different way of thinking about

Russia based on business, not fear. "President Reagan is a big supporter of American businesses working with Russia. We have to, for peace," he said. "Farm boys like you will show them how to do it."

But Mr. Block's efforts were in vain. There was another incident that was very traumatic and had a huge effect on me. In 1983 one of my classmates, Alice Ephaimson-Abt, had completed her undergraduate degree and arranged to go to China to study. She was on Korean Air flight 007 en route to China when the Soviets shot her passenger plane down over the Sea of Japan, claiming it was a spy plane. That was a lie, and so were the other excuses they offered. Alice was one of 246 passengers on board and one of 61 Americans. Everyone on that doomed flight perished. I had never met Alice, but this was the last straw for me when it came to hating the Russians.

I remember President Reagan speaking on television, proclaiming that Russia was an "evil empire." He stunned the world when he said this, and that label would galvanize America's hostile attitude toward Russia for the rest of his presidency. When I heard this, I couldn't agree more. I clearly had no idea I would one day live in the Soviet Union, fall in love with a Russian woman who would become my wife, and come to love a country that was once my sworn enemy.

2

TEAR DOWN THIS WALL

How did driving a tractor on a farm in Ohio prepare me for heading up a major American record label in Russia?

Well, the tractor didn't help me at all. But for those two years before I left for college, my father had turned over summer operations of our family farm to me. My responsibilities included baling hay and straw, which was a big operation, as our alfalfa hay was coveted by racehorse farms in Kentucky. I assembled my best friends into a working team. We weren't Boy Scouts—we worked hard and got the job done efficiently, and then we drank beer and goofed off. After a long day of work and before the sun would set, we'd go out on the lake in our boats and water ski.

My father made a lot of money that summer, and I proved that you could have fun and be a good boss at the same time. I've followed that pattern in every organization I've worked for since then.

Later it would serve me well in Russia, when I was the only American in Moscow working in the music business. People wondered, "Who is this guy?" and "What was he doing in our country?" I gained their trust when they saw how I led my staff. I became friends with these Russians, and they let me lead them.

When I graduated from college, I became a legislative (paid) intern, assigned to two legislators in the Ohio legislature. Based on my interviews for the position, I was assigned to Tom Roberts, a Black representative from Dayton who was chairman of the committee studying homelessness, as well as to a talented, liberal, and progressive politician named Jane Campbell, who would later be elected as the first female mayor of Cleveland. Jane was one of the key state leaders who brought the Rock & Roll Hall of Fame to Cleveland.

Rural Madison County, where I'd grown up, was home to the richest farmland in Ohio and was so Republican that you couldn't get elected dog catcher as a Democrat. But my mother's side of the family were hardcore FDR Democrats. We were an island of liberalism in a sea of conservatism. So it was fitting that I was now working for two of the most liberal Democrats in Ohio.

While working in the Ohio legislature, I figured my career would be in government or politics and that I should get a law degree. I applied to Cleveland State University's School of Law and was accepted. I was trying to figure out when I should quit my job and take a vacation before starting law school. But then one fateful, warm, and sunny spring day, I was at my girlfriend Maureen's house, listening to my favorite rock radio station, WLVQ-FM 96, when an exciting announcement came on that would change my life: "Roger Waters, lead vocalist for the band Pink Floyd, has announced that since the Berlin Wall has come down, he will perform his iconic *The Wall* album in Berlin this coming summer."

I was the biggest Pink Floyd fan in my school—the other kids who were rock fans were more into Def Leppard and Rush—and I was devastated when they'd split into two factions. Waters left Pink Floyd in 1985, and it was during this time that US-Soviet relations were edging closer to nuclear war. My high school teachers especially disapproved of Pink Floyd's biggest hit "Another Brick in the Wall," which had become an antiauthority anthem for school kids in England and America. Waters was always asked when he would perform *The Wall* again, and he would facetiously say, "When the Berlin Wall is torn down."

It was impossible to imagine this happening when he said it, but by 1990, Mikhail Gorbachev's glasnost and perestroika in the Soviet Union had led East Berliners to knock down the wall dividing them from the West. The world watched the images on TV of Germans on the West and the East sides tearing down the wall, section by section, piece by piece. They had sledgehammers, picks, crowbars—anything sharp enough to keep smashing it until it fell. The world joyfully embraced these events.

When it actually happened, Waters kept his word, even if he had meant it as a joke. The concert, with its proceeds going to wartime victims, wasn't going to be held until late summer, but tickets were going on sale the next day at my favorite record store, Buzzard's Nest, the only place in Columbus authorized to sell tickets for this event. As a lifelong Pink Floyd fan, I knew this was a once-in-a-lifetime opportunity that I could not miss. I woke up super early and drove to Columbus to join the throngs who would be in line to buy tickets. I knew it was going to be pandemonium.

I got there at 10:00 a.m., and tickets were going on sale at noon. I was the first person in line. But for the next two hours, I was also the only person in line. I guess there weren't very many people in Columbus who were willing to travel to Germany. As a history buff, I was fascinated with the Berlin Wall and Checkpoint Charlie and no man's land, where people from East Berlin had tried to escape to the West, often with fatal results.

When tickets went on sale at noon, the guy behind the counter looked at me and said, "You do realize this is international? This is not for a show here in Columbus. It's in Berlin, in Germany."

I said, "Of course I know that."

I had never yet been to Europe at this point. Maureen, who was a few years older and wiser than me, had lived in France for a year and encouraged me to go. She also advised me to buy a Eurail pass to travel around the continent by train because I wanted to visit London, Paris, and Stockholm after the concert in Berlin. I wanted to see Big Ben and the Eiffel Tower.

I booked my flight on Lufthansa from New York right into Berlin. When I arrived, I was startled by the difference between West and East Berlin, even with the Wall down. West Berlin was a modern, shining city. East Berlin had not yet recovered from World War II. The city was dark and grungy. It was dirty and it smelled.

One day before the concert, I checked into a youth hostel near the main Berlin train station. It was a chaotic scene in the city, with hundreds of thousands of tourists descending on Berlin just to attend the show. Not everyone could find a room with a bed. People were sleeping in corridors, rec rooms, train stations—wherever they could find shelter.

I found out the rehearsal was going to take place in no man's land, and together with some people I'd met at the hostel, we made plans to sneak in early to watch the dress rehearsal. I knew what to expect, having seen the film *The Wall*. Side four of the album has Waters transform into a fascist dictator running a rock concert. That might play in Los Angeles or New York, but his coming out on stage wearing a Nazi-looking uniform (albeit with hammers in place of swastikas) made me wonder how that would go down in Berlin.

The next day, along with five hundred thousand people in Potsdamer Platz and two hundred million on live TV in Europe, I saw a rock concert that was so much more than a show; it became a celebration of the dawning of a new era in international relations between the East and the West. It was one of the greatest rock concerts in history on the site of one of the greatest symbols of oppression. Waters had assembled an eclectic group of guest artists: Germany's own Scorpions opened the concert; Cyndi Lauper sang the hit single "Another Brick in the Wall"; and Bryan Adams, Van Morrison, and the Band also performed with the East German Air Force Band with the East Berlin Symphony Orchestra backing them. An actual wall was built, brick by brick, on the stage to one hundred feet high, separating the audience from the band. Giant inflatable characters and laser special effects were special moments. In the finale the bricks began falling until the wall came down, and the audience was reunited with the performers.

My fears about Germans having a bad reaction to the fascist imagery were unfounded. And when the wall came down onstage, Waters reappeared, having shed his fascist character for a liberated one, a metaphor for Eastern Europe. Freedom rang out, and it was a great, celebratory night for being free. We could see the world coming together at last.

■

After the show I lost my way going back to the hostel and wandered aimlessly. A chance encounter with two university students from Czechoslovakia, Helga and Olga, would change my life. They were sitting on a blanket, drinking wine. They were laughing and having fun, and they motioned for me to come over.

They offered me some wine, and we managed to communicate through their broken English. They insisted their hometown of Prague was the most beautiful city in Europe and invited me to come see it with them. There was a daily train from Berlin, and they said, "We're leaving in the morning." There was nothing holding me back, my only possession being a backpack at the hostel.

I walked them to the train station in East Berlin, and like the rest of that formerly divided city, it was dirty and run-down. The trains were old-fashioned locomotives. They helped me purchase a ticket for the following day.

There went my plans to travel west to London and Paris. I arrived in Prague, and they met me at the station and found a dormitory for me to stay in. I threw away my Eurail pass. Helga and Olga were right: Prague is the most beautiful city in Europe. I had read about the city in books by Milan Kundera and Franz Kafka, but I never learned much about Eastern Europe in school—superpower enemy Russia always overshadowed it.

Helga and Olga introduced me to their university colleagues, and I was the first American they had ever met. Sitting on a park bench overlooking the Charles River, with white swans swimming nearby and drinking Czech beer, I learned from those students how terrible life is without freedom and that when you suddenly gain it, it is like a rebirth. They were bursting with optimism. The Communists had kept them down for so long, but with the Soviet Union collapsing and the East and West united again, everything was new, and anything was possible for these young people. They were hungry for freedom and capitalism after shedding communism. Eastern Europe was the most exciting place in the world, and I realized that I wanted to be a part of that.

■

The whole experience of the Roger Waters concert and this chance encounter made me feel like it was my destiny to work in this part of the world. The girls spoke Russian, and they told me I should learn the language so I could communicate with anyone in Eastern Europe, as they had all been forced to learn Russian.

At this point, my life's path was clear: the farm would always be there for me, and going to law school would assure a bright and prosperous future. And yet I met two students from Czechoslovakia and threw all of that away to follow a scary and dangerous path.

I was certain my calling was to return to Eastern Europe and help build the bridge between America and Russia. I told friends and family I was dropping out of law school and moving to San Francisco to study business and learn the Russian language. I became an apartment manager in Haight-Ashbury and met some of the wildest hippies and weirdos that the Bay Area had to offer. I bought a motorcycle to get around the city. And the thought that consumed me was that I wanted to live in Russia.

3

DIAMONDS ARE FOREVER ... OR ARE THEY?

I didn't know what path would lead me to Russia, but with that goal in mind, I was enrolled in an MBA program at San Francisco State University. In my final year there, I started sending out my résumés not only to companies in San Francisco but also to businesses in Moscow. My friends didn't understand why I was applying for a job in Russia, but I had my eye on that prize. My specialty was accounting, so I faxed my résumé to an American accounting firm in Moscow—KPMG. It was the first time I had used a fax machine. I remember the beeps and noises sounding like it was sending a message to outer space and then receiving one back. It was crazy high tech at the time.

The very next day, I received a call from their San Francisco office. They wanted me to come in for an interview—that day. They told me I would not be working directly for KPMG but for one of their clients—a high-profile company in Russia. They weren't willing to tell me which company over the phone. I put on a suit and tie and hopped on my motorcycle to drive to their office in an industrial part of San Francisco.

When I pulled up to the building, I got an ominous feeling about the place, like Keanu Reeves' young lawyer in *The Devil's Advocate* feels when he first sets sights on the demonic apartment building. The mysterious headquarters was shaped like a diamond. It was an imposing glass structure in the heart of San Francisco's South of Market area.

I entered the building and encountered the heaviest security I had ever seen. I imagined it was more imposing than what the White House or Fort

Knox had. We're talking eye scans, finger scans, machine guns, and heavy glass doors. Finally, I was allowed into the lobby, where the KPMG executives were waiting for me. "David, it's nice to meet you," one of them said. "We have a new client in Moscow, and none of us speak Russian. We desperately need someone who understands accounting."

I told them I didn't have my degree yet and was still taking classes. They told me not to worry about it and offered me a salary three times what I had made teaching English in China. I said I would take the job. Then they walked me upstairs to meet their Russian clients from a company known as Golden ADA, a diamond manufacturer that was opening a new cutting factory in the Bay Area. It was a mystery to me why these Russians would want to hire an inexperienced young American, but I saw this as a way to get to Russia, so I didn't ask a lot of questions.

Work was fascinating. My Russian bosses were very friendly with American politicians. I saw photos of them with Vice President Al Gore and First Lady Hillary Clinton that were proudly displayed on the wall in the executive suite. The mayor of San Francisco, Willie Brown, was a frequent visitor to our offices. My bosses gifted the city's police department with a Russian helicopter—a massive, dual-propeller, heavy-duty machine designed to fight fires in Siberia.

On the day of the presentation, many local politicians gathered on the roof of our office building. The helicopter was parked on a boat in San Francisco Bay, right near Alcatraz. It took off and flew over the city and approached the rooftop, which was bedecked with Russian and American flags. The rotors were loud, and from our perspective, the copter appeared to be too big to land. Suddenly, it smashed the windows of a neighboring building and had to abort its landing. The near tragedy made the evening headlines.

That was just one red flag (no pun intended).

In my first weeks working for the company, I realized their records were a mess. They weren't translated into English, and many things that should have been there were missing. I attributed it to them being a new company and not understanding our way of conducting business. One of my first tasks was to conduct an inventory of all the property the company had purchased in the United States, like the house at Lake Tahoe where scenes from *The Godfather Part II* had been filmed.

My Russian bosses had made the homeowner an offer they couldn't refuse, paying cash far exceeding its market value. They really wanted it because they were fans of *The Godfather* movies. Because it was a cash sale, I couldn't find any financial records on the house or the other real estate the company owned.

Then my American boss, who didn't speak Russian or understand the diamond business, was asked to wire $20 million to the Moscow office and didn't know why. He asked me to look into it, and when I did, I was told to mind my own business. I was still willing to overlook all of this because I kept asking the company to send me to work in their Russian office.

Three months into the job, they did so, naming me chief of the Moscow headquarters, a job that came with a very large, ornate office very close to the Kremlin. The amenities included my own executive bathroom, a personal chef, and a chauffeur.

One of my main responsibilities was to prepare Russian diamond cutters to travel to San Francisco, which included organizing their documents for the US Embassy. My Russian was still rudimentary back then, and I needed help from the company translator. Her name was Natalia, and she spoke French, English, German, and a number of other languages. She was beautiful and smart, and I was immediately attracted to her, but when I first met her, she wasn't impressed with me. Because her job was company translator, she had met many foreigners; there was nothing special about me.

When I asked her out on a date, she turned me down. I tried again and invited her to a concert by the famous American punk rocker Henry Rollins, who was performing in Moscow. She accepted my invitation. This was the beginning of our love story. She was a lightning-fast translator who could listen to one person while translating out loud what someone else was saying at the same time as she was flirting with me while I was sitting at the other end of the table. I fell hard for her, and we decided to get married. We had a big wedding party in the office with a gigantic smorgasbord and a lot of vodka.

When Natalia became pregnant she stayed home while I continued to work in the office, where I discovered the surprising news that the diamond cutters in San Francisco were running out of stones. Then I found out the Russian government had stopped sending us diamonds. None of this made sense to me until the media uncovered what was really going on inside Golden ADA.

On February 15, 1996, the Associated Press reported:

Russia shipped hundreds of millions of dollars in uncut diamonds to the San Francisco company, which was supposed to cut, polish, and return them. But few, if any, ever returned. Now, up to $400 million in diamonds, gold, and cash has vanished from Golden ADA, and federal investigators suspect the Russian mob stole the riches. The company's Russian owner, Andrei Kozlenok, is also missing. Investigators want to know where the valuables are and why Russia continued to ship them even though the company had failed to pay.

Russia contends Golden ADA illegally sold its diamonds and kept the cash. Some of the money apparently helped buy a stunning array of luxury items, including a Fabergé egg created for Tsar Nicholas II, a $377,000 Rolls Royce, nine speedboats, a $20 million Learjet and a $4.4 million Lake Tahoe estate used in *The Godfather Part II*, outside auditors found.

In America the FBI raided our San Francisco office. In Russia the Ministry of the Interior raided our Moscow office and closed it down. All of the Russians had fled and were in hiding. One morning a police brigade of twelve soldiers armed with machine guns raided my apartment. I wasn't home, but Natalia and our baby were. They ransacked the place and took everything. Natalia stepped away from the police brigade and reached me on the phone at my office.

"Don't come home," she said calmly. She knew they would arrest me on the spot.

"What's going on there?" I asked her, insisting on knowing more, but she wouldn't give me any details.

"There's nothing you can do. The baby and I are fine. You should wait at work."

I was full of anxiety, worried about what was happening in our apartment. I returned home a few hours later, and the raid was over. We sat in our kitchen, worried about what was going to happen to me. Natalia's father came by and told me I might be in big trouble with the Russian government. Sure enough, I was summoned to the general prosecutor's office, where they told me I was under investigation for the theft of $200 million in diamonds and that I could not leave the country.

As I sat across the table from the Prosecutor General, I knew I had to make a case for myself if I was going to get out of the building alive. Words were failing me. I wondered if I should ask for a lawyer or a translator.

I explained that I was simply a twenty-eight-year-old accounting student from San Francisco who wanted only to help Russia and had found this job in Moscow. I knew nothing about embezzlement, had little to do with the company operations, and had never even met some of the notorious new bosses.

It was eerily quiet in the prosecutor's office. Did the officer believe me? Would I be allowed to go home? Did I have enough warm clothes to survive in the Gulag? A lot of innocent people like me were never seen again after a chat in this infamous building on Tverskaya Ulitsa.

The Prosecutor General with icy blue eyes continued to give me a cold stare. Finally, he spoke: "You are free to go until further notice."

I thanked him and jumped up to stumble down the stairs. Outside, I took a deep breath of dusty, smoky air (Russians did not believe in unleaded gas at this point). It smelled like freedom. But I couldn't forget his "until further notice" comment.

Meanwhile, the main Russian culprit in all of this—Andrei Kozlenok—was hiding in Greece. He was tricked into traveling to Italy, where Interpol arrested him. The next thing I knew, he was on the cover of *U.S. News and World Report*, in handcuffs, with the headline "Dirty Diamonds." It was only after his arrest that the Russians understood that American employees had been used as pawns, with no knowledge of any criminal activity. But I still wasn't cleared.

Two years into living in Russia, on my birthday, I received a telegram from the Russian prosecutor general saying I had to come to their main office because they had something for me. "What?" I thought. "A prison sentence?" No. It was a letter.

I opened it up, and it said I was no longer a suspect in the theft of $200 million in diamonds. It was one of the greatest moments of my life. I came to Russia to build bridges, not steal diamonds. Now I could finally go on with my life and not worry about being sent to Siberia.

PART 2

MY MUSIC CAREER BEGINS

4

KETCHUP OR MUSIC?

Under the pressure of the investigations in the United States and Russia, the diamond company imploded. I was out of a job, and I was no longer personally under investigation by the Russian state prosecutor; I was finally allowed to leave the country with my young family. But I didn't run, I stayed. To this day I don't know how I made the decision. I just wanted to get back to my original plan of building bridges between America and Russia. I wanted to raise a family in Moscow. I needed a job.

I had an MBA and was a little more fluent in Russian than when I'd first arrived in Moscow. So I knew my skills were in demand. I needed to pick a company that wasn't going to get me involved in an international scandal. I needed to work for a well-known Western business. Many were trying to open offices in Russia. I needed to find the right one.

I was a regular reader of the *Moscow Times*, an independent, Dutch-owned newspaper that had a "Help Wanted" section in their classified ads. I saw that Heinz was looking for a chief financial officer. I can't say that ketchup excited me, but I needed to move on, and on the plus side, it was the number two job in the company. I sent my résumé and was granted an interview.

Then they offered me the job. I still remember sitting in the kitchen of our Moscow apartment, thinking, "Do I accept this? I mean, it's ketchup."

That morning, I was reading the *Moscow Times*, and I saw a help-wanted ad for PolyGram Records. One of the largest multinational labels, they were looking for an expatriate financial controller for their Moscow office: "Native English a plus."

Hey, I spoke English!

I had a vague idea of what PolyGram was because I owned a Lily Tomlin album that was on their Polydor imprint. I did a little research and discovered that Island Records and Def Jam were part of PolyGram, and the company had an artist roster that included U2, Bon Jovi, and the Cranberries. I figured there would be hundreds of people applying for this job (but then I'd also thought thousands of people would be lining up in Columbus for a ticket to Roger Waters in Berlin). I called the number in the ad and spoke to a headhunter named Michael Page. He asked me to fax my résumé.

That afternoon he called me back and said he had shown my résumé to executives in PolyGram's London headquarters, and they wanted me to fly there tomorrow. They bought me a business class ticket on British Airways, and a hotel room was arranged. I arrived at the company's office in London's St. James's Square and met the financial director for Europe. He marched me upstairs to meet the chief financial officer (CFO) for the world, a tough man from the Netherlands named Jan Cook. He was a Philips man—Philips, as in the Dutch manufacturer of audio equipment.

Philips was also originally a classical record label that was part of the Phonogram company. In 1962 Philips merged with Polydor/Deutsche Grammophon, a German company founded in 1898. The merger of Phonogram and Polydor created PolyGram.

He asked me, "Why do you want to live in Russia? Are you crazy? Aren't you scared?"

He was testing me. He wanted to make sure I wasn't going to change my mind about living in Russia. He had no idea of my complete history, because I never mentioned my time with the diamond company. PolyGram was desperate to find a CFO for Russia because their business there was crumbling, and they didn't know why. And I was eager to land this job and seize the opportunity to work in the international music business.

■

The next step was for me to meet Boris Zosimov, PolyGram's partner in their Moscow office. He was Russia's first media mogul, and he had spent time in New York. He'd worked with MTV to show music videos on his own TV channel and formed a joint venture with PolyGram to open their Russian office.

When I arrived at PolyGram's Moscow office for my job interview with Boris, I was invited into his large office, where I took a seat at a long, beautiful oak conference table, waiting to talk with him, but we were interrupted constantly by some very important visitors. I felt as if I were in a variety show with a cast of characters that represented not only the full spectrum of Boris's power but also his knowledge of how to do business in Russia.

One of these characters, a police colonel, handed Boris a blue siren and told him how to use it on his golden Jaguar parked out front. The blue siren would allow Boris to bypass all security checkpoints and traffic jams. In Russia there are special roads set up in the middle of the main thoroughfares with lines on each side to allow government ministers, important bureaucrats, and the president and his administration to use this road. But certain friends are also granted access, and Boris was a friend of the colonel, so now he could use this special road.

The next guest was Bill Roedy, the head of MTV International. He wanted Boris to open MTV in Russia. Boris has just added PolyGram to his portfolio, and other Western media outlets were pursuing him too. His power and influence were well-known.

After Bill, Philipp Kirkorov, the biggest pop star in the country, made an entrance. He was flamboyant, extremely tall, and dressed wildly on stage—think of Liberace. His first album for PolyGram had dropped on that day. It was called *Ckazi Solncu "Da"* (Say "Yes" Sunshine). The lead single, "My Bunny," was a cheesy, corny, cute little pop song that went right to no. 1, and it was a big day for Boris and his Polygram office. Philipp was beaming with delight.

The next person that interrupted our interview was sales manager Alex Sidorov, a portly, disheveled audio enthusiast who, even though he was usually reeking of alcohol, had an encyclopedic brain about Western rock music. He knew more about Deep Purple than Deep Purple, and he could tell you anything you wanted to know about all of the great rock artists. He had studied them during the era of the Soviet Union and was embracing the job as sales director for a Western record company in the new Russia as a dream come true.

His job was to sell records and, thus, generate profits. But his drinking was so bad that Boris sometimes had to lock him up in a room in the back of the building and keep him there for days to dry out. That is the kind of control Boris had over his staff, which would have been impossible in America.

As sales director, Alex would later educate me about our biggest problem: pirates controlled 90 percent of the market. He asked me if it was possible to convince PolyGram to lower the twenty-dollar retail price for CDs manufactured in Russia rather than to keep importing them from PolyGram's factory in Hannover, Germany. I knew that wouldn't work, because these reduced-price CDs could be exported to Germany and Eastern Europe, ruining price stability in their markets. That for sure would get me fired. Plus, how were we going to trust a CD replication factory in Russia?

Boris's daughter Lena was the next to arrive, and she was a pop star wannabe. She was working hard on her new record, and it was understood by everyone that this one was going to be a hit. Boris would make sure of that.

Finally, a billionaire from America walked in. He was one of the wealthy Zipf brothers, and he was investing in Russia. He and Boris were longtime close friends from New York.

Eventually, we got around to my interview with Boris, and he was very happy to have me joining PolyGram. He wanted me to talk to the Westerners, to the people in London and the Netherlands, where the corporate offices were. He didn't like engaging with them and thought it was a waste of his time. Boris said that would be my main responsibility, which was why he was delighted to bring me into the company.

Boris became my mentor—my introduction to the Russian music industry. I learned so much from this powerful man who was able to balance politics and business (he helped Boris Yeltsin get reelected in 1996 by marshaling MTV and the Rock the Vote movement. The Communists were definitely gaining on Yeltsin and clearly could have taken over the country again, but it was the youth vote that tipped the scales in favor of Yeltsin, thus saving them from a return to the Soviet Union).

As I walked with him out the door with his bodyguards in front and in back of us, we exited the building, and he congratulated me. His blue siren was already on top of his golden Jaguar. He sped off with the Range Rovers in front and in back of him. This man was the coolest man I'd ever met in my life, and now he was my boss. I was so lucky.

Even before my first day on the job at PolyGram in Moscow, I knew something about the music industry in Russia. Years earlier, while traveling in Leningrad (before it became St. Petersburg), I'd seen counterfeit CDs on sale in the streets. That made me wonder how any record label could actually make money in Russia.

I also learned a lot about music in Russia from my wife's father, who told me how, in his younger days, he would bootleg music that wasn't officially released in the USSR. He and his friends would go to hospitals and dig X-rays out of the trash bins. They would record music onto the X-rays and bring them to parties and play them like you would spin a vinyl record. When Natalia would look through her father's record collection and pull out an album by the Beatles, inside there would be an X-ray. She could not only play the music, she could tell if the patient had tuberculosis. And that is not a joke!

One of the first things I did in my new job at PolyGram was to ask the accountants to bring me their books with figures on all of our sales, expenses, and balance sheets. I discovered that not only were we not making money, we were losing $1 million a year. While it was noble to open an office in Russia and release legal music, we weren't going to stay in business if we couldn't make a profit.

What made it worse for us was that other Eastern European countries, like the Czech Republic, Slovakia, and Poland, were on the plus side of the ledger. These countries were quicker to adopt capitalism after the fall of the Soviet Union. It became apparent to me that the London office had hired me for Russia not to keep the company going but to shut it down. They didn't trust Boris and didn't want to keep investing money in a losing proposition. I had just begun this new job, and I was already afraid of losing it.

I reported to two bosses at PolyGram. Jana Fertig was the Czechoslovakia-born financial director for Eastern Europe. Her hatred of Russians dated back to the invasion of her home country in 1968. This would be the first of many times I would struggle with the duality of Russian history; what the Soviets did was evil, and I can't blame Jana for her feelings. But it was the new Russia now; they no longer wanted to take over the Czech Republic. Of course, at this moment, I had no idea what the state of Russian affairs would be in the 2020s. Still, Jana had no time for Boris and was dismissive of any idea that would keep the Russian office open.

The second boss was Thomas Hedström, PolyGram's vice president for Eastern Europe. His goal was to expand to as many countries as possible. He believed in Russia, which was the biggest market but also the one with the biggest problems. He wanted the office there to survive.

When I brought him the idea of issuing CDs with Russian graphics at a cheaper price point, he said we should ask Jon Bon Jovi's manager if they would allow it. Jon's manager agreed, as did Paul McGuinness, the manager of U2. We used Russian graphics on U2's *Pop* and Bon Jovi's *Have a Nice Day*. We sold thousands of copies at a reduced price. Russian consumers were willing to pay four dollars for our CDs over two dollars for the bootlegs. We manufactured more CDs by a variety of artists, including Elton John, Bryan Adams, and the Cranberries, all of which had Russian graphics. Thomas was thrilled with the result and so were the artists, as we were building fan bases for future tours.

The only person unhappy with the result was Jana, because it foiled her plan to close the Russian office.

My idea brought in revenue and kept us afloat. But we were still in the red, and piracy continued. Our lifeline didn't last long, as Jana was more intent than ever on shutting us down. I flew to London to plead our case. But the executives in the United Kingdom had made up their minds. Jana convinced them that it didn't make sense to continue operations in Russia. Maybe they could reopen the office in ten years. Between losing money and their distrust of Boris, the PolyGram executives in London had decided it was game over. I flew back to Moscow, defeated. And Jana followed to complete closure of the company.

5

BREAKING NEWS

Back in Moscow, I was not only dealing with Jana's arrival, I was thinking, "What am I going to do next? Should I continue to live in Moscow? Should I return to America?" I didn't want to do that, especially not to work on the farm again. I didn't want to be an accountant again. My dream of building a bridge between America and Russia was not working out too well. First, the diamond company went kaput, and now the PolyGram office was about to be closed. Maybe I should have taken the ketchup job.

It was my responsibility to inform Boris Zosimov that our Moscow office was going to be shut down. But I knew if I told him and our staff prematurely, everything would collapse. People would stop working, and they would go into panic mode. I kept the news to myself because I thought I could somehow save the company. There must have been something I hadn't thought of.

But there wasn't. The situation was hopeless.

Jana arrived at the airport, and I met her there. She was in a great mood because she had won. She told me, "Your job is to manage the closure. Make sure we don't lose any more money. Take care of all the paperwork with the government. We don't want any hassles with the Ministry of Finance."

She hinted that if I followed her bidding, there might be a place for me somewhere else in the company. But where would that be? Hungary? That wasn't going to happen. So I listened to her orders, but I was extremely unhappy.

Jana disliked our office so much that she wasn't willing to spend any time there. She asked me to meet her at her hotel, the Metropole, on the edge of Red Square, to discuss her plan. We were in her suite, and the television was on, tuned in to CNN. And as we were getting into the minute details of shutting down the company, we heard the anchor say, "Breaking news. Seagram, the alcohol company which owns Universal Music, has just purchased PolyGram."

Jana and I looked at each other, stunned. The news came out of nowhere for us, taking us completely by surprise. Jana got on the phone with her bosses to find out what was going on. She was told the deal was done in complete secrecy, with most PolyGram executives kept in the dark until the news became public.

Ironically, the sale of the company resulted in Jana being let go, while my other boss, Thomas Hedström, kept his job under the new ownership.

So at the last possible moment, the Americans at Universal swooped in and saved my job, our office, and the music industry in Russia. Doug Morris, Edgar Bronfman Jr., and Zach Horowitz at Universal were our saviors. They had decided to keep the office in Moscow, and they hired me to be the chief executive officer (CEO), making me the first American to run a record company in Russia. I had been the lone American in the European world of PolyGram, and I had longed for more American influence in the company.

And now I suddenly had that.

■

Being part of Universal meant that we shared the company's logo, the familiar rotating globe from the company's motion pictures. PolyGram's logo was just the word "PolyGram"; the Universal logo came with drums and an image of the universe. The Russians already knew that logo from Hollywood movies. My business card had the logo. We had T-shirts and large banners with that logo. It was exciting and cool—words you wouldn't usually use to describe a major company.

Despite the new American ownership, I still reported to the Universal office in London. The new owners took over the PolyGram building on St. James's Square. They appointed Jorgen Larsen, who was from Denmark and had been a longtime executive in the European music industry, as the new chairman/CEO of Universal International. The big difference was that

PolyGram was run by people from Philips Electronics. After the merger our top management were music people like Doug and Edgar, who were both executives as well as songwriters. We were no longer being managed by a company that manufactured refrigerators.

The Universal management team was surprised that PolyGram wanted to close the Russian office. Our new owners kept it open because they saw a lucrative opportunity to promote Universal's top-selling artists in Russia. At this point, there was no emphasis placed on signing Russian artists. But I hoped that would change.

The heads of the company in London wanted us to promote British artists first, then the French and a few select German ones. Maybe an occasional Swedish or Italian signing would be encouraged. Our UK priorities were Sophie Ellis-Bextor, Pulp, S Club 7, and Boyzone (from Ireland). S Club 7 was popular in Britain because of their television series, but they had no fan base in Russia, so that was difficult. We had no German artists who were priorities when I'd started, but later, Rammstein would become one of our major acts.

As the only foreign record executive in the country, I knew I needed the help of smart young Russians who understood Western music and, in particular, American music coming from Universal. I assembled an extremely talented marketing team, which was led by a very bold and outspoken woman named Asya Kalaysina, whom I stole from MTV. Her MTV show *S**t Parade* was a satire on music videos; it was a huge hit and a metaphor for a new, modern Russia—confident, arrogant, and not afraid to push buttons.

The old Soviet ways had been abandoned and replaced with an aggressive stance, and if I was going to turn the old Soviet music industry upside down with this modern Russian music industry, she was the perfect copilot.

I needed someone with attitude and who was fearless. She in turn put together the best and the brightest of Russian show business to form a brilliant team, including a radio promoter, print manager, and artist manager. Our marketing department was one of the best in Europe. This was my first smart move as the new CEO.

It was this team that would lead me to all my future successes in the Russian music business. And it was this team that told me they couldn't sell the British artists that Universal had made a priority. They said that Russian kids wanted American music—Nine Inch Nails, Blink-182, the Killers, Black Eyed Peas, and No Doubt.

Meanwhile, I had to fly to London for marketing meetings with the top executives from Europe, where they would bring in their priority artists—people like Sophie Ellis-Bextor and Ronan Keating and Daniel Bedingfield. The only American artist I did meet at a European marketing meeting was Shania Twain, when she was the top-selling country artist in the world. She insisted we come to her in Switzerland, where she was living with producer Mutt Lange.

Then, suddenly, my life and work priorities changed in one day. I was sitting in my office in Moscow when a package arrived from California. I opened it up, and there was a note addressed to me, accompanied by an album with a blank cover and no information. I played it, and I hadn't heard an album that shocked me as much since I'd heard the Sex Pistols' *Never Mind the Bullocks* for the first time. It was a masterpiece by a man named Marshall Mathers, who is better known as Eminem.

I played it for my marketing director and her team, and they were all as enthusiastic as I was. I wanted to do everything in my power to make this album huge in Russia. I spoke to my bosses in Britain, who told me that hip hop was not going to make it in Europe and that I needed to focus on the new S Club 7 album.

Despite that, we leaked the Eminem album to Europa Plus, which was the top radio station in Russia playing American music—specifically, the single "My Name Is." We told the radio folks, "We're not giving this to you. You never saw us. You got this from somewhere else."

It was an instant hit on the radio, and as a result, MTV called us, demanding the video. Filing the sales reports with London was my vindication. Russia was selling more Eminem albums than some of the larger offices in western Europe. Eminem gave us an award, and it was a major achievement for Russia. It proved that I knew what I was talking about and that I had an excellent team.

Most importantly, the success of Eminem opened the floodgates for American hip hop in Russia. And Universal happened to be the dominant hip hop label on the planet, with the Death Row and Def Jam labels. Suddenly, we were selling massive quantities of albums by Snoop Dogg, Dr.

Dre, 2Pac, the Game, and 50 Cent, plus East Coast artists like Jay-Z. We weren't just selling music—we were selling a lifestyle.

Hip hop is a community of like-minded people, and the music translates into other languages, inspiring cultures around the world to build their own hip hop communities. Russian kids took to it so strongly that it exists to this day, and twenty years later, it is still the most popular genre because of its authenticity and the messages in the lyrics.

With hip hop's ascendancy in Russia, artists from the West came to Russia to tour and promote their music. Akon was the first, followed by Pras from the Fugees and then Shaggy. They were all shocked at how popular hip hop was in Russia. They all had preconceived notions about what Russia would be like—bears running in the streets and gangs shooting each other. Akon was very grateful to us for introducing his music to Russians. He and other artists visited Russian radio stations and went on MTV. There were press conferences and after-parties.

■

After this wave of success, when I would attend meetings in London, there was far less pressure on me to promote British artists in Russia. I was able to introduce American pop, rock, country, and hip hop artists to Russians, including No Doubt and Shania Twain.

Selling Eminem albums was a very satisfying achievement, as well as my first real breakthrough in the international music business. But I knew that, in order to be a real record executive, I needed to sign local talent and promote them internationally. All of my mentors were experts at building trust with artists, and I wanted to emulate that in my career.

One of the first record executives to have a huge impact on me was Pascal Nègre, president of Universal France and one of the most successful executives in the history of the French music business. His artist Mylène Farmer was an icon in France. She was performing at a sold-out show in Moscow's Olympic stadium, and he was there to support her. Russia had become Mylène's most important market outside of France. Her very loyal following was made up of rabid fans, many of them gay, who quickly snatched up all the tickets. I was backstage with Pascal and Mylène as she was preparing for the show.

Pascal spoke very kindly of me as he introduced me to her, and he promised Mylène that her music and records were in good hands here in Russia with our Universal affiliate that I managed. I watched them walk over to the corner of her dressing room and have a very intense conversation in French. I couldn't understand what they were saying, but I could see that she was hanging on his every word. Her trust in him was complete, and why not? He had made her wildly successful. Pascal was the kind of executive I wanted to be.

I visited other European territories, including Sweden, which was a great example of how to export domestic artists to the world: think of ABBA, Ace of Base, and Roxette. My boss, Thomas Hedström, who was Swedish, introduced me to Ola Håkansson, the head of Stockholm Records, the label home of the Cardigans. I learned a lot from Ola, whom I've also considered a mentor. He taught me how artists can appeal not just to their own country but to the world. Ola was an expert, as was evidenced by the Cardigans' worldwide success.

One of the most important things I learned in Sweden was the existence of their trade organization Export Music Sweden, which is dedicated to bringing Swedish music to the rest of the world. Music was bringing a lot of money to the Swedish economy. I studied how the music business was impacting Sweden and this effected my strategy for signing a local Russian artist to Universal Music. I realized I wanted to follow the Swedish example of exporting Russian music to the rest of the world.

■

As the new CEO of Universal Music Russia, I was always being asked to speak to various groups, including the American Chamber of Commerce in Moscow. We were the first music company to join the Chamber; most of the members were the executives running the Russian offices of companies like Exxon, J. P. Morgan, Texaco, and McDonald's. I made my debut at the chamber by giving a speech for the members as well as the invited guests from the Russian Ministry of Culture and the US ambassador to Russia.

My topic was the potential for Russia to be like Sweden. I said that Sweden was exporting more ABBA records than Volvo was selling cars to the rest of the world and that Russia needed to protect the music industry like Sweden was doing.

I explained that the potential was unlimited, but there were so many talented young Russian artists unable to make a living because of music piracy. The Mafia gangs controlling the pirate factories in this country were stealing their creative works, and Russian artists deserved to be paid for their work. After some applause, I continued, "Universal Music is proud to be here in Russia, but we are not here just to sell Bon Jovi and Elton John. We're here to find local talent and export them to the world, but in order to do that, we needed a normal, legal market without the criminal element dominating our business."

The reaction from the ministry was positive; at that moment in history, Russians were embracing Americans as well as our know-how and expertise. They considered me credible, and they agreed with me. But of course, they didn't do anything about piracy. It was out of their hands. I would learn that organized crime was more powerful than the government. Until Russia solved its problem with piracy, we couldn't make any money selling their product at home. I needed to find Russian artists that I could export to the West. That became my mission.

PART 3

POP STARS
AND OLIGARCHS

6

THE OLIGARCH'S DAUGHTER

The Universal merger had a huge effect on my career, as I was no longer confined to the accounting department but now truly trusted with the whole company. I loved my job so much and recognized that I was given the biggest opportunity of a lifetime. Being the CEO of anything would be a humongous step, but being CEO of an international record label was beyond my wildest dreams. So many perfect things were happening to me. But the pressure to find a local star was real. I needed to sign an artist I could promote in the West; it was the only way to make money for Universal, as we couldn't compete with the pirates who were manufacturing and selling bootleg CDs. I was desperate to keep the company profitable and open.

I needed to find a pop star. The only bands sending us demos were cool alt-rock groups, but that was a trap I didn't want to fall into, because promoting rock bands was much harder than creating a pop star.

When it was announced that, for the very first time since the purchase of PolyGram, Universal would be gathering all of the heads of labels throughout the world in San Francisco, Max Hole, the company's head of marketing, told me and my Eastern European colleagues that this would be the best chance we would ever have to present local music to Universal executives worldwide. Some of the most famous executives in music would be there: Jimmy Iovine from Interscope, Lyor Cohen from Def Jam, CEO Doug Morris, and Edgar Bronfman Jr., chairman of the Universal Music Group.

"So bring something good!" Max exclaimed.

But we didn't have anything good enough to present. Boris had signed Russian artists who didn't sing in English and couldn't sell records outside of Russia. I wanted to make a statement within Universal that I could bring them artists from Russia that could sell in America and around the world. San Francisco was the opportunity. Of course, the Eastern Europeans were going to present music from their top artists, but in my mind, what they had to offer wasn't good enough for the Americans.

The Czechs had MC Erik and Barbara, a duo with a hit remake of "Summer Nights" from *Grease*—not really unique. Poland and Hungary also had unimpressive artists to present. If we all came with mediocre music, the Americans were sure to write off Eastern Europe, like PolyGram had. I wanted Russia to change that forever. I wanted to prove I was a real record executive, not just a guy in Russia selling Eminem albums.

My goal was to find a Russian artist that Universal executives in America would find appealing. I asked myself, "Who is the most popular Russian in America now?" That was easy: tennis pro Anna Kournikova. Although she didn't win any singles titles, she was a formidable player in doubles tennis, but her stunning good looks and charm is what won her over with Americans. I recalled seeing her on *The Tonight Show with Jay Leno*. When Jay asked Anna if she's a Russian citizen, she answered, "I am, but I moved here seven years ago, so I feel kind of American, you know." The audience loved it, and America loved Anna. I knew I needed to find a Russian pop star version of Anna Kournikova. But time was running out before the start of the Universal worldwide conference in San Francisco.

Then, laying on my couch late one night, I switched on MTV to see what Boris was doing with the channel. MTV was rocking the country. It was the best version of MTV anywhere in the world because of the complete freedom Boris negotiated as well as his progressive young staff. It was a mix of Red Hot Chili Peppers and Mariah Carey, with some Russian stars sprinkled in less frequently. Boris wanted to make sure his version of MTV was the gold standard. So if you were a Russian artist, your video had to be outstanding and competitive to make it on his airwaves, and even then, it could be quickly yanked if it didn't get traction. There were so many Western, especially American, videos vying for TV play. Russian artists had to compete not only with American and UK artists but also with high-quality Swedish pop, some German and French pop, and an occasional Italian video.

As I continued my late-night MTV viewing, suddenly, I felt like I was watching a movie. But it was a beautiful music video that was expensively produced with gorgeous scenes of snow and famous Russian actors. The song was a ballad called "Winter Dream." Then the artist entered the scene, and she reminded me of a younger version of Russian tennis star Anna Kournikova.

Bingo!

I thought, "If she could only sing in English!" Her name was Alsou, and I called MTV to find out more. I learned she was not signed to a label, and MTV said they would ask her manager to call me.

The manager's name was Valeriy Belotserkovskiy, and when we spoke on the phone, he reminded me of a modern-day Rasputin. I could tell from that very first call that he was twisted and sinister and very protective of his client, an opinion that was later confirmed when we met in person, after my head of marketing, Asya, had persuaded him to come to our office. He was not very forthcoming with more information about her but said he'd be willing to discuss a contract.

I asked if Alsou could sing in English, and he told me, "She lives in London. She speaks better English than you do."

I took the insult because I was thinking she might be the one I'm looking for. But Valeriy was refusing to let me meet Alsou. Finally, I told him, "If you don't let me meet her, I can't offer you a contract."

Valeriy consented and brought Alsou to our office—the first artist to visit. Alsou flew in from London to meet me and our marketing team. She had never been inside a record company. When she walked in, it caused a commotion; everyone was anxious to see our first potential Russian artist. Alsou dressed very casually, wearing a cap and sweatshirt. She was friendly, with a bright smile, but a little nervous and shy. She deferred to Valeriy when we asked her about her recording plans. Then there was the matter of signing a recording contract. Valeriy said Alsou was fifteen, and first, her parents had to sign her contract. Of course, I agreed to meet her folks. But we couldn't seem to find a time when her father would be available. Apparently, he was busy with his work.

The next step was to prepare the contract for Alsou, and it was a big deal because it was the first professional Western recording contract ever done in Russia. It was hot off the presses from our London office, and along with our company lawyer, I had to review it to make sure everything was in order. A press conference was arranged, which is where I was finally going to meet Alsou's parents. And our lawyer asked me, "How many bodyguards will Alsou's dad bring to the press conference?"

I didn't know how to answer that. "Bodyguards?" I asked him. "Why would he be bringing bodyguards?"

And the lawyer said, "Don't you know who her father is?"

No, I didn't. Our lawyer informed me: "His name is Ralif Safin. He owns LUKOIL, the biggest oil company in Russia. He is an extremely powerful man."

My first Russian signing could have been anybody—maybe some poor pop singer from a faraway town like Vladivostok. But my first artist had a father who was one of the most powerful—and perhaps most dangerous—men in the country. Yet I was undeterred, because I really believed Alsou was the Russian Britney Spears.

I had never met an oligarch, and this is where my Russian journey took a wild new turn. The rise of the oligarchy in Russia started in the 1990s, when a broke Russian government decided to privatize all the major industries in the country that had previously belonged to the state, before the breakup of USSR. Shares of the companies would be distributed to the workers. Russia's powerful oil companies were on that list. Ralif was able to engineer a takeover of LUKOIL by purchasing the shares of the factory workers. He became a multibillionaire overnight.

I didn't have time to consider the ramifications of signing one of the wealthiest daughters in Russia. I was busy planning a big, fancy, Western-style press conference to announce that we had signed our first Russian artist. We wanted to do something as big as a Hollywood movie premiere with Brad Pitt or Julia Roberts. To make an impression, we chose the Radisson Hotel, the only American hotel in Moscow. It was huge and had a ballroom suitable for us. We made a large banner featuring the Universal globe, and we invited not just the music press, like MTV, but the mainstream news media, including CNN. The hotel was home to most of the international press in Moscow, so they didn't have to travel but a few steps to attend what was not a typical music story but an historic moment.

Asya organized the event. I was there with the contracts, which were so thick they were bound in book form. Everything was laid out on a table on stage, and the media was gathered as we were waiting for Alsou, who was late. Then I saw her entourage arrive at the ballroom. They had their own TV crew filming everything. It was as if Princess Diana had entered the room. I greeted Alsou, and then I got the first glimpse of her father, a tall, impressive man. He was glowing with excitement. He was indeed surrounded by bodyguards, and I walked up to him and extended my hand to shake his.

I told him, "I'm about to sign a seven-album deal with your daughter. It's going to last for years, if not decades. Nice to meet you."

He was all smiles, unlike Valeriy, who was hovering nearby, clearly nervous that I was talking to Ralif directly.

When the press conference began, I told the assembled media about our plans for Alsou, and I proclaimed this to be a history-making day for the company, signing our first Russian artist. I introduced Simon Napier-Bell, the legendary British manager who had been hired to look after Alsou's career. He talked about his experience managing Wham! and its breakout star, George Michael. He told the media that he would make Alsou a star in Europe. I introduced my team, and then Alsou said a few words in Russian and then English. She was extremely shy.

Next, it was Q and A time for the media. The Russian journalists asked tough questions, searching for any kind of scandal. They asked me, "What makes you think Alsou is capable of performing like a Western artist?"

It might have been a fair question because Valeriy had her singing love ballads, dressed in evening gowns. I told the media that we were going to provide Alsou with the songs and the music and the support she needed to compete on the level of a Britney or a Christina Aguilera. The next question came from someone Valeriy had planted in the audience.

He asked Alsou, "Now that you're working with a Western record label, what about your Russian fans? Will you let them down, or will you continue working with Valeriy to develop music?"

Alsou was not stupid. She knew the last thing she needed now was Valeriy harassing her. She told the shill that Valeriy was very important to her and she wanted to be an international star as well as a Russian star. She handled the situation like a diplomat.

Now it was time to sign the contracts. Ralif pulled out his own very fancy pen. I grabbed one of my own, but he handed his to me, which I couldn't get to work. He looked at me like I was an uncultured fool who didn't know how to use a real ink pen, but finally, my name dripped out. Then everything was official, and Alsou was presented with more flowers than she could possibly manage to hold. Photos were taken in front of the Universal globe banner.

By the time I arrived in San Francisco to present Alsou's music video to the Universal executives at the worldwide meeting, I knew I was bringing them the first international pop star from Russia. In the large downtown ballroom where the leaders from the varying international Universal offices were gathered, I was seated in the back, at the Eastern Europe table. As I predicted, the videos from Hungary, Poland, and the Czech Republic were not impressing the Americans. But when Alsou's music video came on the screen, everyone in the room was captivated. Even Edgar Bronfman Jr. was impressed with her, as he let me know through Max Hole. Now all I had to do was deliver results and manage the East vs. West war between Alsou's dueling managers, Valeriy and Simon.

7

IT'S IN THE BAG

The day after the press conference, we had a meeting with Valeriy at his office, located at the Cosmos Hotel and Casino, the preferred destination for Moscow's top gangsters, corrupt generals, and prostitutes. Nothing symbolized the dark underbelly of Moscow's criminal world better than the Cosmos, and this is where Valeriy's management offices were located. Walking up to the mammoth Soviet structure, a black semicircle of steel, iron, and glass, Simon looked at me and said, "You know we might not come out of here alive, right?"

I wasn't sure if he was joking. Valeriy had closed down the casino restaurant exclusively for us. A major buffet of Russian food and caviar and champagne and vodka was prepared. Ralif arrived with his contingent of bodyguards; then Alsou came with hers. Finally, Valeriy made a grand appearance. He wanted everyone to know who was in charge. Simon was smirking; he was not fooled for a moment.

Ralif announced, "We're going to Eurovision."

As an American, I had no idea what he was talking about. I turned to Simon and asked him, "What is Eurovision?" He replied with two words: "ABBA. 'Waterloo.'"

I told him I loved that song, and he explained that ABBA wanted to break out of Sweden, so they entered Eurovision as a way to achieve global success. Their song won, and their plan worked. Now the same thing could happen to Alsou. I told Simon I thought it was a fantastic idea, and then he said, "And no one else ever had the same success out of Eurovision as ABBA."

Valeriy countered, saying, "What about Julio Iglesias?"

Indeed, the Spanish superstar had competed in 1970. He could have also mentioned Celine Dion, who was nineteen when she won for Switzerland in 1988.

Simon said, "Eurovision is kitschy and silly. But three hundred million people watch it. Let's do it. It could go either way—it's a risk. But I will put together the number one team in the industry from stylist to wardrobe to backing vocalists. And I'll find the song."

It was during this time that I learned more about Simon's accomplishments—how he brought Wham! to China and filmed a video there, how he managed the Yardbirds and Marc Bolan of T. Rex, and how he helped write the English lyrics to the Italian song that became "You Don't Have to Say You Love Me," a huge hit for Dusty Springfield. He was clearly a force to be reckoned with, and the smartest thing I could do was support him and shield him from Valeriy, who, in a rare moment, did say, "I will leave you guys alone, but you better deliver results." We knew that if we failed, Valeriy would take back complete control of Alsou and she'd be back to singing ballads in Novosibirsk.

So the pressure was on.

Ralif remained above it all but never let go of his mission to make Alsou an international star. That was the entire reason he let her be signed to Universal, overruling Valeriy, who wanted to keep her confined to Russia. Ralif expected me to deliver results and made it clear money was no object as long as I came through. If I didn't, I knew it was going to be very dangerous for me. This was a risk that the mentors I'd admired from afar, like Clive Davis and David Geffen, never had to take with their artists. They never had to worry that if they didn't make an artist a star, they would disappear.

■

We had a few months to get it all together before Eurovision was going to be held in Stockholm in May 2000. Simon found the song "Solo," which was written by two Americans—Andrew Lane and Brandon Barnes. The producer was Steve Levine, famous for his work with Culture Club. Simon lined up the choreographer and found the backing vocalists, including Clare

Torry, who had worked with Pink Floyd. A true genius, Simon ran the campaign like a military operation. We filmed a music video in London and sent Alsou to Moldova, Romania, Estonia, and Latvia, all countries that would be voting in Eurovision. She made local TV appearances and did interviews, and it all worked. People all over Europe were talking about Alsou.

In May we loaded up a plane in Moscow for our flight to Stockholm. We were truly an East-West delegation, made up of a dozen people on Simon's team from the United Kingdom, including the costumers, makeup artists, and two dancers, as well as a lot of Russians, like Alsou's immediate family and her relatives from Tatarstan (where she was born), plus Russian media. We were going to be in Sweden for a week, based at the Globen, a spherical indoor arena built in 1989.

The schedule for the week included multiple rehearsals, two official press conferences, and a party at the Russian Embassy in Stockholm. Every time Alsou stepped out in public, whether it was to buy a snack at a local convenience store or to do a media event, Simon made sure she looked gorgeous. She had a different dress for every appearance. Alsou loved that; she had hotel rooms filled with different costumes and two people to oversee her wardrobe.

The Russians were counting on her to win. Russia's performance at Eurovision had been spotty up until this point. Russia had first entered in 1994 and placed ninth. Then there were years where Russia didn't qualify for the final. So it was up to Alsou to bring glory to the homeland for the first time.

Valeriy kept out of Simon's way. Valeriy may have been jealous of Simon, but he knew the Britisher could pull it off. It was as if Valeriy and Simon had declared a truce. Simon carried most of the load, and Valeriy built up interest in Russia, telling everyone that Alsou was going to win the contest. In Stockholm Valeriy's only real contribution to the whole event was organizing a previctory party at the Russian Embassy, where he had legendary crooner Lev Leshenko belt out the song "Victory Day" to a crowd of Russians and the embassy staff. It was a famous World War II song that is known to every Russian and normally sung every year on May 9 to celebrate victory over the Nazis. Simon and I watched in amazement, and I thought it very strange that we were singing a World War II song prior to a song contest. It felt like we were preparing for battle instead of a pop music competition.

On the day of the event, there was an afternoon dress rehearsal—the third dress rehearsal in two days. Alsou was perfect. But for the live broadcast on Saturday night, Simon and I were backstage with her, and just as she was about to go out on stage, she had a stomach contraction—perhaps from nerves—and she missed her first note. Simon and I stared at each other, thinking, "Are we going down in flames?" But somehow her stomach settled itself, and the rest of her performance was fine.

Now it was up to the voters. Half of a contestant's score is from a professional jury in each country, and half is from public televoting. Each country announces its points in turn. Alsou received the top score of twelve points from four countries (Romania, Cyprus, Malta, and Croatia), and each time, the camera showed us in the green room, gleefully reacting to our high marks.

As the votes came in, the leaderboard changed hands several times. There were moments when we were in the lead, and for a brief second, I thought we could actually win.

When all the votes were tallied, Denmark had won the competition and Russia placed second—the country's best finish to date—but it was not a win. I was worried what the reaction would be from Ralif and the state-controlled television channel ORT, which broadcasted Eurovision in Russia.

It turned out they were just hoping to end up in the top five.

We left the Globen and went out on the town at some fancy clubs, drinking champagne. Alsou was finally able to relax and party with her friends. She was back to being a teenaged girl having a good time on what she said was the greatest night of her life.

The next day we flew back to Russia. The pilot came on the PA system and announced that Alsou was on board, and the crew was honored to be flying a champion home. When we were back in Moscow, Alsou was invited to the Kremlin to meet President Putin. I was not on the guest list.

It would have been fun to go, but it really didn't bother me to not be included. I was back in the office, and everyone was congratulating me for being on TV. Then I had a phone call from Ralif's secretary. He wanted me to come to his office at 2:00 p.m. It was not a request; it was a command.

I headed over to LUKOIL's office in one of the oldest areas of downtown Moscow. It was a beautiful space, and their building was one of the tallest in the city. Ralif's office was on the top floor, and security was as tight—or tighter—than at the Kremlin. It was like a minifortress, and they sent some-one to the lobby to escort me up.

I didn't know what to expect from Ralif. As I entered his office, his sec-retary asked me to surrender my cell phone—standard operating procedure, nothing personal. As I handed it to her and waited for Ralif, I wondered if he was angry that Alsou didn't finish in first place at Eurovision. If he was, he could easily have LUKOIL's vast and secretive security force whisk me out of the building, never to be seen again. Then Ralif appeared and pulled a brown paper bag out of his desk, saying, "Helluva job, David. Helluva job. Thank you."

And that was it. I didn't open the bag yet; I just took the elevator back down to the lobby. That's when I looked in the bag and saw stacks of hun-dred dollar bills. I stuffed the bag in my coat and didn't count the money until I was safely back in my office.

Ralif had given me $20,000.

8

ENRIQUE IN
THE KREMLIN

Sitting in my office with Ralif's unexpected gift, I realized two things: I had to tell my bosses about this. And since this was Russia I was dealing with, I never knew if I was being set up. So I immediately called the people in charge at the Universal office in London and told them, "I've just been given $20,000 in a brown paper bag. What do I do with it?"

That created quite a discussion among the executives in the United Kingdom. They were mainly asking themselves if I should keep it or give it back.

I knew I wasn't the first music executive to be offered cash, but I was probably the first one to admit it. The folks in London ultimately decided I should keep the money and shut up about it.

Now I had to decide exactly what to do with it. I hid the money in my apartment for a while and then eventually imported a Volkswagen Golf from Lithuania that may or may not have been stolen in Germany as part of an insurance scam, a common practice at the time. Russian cars were terrible. I was driving Natalia's father's Lada to work every day, and it was a miserable experience.

The money wasn't the most important thing on my mind. I was more concerned with Alsou's career and what the next step should be. After the performance at Eurovision, Howard Berman, President at Universal's Mercury Records in London, signed Alsou for the UK. "Solo" entered the top twenty on the British singles chart. Her video went to no. 1 on the UK channel the Box. Since Alsou lived in London, it meant a great deal to her to be successful in Great Britain. Mercury Records, one of Universal's most prestigious sublabels and home to Bon Jovi and Elton John, was the perfect home for Alsou. She was Mercury's first Russian pop star in the British charts.

"Solo" also became a big hit in Russia. It was a source of pride for the Russians not only because Alsou did so well but also because it proved Russia could produce songs that the world—or at least Europe, at this point—would embrace. Next, "Solo" debuted on the German charts. The French were interested too. Just before "Solo" was released there, Alsou was invited to perform at a United Nations Educational, Scientific and Cultural Organization (UNESCO) concert in Paris, where it was a big deal for her to represent Russia. Pascal Nègre at Universal France was going to promote Alsou. Everything was going our way.

And then there was a change in management at Mercury. Alsou's main supporter, Howard Berman, was fired. Howard's team was let go too. A new leadership team replaced him, and they were not interested in any of the artists supported by the outgoing team. Alsou's progress immediately slowed. The British were no longer interested in her, and so Universal France became hesitant. The Germans were counting on Britain to turn Alsou into a major star, and now that wasn't going to happen.

She continued to do well in Russia, but that didn't matter much to me. The idea was to make her a global phenomenon. I had to come up with a plan, and once again, an American angel came to my rescue. I got a call from Max Hole, Universal's worldwide head of marketing in London.

He told me, "Enrique Iglesias is coming to Moscow for two shows, and you did such a fantastic job with Eminem. Do you think you could do something really big for Enrique?" Interscope head Jimmy Iovine had shelled out millions to sign Enrique and wanted to make him bigger than Ricky Martin and Marc Anthony. I said we would be glad to help.

My idea was to ask Enrique to record a duet with Alsou. Max forwarded the request to Enrique's management, and I'd be damned if I didn't get a positive response—but there was one condition. I had to promise that their duet would go to no. 1 in Russia and that Enrique's album would also top the chart. And most important of all, I had to ensure that Enrique would be a bigger star in Russia than his father, Julio. That was Enrique's wish, which he personally expressed to me while backstage at the Kremlin Palace during rehearsals.

Enrique agreed to rerecord his song "You're My #1" as a duet with Alsou. We went to Alsou with the idea, and she said yes, but she didn't understand why her main supporter in the United Kingdom, Howard Berman, was gone and why Universal London wasn't interested in promoting her any longer. What was worse for me was explaining the situation to Ralif, the man who had just given me $20,000.

"I don't understand, David," he told me, his anger building. "She does so well in the charts in England, and they won't call you back. How can they be so rude to my daughter?" I did my best to keep everyone positive and looking forward, but Valeriy was eager to pounce at any perceived failure on Simon's and my part. We had a very limited amount of time to turn this around, or I would lose Alsou to my Rasputin-like nemesis.

There was no lack of drama in the situation. The show was to take place at the Kremlin Palace, a massive hall located inside of the Kremlin walls that had been the site of the Congress of the Communist Party meetings since Stalin. It was now the premier music venue in the country. Later, while walking around backstage during rehearsals with Enrique and Alsou, I could feel the ghosts of Stalin, Khrushchev, and Brezhnev. I wondered what they might think about two pop stars appearing on this stage now, one of them being a star from the West who had sold out two shows in the hall.

There was more drama from the promoter of the concert, who was diabolical and a friend of Valeriy's. There was no Ticketmaster or Live Nation in Russia yet. At the time, the promoter would pay the artist(s) a lot of money up front because artists from the West didn't trust the Russians and wanted their money first. After the up-front money was transferred to the artist, the promoter would become all-powerful, and this one had a huge ego and wanted Enrique at his dinner table.

Enrique was already very popular in Russia, thanks to his worldwide hit "Bailamos." He had filmed a music video with Anna Kournikova, which was ironic, as it was seeing Anna on *The Tonight Show with Jay Leno* that had inspired me to find Alsou. We were two weeks out from Enrique's pair of sold-out shows in Moscow when I received a call from Interscope in LA. They needed Alsou to go into a recording studio in London to cut her part of the duet. She did that, and now we needed a music video. We hired a director to film Alsou and Enrique meeting for the first time, at the venue on the night of the first concert. They were introduced to each other backstage. The show itself was a triumph, but there was more drama to come. Ralif was very happy, but his wife, Raziya, was not. She came up to me after the show and accused me of turning her daughter into a backing vocalist for Enrique. Raziya was always on Valeriy's side and wanted her daughter to just sing Russian ballads. She thought Enrique was too sexual and that he was making Alsou one of his "babes." I assured her that wasn't the case—the song was simply a nice duet. She wasn't convinced.

I was very conflicted the next day. Ralif was very happy, but I had never had that kind of feedback from Alsou's mother before. All of that confusion washed away as I was driving to the office, listening to the most important radio station in the country, Europa Plus. The deejay announced he was about to play a history-making duet by "our very own" Alsou and "one of the biggest pop stars in the world," Enrique Iglesias. He said this was a sign that the Russian music industry was changing.

The song came on, and I had to pull off the road because it was such an emotional moment for me. I wasn't the artist, but I did tear up. I was so proud to hear the song on the radio and to know that we'd done something that really mattered. Two weeks later, the video went public on MTV, and it was visual proof that Alsou belonged on stage with the biggest star in the world. This was a turbocharge for her career. The single went to no. 1 in Russia and ultimately was the best-selling single of the year.

Thomas Hedström and I flew to London to meet Enrique backstage at *Top of the Pops,* a long-running weekly TV series that featured the top artists and songs of the day. It was a very proud moment for Thomas as VP of Eastern Europe for Universal, as this was his biggest success yet by any of his labels in the territory. This was the turning point where Russia finally became more important to the company than Poland or the Czech Republic. Backstage in the BBC studio, I presented Enrique with a platinum disc for the duet. He was the friendliest of all the international artists I had worked with. It didn't hurt that I helped him fulfill his goal of becoming more popular in Russia than his father, something I reminded him of when I made the presentation, as this platinum award was proof that we'd done it—Julio never achieved platinum status in Russia. This success gave Simon and me more time in the hourglass to keep Alsou away from Valeriy and to have another go at an international breakout.

We were busy figuring out our next steps, but so was Valeriy. We wanted to go on a promotional tour of Europe, but he organized a big homecoming concert for Alsou in Bugulma, a tiny little village in Tatarstan that she hadn't lived in since she was three years old. It was to be a free concert where she would sing her Russian songs, "Solo," and her hit duet, but with a local Russian singer. Valeriy invited government VIPs, and Ralif was there, too, because he was thinking of running for governor of Tatarstan and expanding his political profile.

Simon and I attended, and we had a great time meeting Alsou's grandparents and other family members. A hundred thousand people gathered in the outdoor air for this concert, and it was the biggest event of the decade in this small town. But we also realized this was a dress rehearsal for a year-long tour of Russia, and Alsou would not be available to travel internationally.

To counter Valeriy's plans, I came up with the idea to take Alsou to New York to see if one of the American-based Universal labels would be interested in signing her. Mercury's sister label in America was the legendary Def Jam Records. I decided to start there. Boris Löhe, who headed up the Mercury label in Germany and who had promoted "Solo" and supported Alsou, helped me and Thomas Hedström get a meeting with the head of Def Jam, Lyor Cohen. Boris and Lyor had coproduced a very successful album called *The Rapsody Overture: Hip Hop Meets Classics*, which, for the first time, combined hip hop artists with classical musicians and opera singers.

Lyor was considered to be one of the founding fathers of hip hop in America due to his managing Run-DMC and signing some of the original and most influential rappers to Def Jam, including LL Cool J, the Beastie Boys, and the label's biggest-selling artist, Jay-Z. He was quite taken with Alsou and clearly wanted to impress her and get her excited about what he could do for her. I could tell she was more nervous than excited.

Lyor told Alsou, "I'm going to work with you. We're going to dirty your style up. I checked out your videos and your duet with Enrique, but that's too slow for Def Jam. We have to change your image."

I thought that this was fantastic. One of the most successful record executives in the world was excited about our artist.

Lyor wanted to know if she was willing to go for it, and so he asked her, "Alsou, are you hungry?"

She replied, "No, I had a muffin this morning. I'm fine, thank you."

And I could feel all the air just vanish from the room. Everyone's jaws dropped. Did Alsou just sabotage any chance for her to achieve international stardom?

9

DID WE HAVE FUN AT THE AFTER-PARTY?

Alsou did indeed have a muffin earlier that day. But something was lost in translation when she misunderstood Lyor Cohen's question. Still, it was symbolic of our struggle with this Russian teenager. She wasn't desperate for stardom. She wasn't as hungry as some starving artists who had nothing else going on and no other options for a career. If her father wanted to, he could buy Universal.

I'm certain that Simon Napier-Bell, Thomas Hedström, and I thought Lyor's reaction to Alsou's answer about being "hungry" was a thousand times worse than it really was, because, in truth, he was undeterred. Even after her gaffe, he said, "I know you're in town for a show."

He was right. Alsou was scheduled to perform at the Taj Mahal in Atlantic City for an annual event organized by Igor Krutoy, a Russian media mogul who was also a singer/songwriter. He would only invite Russia's top pop stars and legends to perform. Russians from all over the East Coast would attend, with a heavy concentration from the Brooklyn neighborhood of Brighton Beach, where a majority of Russian immigrants lived. Atlantic City's casinos reminded them of Moscow.

It was a real honor to be invited to perform at this event, and Valeriy wanted Alsou to only sing her Russian songs—more prep for the Russian tour he was "secretly" planning. Simon managed to sneak in "Solo" for the New York Russians, who were as proud of her Eurovision triumph as the Russians back home.

We were surprised Lyor was interested enough to travel to New Jersey. He told Alsou, "We're coming. I'll call Edgar (Bronfman, Jr.) and ask for the company helicopter, and I'll call my friend Donald Trump to book a ballroom at the hotel. I'll organize an after-party."

We were still in his office when he connected with Trump on the phone, and I heard Lyor ask him, "Can we get a room for a buffet and champagne? And I want a big ice sculpture centerpiece."

I was thinking that Lyor was one of the most powerful men in the music business and in all of New York City. I was rolling with the bigwigs now. And throughout our meeting with Lyor, he was on several phone calls about Jay-Z's latest album, which had been released that day. Lyor was nervous about it debuting at no. 1, like his previous albums. He was getting constant updates on sales, and I was in awe. Lyor was the founding father of hip hop, and I couldn't believe he was talking to us while also in conversations with his most important artist, one of the greatest rappers in history. It was all surreal. And I mean—helicopters, limos, the Taj Mahal. This was show business! What could possibly go wrong?

I was worried that Lyor had no idea of what kind of people would be coming to his after-party. Ralif's friends included a wide range of oil executives, corrupt government officials, greedy bankers, and the most powerful Russian gangsters on the East Coast.

Alsou had to head over to the venue for rehearsal, so later that evening, Simon, Thomas, and I met Lyor at the Universal helipad. The interior of the copter was very luxurious, complete with a bar. We landed near the Taj Mahal, and a limo picked us up. We were greeted by Lyor's assistant Julie Greenwald, who would later become one of the most powerful women in the music industry, first, as the president of Warner Music, then as the chairperson and CEO of the Atlantic Music Group.

We walked into the hotel with Lyor. Here in Atlantic City, on a night when Russians had taken over, he was unrecognized, as no one knew who Lyor Cohen was. After Alsou performed, we made our way to the afterparty. Ralif gave a speech in Russian, and I introduced him to Lyor. And the first thing Ralif said was: "Why did you guys stop working with my daughter in England?"

Lyor gave me a look. He had nothing to do with the Mercury Records debacle and had no idea what Ralif was talking about. People nearby were staring at us—not just ordinary people but big, tough, scary thugs. Lyor is a tall man, but Ralif is bigger, and in this battle of titans, Ralif was winning. We made some uncomfortable small talk, and then Ralif told Lyor, "I could buy this whole company if I wanted to. I don't know why we need to come here and beg you to help my daughter."

It could not have gone more wrong. I headed back to Manhattan with Lyor on the helicopter for an awkward ride, and he was busy on the phone, talking to other people about other things. Julie told me how cool and fantastic the evening was, but I knew it was a disaster. Sure enough, Lyor lost interest in Alsou, and the deal never happened.

I returned to Moscow and got the news that Ralif had fired Simon, and Valeriy was now in complete control. Alsou flew from London to Moscow to record new songs for me and prepare for a big tour. I was still supportive of her career and wanted her to be the biggest pop star in Russia. But any chance for international success was gone.

The bright future I'd planned for Alsou never happened. We released two more albums, and they sold well in Russia, but they were nothing close to the Pan-European sales of her first release. The pressure on me subsided because they knew I disagreed with firing Simon, and Ralif and Valeriy were only interested in her Russian career from that point on. Ralif was busy running for governor, a position he did not win. He was appointed senator, and Alsou continued to make music. Valeriy managed her for several more years, until she'd had enough of him. In March 2006 Alsou got married, and her husband became involved in her career. I was long out of the picture by that point.

I'd so badly wanted Alsou to become an international star, and so many times, I felt like we were close: Eurovision, the Mercury UK deal, Enrique, Lyor. But it just wasn't meant to be. It felt like the record industry let her down. She should have been Russia's first international pop star. I sincerely believe she was Dua Lipa but twenty years too soon. She was an amazing talent who could sing Celine Dion-like ballads that would bring tears to my eyes. Simon and Lyor wanted to "dirty her up," but in the end, maybe Valeriy was right about her singing ballads.

But Valeriy was a curse, and working with him showed me the ugly side of Russian show business that had carried over from Soviet times. He was not willing to embrace Western management style practices. It was all about Valeriy and his Russian tour ambitions, not Alsou and developing her true talent internationally. It was an East-West conflict that doomed Alsou's international career. At least Ralif didn't kill me.

■

After Alsou, I didn't give up. It was back to the drawing board to continue my search for a Russian artist who could become Russia's first worldwide star. I had to keep looking; I was never going to prove that I was a true record executive until I had that first breakthrough. Even legendary executives Jimmy Iovine and Lyor Cohen had to start somewhere. It wasn't long after the Atlantic City fiasco that an opportunity presented itself.

I had been monitoring MTV Russia for new talent. One night, at 2:00 a.m., I saw a video with two schoolgirls standing on one side of a fence, with their teachers and the rest of society on the other side, scolding and shaming them. And what do the two girls do? They turn and look at their tormentors, and then they kiss. The song was called "Ya Sashlo Suma" (translated in English as "I'm Losing My Mind").

It was a controversial move in a socially conservative country where promoting homosexuality was a crime. It was shocking to people who had lived through the Communist era, when being gay was punishable by imprisonment. It was also provocative for people who had embraced the Russian Orthodox Church, which had become the predominant moral authority after the fall of communism.

As provocative as the video was, the song itself was what got my attention. It had an irresistible melody and rhythm, and I strongly believed it could be a radio hit if it were recorded in English. I felt the power of the video and showed it to my team. They saw trouble. I saw two talented Russian girls who would achieve the international breakthrough I was dreaming about.

PART 4

THE MOST DANGEROUS BAND

10

THE KISS HEARD 'ROUND THE WORLD

I knew the Moscow-based duo t.A.T.u., with teen vocalists Julia Volkova and Lena Katina, was going to be my international breakthrough from the very first moment I saw their controversial video. I loved their music. Julia's dynamic vocals were haunting, and the music had an infectious dance beat. The lyrics were provocative.

There was no act like them anywhere in the world. But I had to convince my Russian marketing and sales team to support me. An act like t.A.T.u. was going to be a risk for everyone. Russia was still a very intolerant society, despite the Soviet Union being long gone. This band would be pushing boundaries. I asked Asya to get a hold of the video for "Ya Sashlo Suma" from MTV. I gathered the team in my office, plugged the VHS tape into my TV hanging on the wall, and we watched it together. Everyone's mouth dropped while watching the infamous scene where Julia and Lena kiss.

"No! You cannot sign them. Are you crazy, David?" shouted Asya, my very wise marketing director, who had just stood up. "We are going to catch so much hell for this, from everybody!"

I argued, "Don't you love how they're rebelling against authority? That's all that kiss is. They're teenage symbols of a new Russia, leaving the past behind."

That's when my excellent radio promoter Sasha Rodmanich spoke up: "The song is a hit."

At a record label, that's all that matters. So with Sasha's promise that the song would be a hit on the radio, I was able to rally the team, including

Asya, who would have to carry most of the burden. We were going to pursue signing t.A.T.u. But she was right to be cautious since I was taking Universal into uncharted territory.

Homosexuality was a crime in the old Soviet Union, and under Russian law, promotion of LGBTQ issues was considered propaganda punishable with time in prison. Gay Russians have always been treated as outcasts and subversives by the authorities. So when Julia and Lena openly embraced gay rights and kissed in their first music video, I knew I had to make a quick decision that could change my music career forever: Should I sign the most exciting new music act in Russia (and maybe the world) to Universal, even if it meant risking my visa status as an American working in the country or even possible jail time because I would have angered the two most powerful institutions in the country—the Kremlin and the Russian Orthodox Church? Both frowned on all things LGBTQ. Or should I shy away from the controversy and miss the best opportunity I would ever have to promote a Russian act around the world, perhaps achieving my wildest dream of being the first record executive to promote a Russian band in America? There was no way I was going to pass on this. I kept my fingers crossed that I wouldn't end up in a Russian prison.

To sign t.A.T.u., I had to deal with Ivan Shapovalov, a former advertising executive and a high IQ provocateur in the mold of Sex Pistols manager Malcom McLaren. He was a manipulative, edgy person, whose eyes would pierce you while you were in conversation. The band was his idea, and he'd brought in songwriters, including his girlfriend Lena Kiper, to craft the anarchistic message. The infectious music was written by a young unknown composer named Sergey Galoyan, who was working out of his Moscow apartment. Ivan had auditioned many girls and ultimately chose two Moscow teenagers: Lena Katina, a fiery redhead with a head of wild curls who was considered the reasonable one, and Julia Volkova, the sassy, manga-comic-looking, foul-mouthed, and funny brunette one. Both had worked in television and music projects as child actors.

I didn't know what to expect from Ivan, because negotiations in Russian show business were never predictable. After the fall of the Soviet Union, Russia was chaotic, corrupt, and dangerous, like Chicago was in the 1930s, when Al Capone was declared the FBI's public enemy number one. Russia was the wild, wild East, and their music industry had no rules or standards.

Common Western business practices like royalty payments and songwriter copyrights were foreign concepts. Payola was rampant to the extent that even music television channels took bribes from wealthy businessmen to put their wives' music videos into heavy rotation. The government was corrupt through and through and didn't support the music industry or musicians' rights.

Ivan was a tough negotiator, and he knew how badly I wanted to sign the band. My rival, Sony Music, had caught wind of my efforts and started courting him while I was trying to close the deal. I knew I had to play to his ego, so when he arrived at our Universal office to discuss a record contract, I made sure Asya gave him a tour of our marketing and sales department, where large cutout posters of Elton John, U2, and Bon Jovi's new album releases were hanging on the wall along with dozens of other posters of Universal's vast roster of superstars, demonstrating that we were an international label, not a small Russian one. That was my best leverage for negotiations.

"Why should I give you the rights to t.A.T.u.?" Ivan asked, staring at me with his wild eyes. "I don't need a record label; the pirates will steal the music from you anyway."

He was right about that; piracy would limit our sales. But I knew the real prize was to sell t.A.T.u. internationally. I told Ivan, "If you sign with me, I guarantee that t.A.T.u.'s album will be promoted by Universal not just in Russia but also internationally."

That persuaded him. Universal was one of the most prestigious American brands in the world and the largest record company, and he wanted t.A.T.u. to be associated with the best Western artists.

Ivan demanded $100,000 for the rights to t.A.T.u., which would have made it the biggest record deal in Russian show business history. He was adamant that he couldn't accept anything less. I didn't believe him until I discovered that he had already sold the rights to the first single, "Ya Sashlo Suma," to a record label controlled by Russian gangsters. My sales manager then stormed into that meeting with Ivan and revealed that the gangsters had already manufactured the first single.

I got angry with Ivan, and he told me that he had made a mistake, that he was new to show business and didn't know anything about song rights. The gangsters had initially paid him $5,000, but now that he was in talks with Universal, they wanted significantly more before they would give back the rights. I didn't have much choice, because this wasn't just any song. This was the hit single with the notorious music video that would launch t.A.T.u. internationally and top music charts worldwide. If I didn't get the single's rights back from the gangsters at that exorbitant price, there would be no t.A.T.u.

I had to keep my bosses at Universal's headquarters in the dark about some of the unsavory aspects of the deal. Luckily, they thought I had done a good job selling American rap and hip hop music in Russia, with Eminem being my biggest success. They also saw Alsou perform at Eurovision for three hundred million people and break into the UK charts, so they knew I could spot talent. Still, $100,000 was outrageous for an artist from that part of the world and would be the biggest payout in Russian and Eastern European history. None of my colleagues who ran Universal subsidiaries in Eastern Europe had ever requested that much. Ultimately, my London bosses agreed to the amount, and I used the money to pay Ivan, who paid off the gangsters.

The duo t.A.T.u. now had a deal for their album and video rights with a legitimate record label. With Universal Russia behind the duo, t.A.T.u.'s debut album, *200 Po Vstrechnoy*, got wider distribution and became a phenomenal success in every Russian city and former Soviet republic, including Armenia, Georgia, Kazakhstan, Belarus, and Ukraine. Julia and Lena topped the charts everywhere in the region, and t.A.T.u.'s first song and video hit no. 1 simultaneously on pop radio and MTV in 2000.

Their music first appealed to gay and lesbian youth, then spread to a much larger audience of disaffected teens. They took off like a wildfire throughout the former USSR. Stadiums were sold-out, and crowds of fans were worked up into a frenzy with Julia and Lena's confrontational performances. It was Russia's version of Beatlemania. My Eastern European colleagues took notice of that because they all had sizable teenage Russian-speaking populations in their countries, and they sensed a hit for their markets. On that score t.A.T.u.'s album delivered, topping the charts in Hungary, the Czech Republic, Slovakia, and Poland. It was a tidal wave.

With its substantial Russian-speaking population, East Germany was an obvious next target for t.A.T.u. We were getting ready to release *200 Po Vstrechnoy* there, but I stopped that from happening. I knew that t.A.T.u. would never go beyond Russian-speaking audiences in Eastern Europe unless they recorded in English for the Western markets, including Germany. I gambled on t.A.T.u. appealing to a much larger audience than just Russian speakers.

We needed a partner to help make a t.A.T.u. album in English. We needed to rewrite and rerecord the songs, and we needed a bigger, more powerful ally inside of our parent company, Universal Music Group, to shepherd us through the process. Universal Russia was too small to manage a global release, plus it had never been done before by a label in Eastern Europe. I wanted Universal's full weight behind the release and knew that without a powerful partner, it would be impossible to break t.A.T.u internationally.

So with my team, I went on a road tour of all the company's offices in search of help. We told everyone that t.A.T.u. was on the way up, selling out concerts everywhere and climbing the charts in Bulgaria, Poland, and Hungary. If they had an English-language release, I said, they could become a global act. Unfortunately, nobody was interested in partnering with us. Wherever we went—New York, London, anywhere Universal had an office—the answer was always no.

Part of the problem was that Lena and Julia had a reputation for controversy. When people from the label saw footage of them kissing onstage, it made them uncomfortable, and when Lena and Julia invited boys onstage to do the same, my colleagues became too nervous to support us. No band had done anything like that onstage before.

Another issue for the executives was my goal of breaking t.A.T.u. into the American market. They would have to compete with American pop stars like Britney Spears and Christina Aguilera, boy bands like the Backstreet Boys and *NSync, and big pop acts from the United Kingdom. The odds weren't on their side—few international artists had succeeded in breaking into the US market, and the handful that did were not from Eastern Europe or Russia. My colleagues arrogantly dismissed the potential for a band not from America or the United Kingdom to have a hit in their market, and they didn't want to take a risk on what they viewed as my pipe dream.

My road tour was a bust, so I went back to Moscow and mailed packages with the Russian album and videos out to all the remaining labels in the Universal Music Group that we hadn't visited to get them to work with us for the release. That didn't go any better, and we kept getting turned down. It felt like we would never find a partner—until suddenly I received a phone call from Interscope Records in Los Angeles, a subsidiary label of Universal and the hottest record company in America.

I was surprised that Interscope was interested. Their roster included No Doubt, Marilyn Manson, the Black Eyed Peas, Snoop Dogg, Dr. Dre, 50 Cent, Eminem, Mary J. Blige, Nelly, and Blink-182—some of the most popular acts in the world. They really didn't need us. Still, I had done well selling their artists in Russia, so there was already a symbiotic relationship in place.

Asya had sent our package to the label's cofounder, Jimmy Iovine. He was the most powerful record executive in the world, and before forming the label, he had produced some of the most prominent artists of all time, including Tom Petty, U2, and Stevie Nicks. He sent t.A.T.u.'s Russian-language CD to British producer Trevor Horn, who had helmed very successful records for artists like Seal and Yes. He had also been in the Buggles, whose song "Video Killed the Radio Star" was the first video ever shown on MTV.

He loved the t.A.T.u. CD and was very enthusiastic about working with Julia and Lena. He had been a groundbreaking pioneer in the UK music industry, producing the openly gay act Frankie Goes to Hollywood. I suspected that t.A.T.u breaking through boundaries in Russia and Eastern Europe had hit a nerve with him. He just had one question for Jimmy Iovine: "Can they sing in English?"

11

FIFTY-FIFTY

With the opportunity of working with one of the most famous music producers in the world, Trevor Horn, right in front of us, I told Jimmy Iovine that t.A.T.u. could certainly sing in English. But I had no idea.

I had never asked the girls, but I knew we had to make it happen. They would have to sing in English in order to sell their records all over the world. We couldn't record, promote, and sell t.A.T.u. internationally without an English-language album and without a muscular label like Jimmy Iovine's imprint. We were the mighty Universal Music in Russia, but in the big picture of an international business, we were too small to be taken seriously. After being turned down by so many labels within the company, Interscope was our last chance. So I told Jimmy and he told Trevor, "Yes, for sure, they can sing in English."

Based on my assurance, Trevor told Jimmy Iovine that he wanted to produce an album of the Russian songs rerecorded in English with the girls. He thought t.A.T.u's songs in Russian were so good—and would sound even better in English—that there would be no need to record new songs. The label's head of international marketing called me in Moscow to let me know that Interscope wanted to release the album worldwide. It was a joyful moment for everyone in my office. I hugged Asya because it was her tenacity that had made this happen. After everyone else had given up, she'd sent the package to Interscope that hooked Horn.

The partnership between Universal Russia and Interscope was history making; no such deal between a tiny upstart label like Universal Music

Russia and a giant in the music business like Interscope had been made before. All of the sister labels within the company that had turned us down had to explain why—just like, I imagined, the guy from Decca Records in the 1960s who turned down the Beatles had to do to his superiors.

Because our partnership with Interscope was so unprecedented and potentially very lucrative, it made my boss in London a little nervous that we weren't prepared. John Kennedy at Universal Music International was excited for me but nervous that our contract with Ivan wasn't strong enough. Before joining PolyGram in the pre-Universal days, John had been Bob Geldof's lawyer and negotiated the deals for the Live Aid event in 1985, so when it came to contracts, he knew what he was doing.

I had negotiated a Russian-language contract with t.A.Tu., drawn up by our in-house lawyer in Moscow. It was perfect according to Russian law, but now tens of millions of dollars were on the line, and Kennedy wanted a tighter Western recording contract. Our lawyer felt insulted, but the powers that be were insisting on it.

Ivan pretended to be blasé about the deal with Interscope because he never believed I would make Julia and Lena international stars and because his goal was to cause disruption in Russia. He wanted us to believe that he didn't really care about the rest of the world. However, when Interscope became our partner, the possibility of worldwide exposure went to his head, and he stopped working with me and my marketing team and insisted on working only with Interscope directly.

When Kennedy asked me to offer a new contract to t.A.T.u., I wanted to help the girls be more independent of Ivan, so I inserted Julia's and Lena's names on the contract signature lines as third parties instead of them being subordinate to Ivan, like the old contract stipulated. This allowed the girls to be paid their royalties from Universal directly, instead of through Ivan's company. Ivan would always resent me for this.

But I had a big problem with the new contract. Interscope not only insisted on a fifty-fifty split of the future profits from t.A.T.u's album sales with Universal Music Russia, they also wanted to be in charge of all decisions about the band going forward. I had to agree to hand over control of the band to Interscope; their ability to promote artists worldwide was the best in the music industry. I figured that if they were to promote t.A.T.u. like they'd done with Enrique Iglesias and Eminem, it would be better for t.A.T.u. and for Universal Music Russia. Ivan was happy that he would only talk with Interscope directly and no longer have to deal with me or the office in Moscow. But I worried about whether or not Interscope understood what they were getting into with Ivan and if they would be able to control him.

We were cut out. Decisions like changing the cover art from the rebel image of the girls' mugshots that we'd cultivated in Russia to a sexier image of two girls on a motorcycle were out of my hands. Interscope didn't ask for my thoughts on the image change, and I didn't like their decision. When I was in London, I complained to Max Hole, but he sternly reminded me that I was a very lucky guy to have the most powerful label in the world, Interscope, and the most famous label president, Jimmy Iovine, supporting my act.

I shut up after that.

But by allowing the girls to be plugged into the well-running, super-charged promotion arm of Interscope, I was able to sit back and watch t.A.T.u. become global superstars. And more money from overseas royalties came into Universal Music Russia than in the entire history of the company.

I had finally saved the company once and for all and proved that I was a legitimate record executive. But I lost complete control of t.A.T.u. from that day forward.

■

It turned out that Lena was proficient in English as far as recording, but Julia was not. Luckily, Trevor Horn was a master producer, and he would sit in the vocal booth with Julia and help her pronounce the English words that gave her trouble. It was a long process, but it was worth it. Julia's vocal range and ability to hit those unbelievably high notes were crucial to the success of the songs.

With Interscope and Universal behind them, I hoped that the rest of the world would see what I saw in t.A.T.u. and appreciate them for who they truly were. Despite their reputation for controversy, there was much more to them. They were natural entertainers who had performed for the public ever since they were children, and they were gifted musicians. Julia was a classically trained pianist, and I remember her playing Rachmaninoff flawlessly between soundchecks. They may have only been sixteen when I signed them, but they were already savvy about their careers and the music business.

After several grueling weeks of recording in Trevor Horn's London studio, the new t.A.T.u. album in English was ready for release in a few select European countries, starting with Italy. Interscope's international marketing department was directing the album rollout. That staff had been very successful in building international careers for No Doubt, Enrique Iglesias, and the Black Eyed Peas. Now they were promoting t.A.T.u. on the same level as the company's top domestic artists. They had selected the legendary Sanremo Festival in Italy to debut the album and booked t.A.T.u. to perform live for the first time in western Europe during the festival finale.

An LGBTQ-supporting pop band from Russia singing live on the most watched television show of the year in the heart of Catholicism and the shadow of the Vatican—we should have predicted the headlines this would create.

While the girls were performing at Sanremo, I was in a London hotel, attending the annual European meeting of Universal executives. All of my colleagues were there, including the CEOs of Universal Music's offices in each European country. We were there to discuss the company's performance and listen to the new releases. It was the most important conference of the year, where we would meet artists like U2, Bon Jovi, and Elton John and listen to their new music months before their albums would come out, then plan how we would promote them in our respective countries.

I walked into the morning meeting and sat next to my Eastern European colleagues, the CEOs of Hungary, Poland, the Czech Republic, and Slovakia. The pecking order of the territories was reflected in the seating arrangement, with major markets like the United Kingdom, France, and Germany at the head of the table with Jorgen Larsen, chairman/CEO of Universal Music International. The tiny Eastern European countries were seated at the far end because our territories were traditionally the least important to the company's bottom line.

I was worried about t.A.T.u. launching at Sanremo at the same time as the meeting, as the marketing plan depended on them performing well enough in Italy to have a chance for their album to also be released in Germany and France, two of the most important markets in Europe. If they flopped, there would be no promotion in Europe, and we would lose the support of our

French, German, and Italian colleagues. That would have been a mortal blow to my dream of making t.A.T.u. global superstars.

Suddenly, there was a commotion on the other side of the table. The Italian CEO had just entered the room holding up the front page of *la Repubblica*, the most influential newspaper in Rome. There was an above-the-fold photo of Julia kissing Lena. The headline screamed, "Scandalo!" because the Vatican objected to their performance on the grounds that they were promoting homosexuality.

The CEO from Italy demanded, "Who is David from Russia?"

He rushed all the way around to my side of the table. He gave me a big hug and thanked me. The entire room burst into applause, and I saw that the situation was the exact opposite of what I had feared. The CEO was delighted that we were on the newspaper's front page because, to his way of thinking, the publicity would push t.A.T.u. to the top of the Italian music charts.

That was the beginning of the launch, and it turned into a wildfire that spread faster than I had ever imagined. Suddenly, t.A.T.u. was no. 1 in France, Germany, and Belgium, and they topped the UK singles charts for four consecutive weeks. The success sent a clear signal to the rest of Europe that t.A.T.u. was a major international act to be reckoned with, not just some flash-in-the-pan girl group from Russia.

Controversy followed the band and helped sell albums, but their talent as performers gave them staying power. At Sanremo they worked the crowd into an absolute frenzy. In South America we didn't even need to promote them. Young, gay audiences in Brazil and the rest of the continent loved them because their performances resonated. You can fake almost anything on television, but you can't fake it to a packed stadium, and they filled those venues to the rafters every time they played. The fans responded to something authentic, something you couldn't manufacture, and something with more lasting value than any controversy. The rabid reaction of fans started in the gay community but quickly went far beyond it to dominate the mainstream pop music scene in each country they visited.

We were selling hundreds of thousands of CDs every week around the world. When t.A.T.u.'s album was released in Japan, it debuted at no. 1, the first time in history a foreign duo or group had done that, an accomplishment even the Beatles hadn't achieved.

With all this success, my attention turned to promoting them in America. That had always been my dream scenario, but initially, I'd thought the chances were remote. But the album kept selling, and t.A.T.u. kept getting more well-known throughout the world, so what had seemed a distant possibility now was within our reach. I was going to be the first American record executive to promote a Russian band to the top of the charts in America.

Bringing t.A.T.u. to the United States was also risky. When I signed them to Universal Music Russia, I knew that all the way to the Vatican and beyond there would be a lot of controversy surrounding this band from Russia. But Interscope was able to open doors in the American market that would have been closed otherwise. Jimmy Iovine had a secret weapon in his promotion department—Brenda Romano, the best radio promoter in the business. Jimmy also used his influence to get t.A.T.u. on television shows like the *Billboard Music Awards* and *Total Request Live (TRL)*.

Then the biggest door of them all opened. When we were in New York for *TRL*, we learned that Interscope had booked the girls on *The Tonight Show with Jay Leno* and they needed to travel to Los Angeles to appear on the show at NBC Studios in Burbank. If only I had known then that their appearance would lead to one of the biggest scandals in the history of network television. It wasn't about kissing or gay rights but, unexpectedly, something else entirely.

And it would jeopardize everything with Interscope.

12

BROADCAST STANDARDS

I was thrilled with t.A.T.u. being booked on *The Tonight Show*. Everyone in the music industry knew there was no better way to promote a new music artist in America than with an appearance on network TV, but Lena and Julia didn't see what was to be gained by being on Jay Leno's show. I was scheduled to fly back to Moscow to talk to the US ambassador regarding music piracy, a meeting I had been trying to arrange for a long time. Before heading to LAX, I met the girls in their hotel room and explained that appearing on the show was a huge opportunity that could turn them into household names in America. I pleaded with them to take it seriously.

I told them how the Beatles and the Rolling Stones had broken through in America by performing on *The Ed Sullivan Show*, and they could do the same thing by appearing with Jay.

They weren't impressed.

They had grown up seeing the Russian government manipulate television for propaganda purposes, and for them, MTV was the only safe space from the Kremlin for Russian musicians, so they didn't understand how being on *The Tonight Show* might benefit them. Still, I stressed that this appearance was in their best interest and would go a long way toward making them famous in the United States. As I departed, Julia winked and promised they wouldn't let me down.

I thought my job was done, so I flew back to Moscow while they prepared for their American television network debut. Although I would have liked to have been backstage at the NBC studio with the band and perhaps be introduced to Jay Leno, the meeting with the US ambassador to discuss the pirate organizations and to explain how they were hurting the record industry was too important. The flight from LAX lasted about twelve hours, and I couldn't get any phone calls while in the air. When I landed at Moscow's Sheremetyevo Airport, I checked my phone. There were fifteen missed calls. Something terrible must have happened.

By the time I got through customs, it was about five o'clock in the morning in Los Angeles. So I had to wait to talk to anybody.

When I finally did, I learned what happened. In their live performances, Julia and Lena's provocative kiss would take place during the instrumental breakdown about halfway into their song. *The Tonight Show* expressly asked them not to do so, and our whole team had agreed to that request. They did it anyway, which was a daring move, but the camera cut away as they approached each other and focused on the backing band instead. Since viewers at home did not see the kiss, it was not a big deal and not the problem—not that it would have been.

At this point in time, despite the show's request, same-sex kisses were common on NBC's hit comedy series *Will & Grace*. And in the closing moments of *The Tonight Show* episode on February 25, 2003, Jay Leno chatted with the girls onstage and called out the show's other guest, Arsenio Hall, who surprised the host by kissing him on the lips in a nod to the unseen t.A.T.u. smooch.

I was told that after the speech I gave them in the hotel, Lena and Julia made a spontaneous decision. If being on this show was the big deal I had said it was, Julia thought they needed to shock the audience: the girls went onstage wearing white t-shirts with "Khuy Voyne" written on them in black marker. I guess no one at NBC bothered to translate the Russian words.

But after the show, NBC received a lot of complaints from Russian immigrants in the United States, who very well knew that "Khuy Voyne" in English was "Fuck War" and were offended by the vulgarity. The girls were ratted out by their own people.

This was in February 2003, when the American invasion of Iraq had broad support in the United States but was very unpopular around the world. Russians had rallied around the United States after the attacks on 9/11. President Putin was famous for being the first foreign leader to reach out to President Bush to offer condolences and help. But by the time the

US invasion of Iraq occurred two years later, the Russians had turned on America and no longer supported our war on terror. Russian foreign policy had been more in sync with the United States during the final years of the Soviet Union, under Gorbachev and after the collapse of the Soviet Union; this strong relationship continued through the Yeltsin years. Under Putin, Russia began to take an independent path. Russia was against the US war in Iraq, and t.A.T.u. took the opportunity to demonstrate it on network television in America. Their symbolic gesture went viral worldwide, making them heroes to the antiwar movement.

Saying "Fuck" on network television was the biggest no-no in the book. Networks could be heavily fined by the Federal Communications Commission (FCC) if the expletive was heard on the air and their privately owned television stations could lose their broadcasting licenses, so the matter was not treated lightly.

The "Fuck War" T-shirts got t.A.T.u. permanently banned from ever appearing on *The Tonight Show* again, and the executives at Universal were furious at me for a minute. They were worried that other Universal artists might get banned from future bookings as a consequence. But t.A.T.u.'s album sales skyrocketed, and they got booked on *Jimmy Kimmel Live!* the day after Jay Leno banned them. On *Saturday Night Live*, Lindsay Lohan and Rachel Dratch performed a sketch where they played a Russian lesbian duo called d.A.D.i. The Jay Leno scandal got t.A.T.u. noticed in America. Soon the album was topping the *Billboard* charts, fulfilling my wildest dream.

In an interview with *Billboard*, I said, "It was just ten years ago that Americans and Russians had missiles pointed at each other. Now we've got Russian CDs on sale at Tower Records in Los Angeles."

I felt like we had dodged a bullet. I didn't lose my job, and t.A.T.u. didn't get banned from any future bookings, nor did any other artist on Universal's roster. That would happen later.

But there was one lasting effect of the whole incident: t.A.T.u.'s antiwar stance made me rethink my feelings about the Iraq War. Like so many Americans, I'd gotten caught up in the visuals on TV of the shock-and-awe campaign in the initial invasion. The reporting on CNN made it seem like a sporting event, but as the war started to go badly and I found myself living in a country that opposed the war, I asked myself, "Why is the world against the United States?" Julia and Lena's stunt on *The Tonight Show* forced me to confront this head on, and I stopped supporting the war after the Jay Leno scandal. To go into the heart of American TV, in Hollywood (technically Burbank), and make such a bold pacifistic statement against the US invasion of Iraq had to be considered one of the bravest antiwar statements ever made on network television, even dating back to the Vietnam War.

13

"GET THEM OUT OF MONACO!"

After *The Tonight Show* ban, I started traveling with t.A.T.u. more frequently to prevent them from getting into more trouble. It wouldn't be long before their next big controversy. It was October 12, 2003, and we were at the World Music Awards, an annual charity event hosted by Prince Albert II of Monaco in a fancy casino right on the French Riviera. It looked like something out of a James Bond movie. In attendance were some of the wealthiest people in the world, and there were diamonds, pearls, and white tuxedos as far as the eye could see. At the time, t.A.T.u. was the world's biggest selling artist, so they were invited to perform that night and to receive an award, all of which would be broadcast on European television.

Julia and Lena wanted people to give money to the charity, but they had an unorthodox idea of how to go about it. Rather than give a passionate speech describing the charity's vital work in the developing world, they brought toy AK-47s and planned to take donations from the audience at gunpoint.

It was only two years after 9/11, and terrorism still weighed very heavily on people's minds, so it was unlikely that the audience would take this plan in good humor. Before Julia and Lena could go onstage, security blocked their entrance with the toy assault weapons. Julia and Lena refused to go on without them, and they ended up missing their entire segment. I still remember being backstage, trying to explain to Melissa Corken, the executive producer of the World Music Awards, that Julia and Lena had only wanted people to donate to the charity.

She was furious and screamed at me, "Get them out of Monaco!"

She chewed me out in full view of the show's host, tennis megastar Anna Kournikova. I was worried that Anna might get upset with me, too, because she was married to Enrique Iglesias, the most prominent artist I had worked with up to that point. Luckily, she didn't. But t.A.T.u. was sent home, and I was no longer welcome in Monaco.

We were all on the same flight back to Moscow. Julia tried to make light of the situation, but the rest of their entourage was in shock at what had happened. I sat in the back of the plane just to get away from the girls. I was seriously worried that this was going to be bad for them and bad for me. But once again, it wasn't.

However, the worst was still to come.

■

It was 2005, and t.A.T.u. had gone to Tokyo to perform on *Music Station*, a popular Japanese show on the TV Asahi channel.

Ivan, t.A.T.u.'s manager, reappeared after the American tour ended. He hadn't accompanied the band to the United States, but he did go to Japan for their promotional tour. Since I was no longer responsible for the band—Interscope was—I hadn't had any contact with Ivan in months, but I was hearing from people close to him that he was getting increasingly erratic. I assumed Interscope had him under control, but we would soon find out they did not. He was watching the show live from his hotel room and saw that Bridgestone, the Japanese tire company, was sponsoring the group's appearance. He thought that Bridgestone should have paid him for the performance too. That's not how it works, but it was what he believed, so he called the studio and told Julia and Lena not to go on.

The network came back after a commercial for what was supposed to be t.A.T.u.'s segment, but instead of seeing an energetic performance, the audience saw thirty seconds of dead air: Julia and Lena were not there. If I had been there in person, I might have been able to salvage the situation, but I was in Moscow. I had to rely on Universal's Japanese representatives to smooth things over, but there were Japanese-speaking people and Russian-speaking people there, with no one to negotiate the language barrier.

After that I spent weeks apologizing, but it didn't help. The head of the station was deeply offended by t.A.T.u.'s actions—t.A.T.u. was banned for life from the show, and every other Universal artist who had been booked was banned for the rest of the year. That included Bon Jovi, and nobody bans Bon Jovi! A big release for Rihanna was coming up, but it was bumped because she wasn't allowed to appear on *Music Station*, and I was blamed by the people at her label, Def Jam, for that. Universal artists were allowed back on the show the following year, but the six-month ban took a toll. That show was the most crucial promotional tool we had in Japan, and being locked out of it for half a year cost us money in the form of music that we couldn't sell, because we couldn't promote it. It was an expensive scandal.

Controversies like these caused me some stress when they happened, but they always blew over, and they were vastly outweighed by all the good that came from signing t.A.T.u., particularly since their success came at a time when Universal badly needed it. Luckily, the t.A.T.u. album came out of nowhere and sold five million copies, generating nearly $100 million in revenue for Universal. It set records in twenty-seven countries, where it went gold or platinum. It's one of the most profitable record deals ever made.

The duo t.A.T.u. made history by being the biggest-selling act from Russia of all time, but there's more to their historical run than album sales. They came from one of the most repressive countries for LGBTQ youth, and being the first Russian music act to talk openly about gay rights took bravery, giving them an authenticity that spoke directly to the hearts of gay youth worldwide. From Brazil to Japan and everywhere in between, Julia and Lena were seen as champions of the gay community, and that's their most lasting impact today.

The success of t.A.T.u. also came when US-Russia relations were at their highest peak since the end of the Cold War. America and Russia were working together on many fronts, including developing the Russian music industry, and t.A.T.u.'s success made a significant contribution. Our partner, Interscope Records, shepherded t.A.T.u. through the same marketing and promotion machinery that made American artists like Guns N' Roses and Eminem global superstars. Universal Russia could never have promoted t.A.T.u. further than Russia and Eastern Europe without Interscope.

It was a true Russian-American joint venture, and even some Russian government officials came around and started bragging about the success of their homegrown global stars Julia and Lena. The US ambassador in Moscow would point to t.A.T.u. as a prime example of successful business cooperation between the two nations. As an American in Moscow, I had never felt more pride for my country or more optimistic about the future. I was very proud that I had helped build a bridge between Russia and America.

∎

On a personal level, t.A.T.u.'s success dramatically altered my career trajectory. Universal promoted me to VP of Eastern Europe. I started opening new record company offices throughout the region for Universal, including in Ukraine. This promotion elevated me to the level of the music industry's most elite players, and for a moment in time, I became one of the most successful record executives in the international music industry. I had proven myself to my Russian music industry colleagues too—a difficult task after a lot of early resistance and doubts that an American could run a successful record company in Russia. I had the Russian music industry's hardest-working marketing and promotion team, a staff of forty young and talented Russians who made Universal Music the market leader. Even though I was a foreigner, they believed in me, and it was very gratifying to deliver for them.

Julia and Lena eventually fired Ivan and took control of the t.A.T.u. brand. You can trace their path to finding their own voices and power back to the Jay Leno incident. They made their antiwar stance on their own, without Ivan. *They* were the disrupters, not their chaos-driven manager. When John Kennedy of Universal had insisted on a stronger new contract for t.A.T.u., it gave me the chance to write Julia's and Lena's names into the document, which gave them the power to do this. If that hadn't happened, the band would always have belonged to Ivan.

They would record a few more albums before they eventually split to pursue solo careers. In 2023 t.A.T.u. celebrated the twentieth anniversary of their American debut, and to this day, they are still the only musical act from Russia to achieve worldwide success.

Unfortunately, in 2022, the clouds of war plunged this region of the world into darkness again, something not seen since the end of the Cold War. At the beginning of this millennium, Ukraine was the first country outside of Russia to invite t.A.T.u. to perform, marking their first international success, and the largest crowds found were in stadiums in Kyiv and Kharkiv, both of which are now, as of this writing, located in war zones. Ukrainian teens, like Russian teens, voraciously embraced t.A.T.u.'s lyrics about love, equal rights, and freedom. They quickly became the most popular band from Russia ever seen in Ukraine.

My heavy heart for the people suffering in Ukraine was lifted slightly when I saw an image on TV of two Ukrainian girls wearing t.A.T.u.'s infamous "Fuck War" T-shirts, the same ones that got them banned from TV in America. I smiled and thought, "Maybe this is t.A.T.u.'s lasting impact."

It's a message that's more vital today than ever before.

Now adult women, Julia and Lena still generate controversy. There has been much speculation that Julia and Lena are not really gay, despite their caressing and kissing onstage. They have both said they never claimed to be lesbians. I do not know if they were faking their sexuality, but they were definitely not faking their support of LGBTQ rights in Russia and world-wide. They were the first pop stars in Russia to take a stand on these issues. Since t.A.T.u.'s phenomenal run of success, Russia has become much more repressive toward LGBTQ rights and has passed laws forbidding the "spread of gay propaganda." If those laws had been in effect in 2003, Julia and Lena—and possibly I—could have ended up in a Russian prison or been sent to a labor camp in Siberia. It's a great irony that t.A.T.u. was invited to reunite and perform at the 2014 Olympics opening ceremony in Russia, even though their music was in violation of the propaganda laws.

The other great irony about t.A.T.u. is that, despite making one of the loudest antiwar statements ever on American TV in 2003, today they are silent as their country invades its neighbor Ukraine. Like so many contemporary Russian artists, they have been cowered into silence for fear of repression by the government. There are a few brave artists willing to speak out against the illegal invasion, but Julia and Lena are not among them.

INTERLUDE

BUILDING THE RUSSIAN MUSIC INDUSTRY

Russia was broke and in chaos in the 1990s. Contract killings, Mafia warfare, and political assassinations were an everyday occurrence. "Gangster capitalism" was a common phrase used to describe this period of transition from a centrally planned economy to a free market one. The Russian music industry was also in terrible shape before I arrived in Moscow. I didn't know if I could make a difference, but this is what inspired me to come to Russia in the first place. I was born to do this.

Decades of central planning and communist ideology meant that basic Western business concepts, like sales and marketing, were totally foreign ideas to Soviet citizens, unless you were involved in selling something outside of the state or marketing something unapproved by the government, which meant you were working on the black market—and that was illegal. That would mean imprisonment in Siberia, for sure.

There had been only one record label in the Soviet Union: the government-owned Melodiya. And if you weren't a useful artist for the Kremlin and their state propaganda purposes, you didn't get a deal with Melodiya.

There was no organization of producers or songwriters, just a very scattered network of government employees who produced music acceptable to the Kremlin. At the same time, there was a vast underground of black market bootleg albums pirating popular artists from the West, like the Beatles and Pink Floyd. The black market was illegal, but at least it did understand the principles of supply and demand and marketing.

This was allowed, as government officials looked the other way as long as music from the West wasn't fomenting protests among Soviet citizens. Some bootleggers were busted and sent to jail, but overall, this market was not easy to control.

This was the state of the industry when I started in the finance department at PolyGram, and I was eager to build a modern music industry in Russia, as piracy was killing the industry and the labels were in disarray. Something had to be done. I learned the basic rules of the American music industry as quickly as I could. I had an MBA and understood business practices very well. I learned about royalties, songwriter rights, and master recordings—all the mechanics of running a record company.

But none of that was of any use unless the problem of music piracy could be solved. Nine out every ten CDs sold in Russia were counterfeit, depriving record companies of desperately needed revenue to survive. When I became CEO of Universal Music Russia, I was called to headquarters in London. Richard Constant, the head legal counsel for Universal International, a curmudgeon-like character who spoke like Winston Churchill, gave me marching orders to go back to Moscow and take the war to the pirates. I was to start by organizing an industry trade group to unite the industry in the fight against piracy. I felt like James Bond getting an assignment from M—I didn't want to let him down. It was exciting and cool. No other record executive was chosen for an assignment like this.

I knew I needed to create a core group of record companies to get behind me, so when I got back to Moscow, I started inviting my colleagues from the other major Western labels in Russia: EMI, Sony Music, Warner Music, and BMG. I knew they would join this new national group because they had no choice; their head office would insist, just like mine had. We had once been the only American record company in Moscow, but after our success, we were joined by the other majors.

Our mission was to be a part of the worldwide trade organization, the International Federation of Phonographic Industries (IFPI), which is based in London. In the United States, the trade organization for the music industry is the Recording Industry Association of America (RIAA). There are counterparts in many countries, but there was no such association in Russia. That was a huge disadvantage, and I saw the need to have one and worked hard to create an organization that would be part of the IFPI with the ability to lobby the government to protect the music industry, including intellectual property rights. We would fight piracy and be an effective force, much like the RIAA.

The folks at IFPI headquarters in London agreed to set up the structure for a group that would exist in Russia—a group that would include all of the legal record labels existing in the country. After convincing the major record labels to get on board, a bigger challenge would be convincing the local Russian record labels to join; I expected them to be skeptical about teaming up with the Western record companies, as well as distrustful of me—a competitor. In 2000 new Russian labels besides Melodiya were opening offices. There were different kinds of labels: some were connected to the government TV channel, while others were secretly connected to a Mafia group or a pirate factory, with a label as their façade. There were labels owned by legendary artists of the Soviet era who wanted to do business in the new Russia. These musical veterans were sometimes connected to oligarchs or organized crime.

The most famous was a singer-songwriter named Igor Krutoy, who owned a record label and a TV channel called Muz-TV that broadcast Russian-language music videos on a pay-for-play basis. It was totally transparent, like legalized payola, and the ultimate vanity project. Oligarchs would pay for their wives' music videos, which would then go into heavy rotation.

I had to recruit enough labels from this surly bunch to form a national trade group in Russia. None of them trusted each other or me. The whole experience made me feel like I was in *The Godfather* movie, acting on behalf of Universal and the entire music business.

When we gathered the leaders of all the big and small record labels around a long table in IFPI's downtown Moscow office, it made me think of the famous scene when Don Corleone brings together the heads of the crime families to make peace and fight a common enemy. I explained the benefits of being an industry organization, emphasizing that we could fight piracy in a more effective way if we were united. I asked Igor Pozhitkov, the local IFPI representative and a legal scholar, to present his plan to lobby the Russian government to do something about fighting piracy and protecting intellectual property rights. He described IFPI's commitment to helping us fight for new laws. But the Russian label heads were skeptical and didn't understand why they would have to pay dues or what good would come from lobbying the government, which they considered to be corrupt.

After the speeches it was time to take a vote. Who would sign up for this new music industry group? I already knew that the Western labels would agree to join; if Universal was going to be a part of this, they also wanted in. The smaller Russian companies were the first to sign up because being associated with a worldwide group enhanced their status. It was a surprise when Real Records, the label connected to the government, wanted in, as I knew they didn't trust me. I'm certain they joined so they could keep an eye on me.

The head of that label, Alyona Mikhailova, was one of the toughest women I had ever met in Russian show business. She had to be since her bosses were in the Kremlin. She didn't like me and how well I was doing with Russian artists. After Alsou's success at Eurovision, Alyona accused me in the press of stealing her away from Real Records, but that wasn't true. I later found out my old Rasputin-like nemesis, Valeriy, was secretly behind the negative attacks on me. In any case, Alyona was a patriot, and she thought I should stick with international artists and keep away from Russians. It was very important that her label join our organization because it would make us stronger. But they were dangerous and a direct connection to the Kremlin.

Some of the pirate labels also wanted to join our nascent organization but were politely declined. They thought they could sneak in disguised as legitimate record labels, even though we knew their backers were organized-crime groups. They were insulted, but we only wanted businesses that were legitimate and honest. Now that we were finally ready to have our own trade organization, we had a healthy mix of Russian and foreign labels.

It was time to choose a chairperson. I did have the trust of many of the members, and the ones who didn't trust me didn't want the leadership re-sponsibilities. As much as they wanted to shut down the pirates, they didn't want to be the public face for that fight. So I received the most votes and was elected chair.

We hired a general manager, Alexey Urgrinovich, a no-nonsense Russian with law-enforcement connections, who did the day-to-day work, which included keeping our members focused on fighting piracy—and not each other. We called ourselves the National Federation of Phonographic Producers (NFPP)—a terrible name, but at least we had a viable trade association with our own office and staff.

■

It was an honor to be voted the first chairman of the NFPP and to officially represent the Russian music industry group. I got my first chance to fulfill these duties when I attended a worldwide gathering of record executives at an IFPI conference in Washington, DC. While I was there, I met with Yuri Ushakov, Russia's ambassador to the United States, to enroll him in our fight against piracy. The Russian Embassy is a mammoth structure behind a huge iron gate that wraps around a large territory and is mounted with cameras and security guards. It looks entirely impenetrable.

I walked into this fortress to plead the case for saving the Russian music industry. One hurdle was that the Russian government didn't take the music industry seriously as a potential tax revenue base. One major difference between the American and Russian music businesses in those early days was that in the Unites States, record companies made their money by selling records. In Russia the main source of money for the music business was live performances. In Russia a lot of business was done in cash to avoid taxes. I couldn't do that. I had to have contracts and be totally transparent.

We had to be clean and honest, and at first, that was a disadvantage. But that began to change when artists realized that if they signed with Universal, they were not going to be cheated out of their earned income. So the best talent in the country wanted to sign with us. Because we were an American company, I knew we were under greater scrutiny, and Russia's black market—where everyone avoids taxes—was going to be a trap. Artists would have to get used to dealing with a legitimate record label that pays its taxes.

I took the opportunity to give the ambassador my quick speech on why Russia should look at Sweden as the best example of helping the music industry generate export revenue. I think my statement that more ABBA records are sold than Volvos made an impression on him, although he would do little to help us other than to send a cable back to Moscow suggesting they keep an eye on us.

Back in Russia, *Billboard* was opening an office, and we made a deal with them to manage and publish an album sales chart for the country. The InterMedia news agency—run by two capable veterans of Russian show business, Eugene Safronov and Alexander Tikhonov—agreed to certify our gold and platinum discs. Presenting these awards to artists and songwriters, something unheard of in the USSR, was another step forward in building a modern Russian music industry.

I was always impressed by seeing gold and platinum awards on the walls of Western record companies—I even received one from Eminem once, which was very motivating.

I had been to the *Billboard Music Awards* in Las Vegas with t.A.T.u., which inspired me to create an awards show for Russia. *Billboard* wasn't ready to be involved with such a project, so we teamed with Pepsi and some other sponsors. That created a lot of tension between the major Western labels, as Universal was selling more records than anyone else, and we were going to win most, if not all, of the awards. That wasn't going to fly. The Russians wanted to win awards as well, and for the first time, our trade group was in danger of imploding.

So we created specific awards for Russian artists. Many of my international Universal acts weren't interested in performing on the telecast, so the guest artists were all Russian.

Unfortunately, the end result was a very lame awards show; it was so bad that no TV channel picked it up, and it was not broadcast. It was held at a theater in a casino in Moscow, and tickets were distributed to families and friends. The awards show was a great way to keep the national organization from falling apart, but the only thing that really mattered for the survival of our industry was fighting piracy. We had to stop piracy or go out of business.

Two Americans were integral to that battle. The first was Jay Berman, the head of the RIAA who became the leader of the IFPI. He made several visits to Moscow to encourage our members to fight piracy and protect artists. The second was Neil Turkewitz, the main lobbyist at the RIAA. He was pushing for a tough response to piracy in Russia, lobbying members of Congress in Washington, DC, to put an end to this criminal practice.

But our model of fighting piracy by lobbying the Russian government was going to take a long time, and the music industry couldn't afford any extra time; the situation was desperate. There was always the threat of the national group potentially falling apart, and the rate of 90 percent of albums being pirated was choking the business. We had to employ a stronger model quickly, or there would no longer be a Russian music industry.

Our role model was the movie industry since they were more aggressive than we were when it came to shutting down movie and DVD piracy. They had strong support from Jack Valenti and the Motion Picture Association of America (MPAA) in the United States. I knew we needed to take extremely strong action, but I had no idea how dangerous this path would be.

I was certain we had to succeed, but I did not want to die for Elton John's royalties.

MY FATHER

OUR FAMILY FARM IN OHIO

MY LITTLE SISTER JILL

MY FIRST TIME ON RED SQUARE, 1993

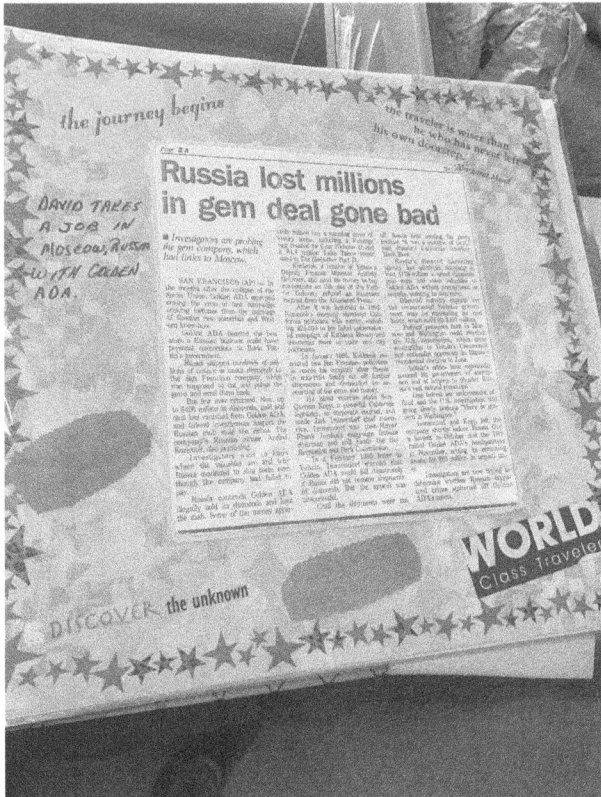

MY FIRST JOB IN RUSSIA WITH GOLDEN ADA ENDS UP IN AN INTERNATIONAL
DIAMOND SCANDAL

ДЭВИД ДЖАНК
ГЕНЕРАЛЬНЫЙ ДИРЕКТОР

UNIVERSAL MUSIC
121096 Москва, ул. Кастанаевская, 14А
ТЕЛ +7 095 737 0090 ФАКС +7 095 737 3322/3655
E-MAIL David.Junk@universalmusic.ru www.universalmusic.ru

UNIVERSAL MUSIC BUSINESS CARD

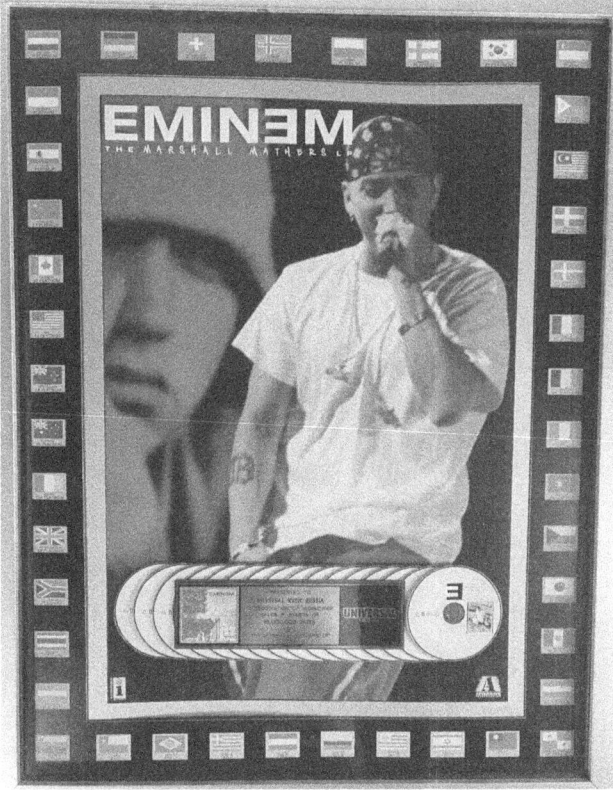

EMINEM DISC FOR TOP SELLING COUNTRIES IN THE WORLD

MY MOTHER AND GRANDMOTHER VISITING ME IN MOSCOW AT UNIVERSAL MUSIC'S OFFICES

BACKSTAGE WITH DIANA ROSS AT THE HERMITAGE OPERA THEATER IN MOSCOW

RONAN KEATING, LUCIAN GRAINGE, MAX HOLE, AND COUNTRY EXECUTIVES FROM UNIVERSAL MUSIC IN EUROPE. I'M IN THE BACK ROW 2ND FROM RIGHT.

ALSOU ON STAGE IN MOSCOW

MY FIRST SIGNING. ALSOU PRESS CONFERENCE.

"SOLO," ALSOU'S SONG FOR EUROVISION, IS HER FIRST HIT RECORD.

AWARDING ENRIQUE IGLESIAS A PLATINUM DISC FOR HIS DUET WITH ALSOU, THE BIGGEST SELLING SINGLE IN RUSSIA

JULIA VOLKOVA AND LENA KATINA FROM t.A.T.u.

t.A.T.u. WINS THE IFPI PLATINUM SALES AWARD, FIRST TIME EVER FOR RUSSIA. [L TO R] JOHN KENNEDY, UNIVERSAL MUSIC; THOMAS HEDSTRÖM, UNIVERSAL MUSIC; LENA KATINA, IVAN SHAPOVALEV, PRODUCER; t.A.T.u.; JULIA VOLKOVA; ME; JAY BERMAN, IFPI

SMASH!! ON SET FOR THEIR FIRST MUSIC VIDEO FOR "BELLE"

DOLPHIN

DETSL

CHAIRMAN OF THE NFPP PLAQUE

COLLEAGUES FROM RUSSIAN OFFICES OF SONY, WARNER, AND EMI

POP ICONS IN RUSSIA, AVRAAM RUSSO AND PHILIPP KIRKOROV

CONCERT PROMOTER NADIA SOLOVIEVA

MY MARKETING DIRECTOR ASYA WITH METALLICA IN KIEV

UNIVERSAL

UNIVERSAL MUSIC INTERNATIONAL
NEWS RELEASE

UNIVERSAL MUSIC RUSSIA MD DAVID JUNK ASSUMES RESPONSIBILITY FOR EASTERN EUROPEAN LICENSEES

MOSCOW, 22 APRIL, 2003 – David Junk, Managing Director of Universal Music Russia, is extending his management responsibilities to include Universal Music International's licensees in the former Eastern Bloc. The new duties were announced today by UMI President and Chief Operating Officer John Kennedy, to whom Junk reports, and take effect immediately.

The Eastern European countries with licensees now within David Junk's remit are Bulgaria, Estonia, Latvia, Lithuania, Ukraine, Romania, Serbia, Slovenia and Croatia. In addition, UMI's exclusive licensees in Iceland, Malta and Gibraltar are now accountable to him.

Junk will continue to manage Universal Music Russia, building on the worldwide success of t.A.T.u., the locally signed act developed in partnership with Universal Music Group's Interscope Records. The female pop duo's single *All The Things She Said* has topped the charts in nine countries to date, while their *200km/H In The Wrong Lane* album has sold 2.5 million copies globally. They are the first act from Russia to achieve this level of global success: *200km/H In The Wrong Lane* recently hit No. 1 in Japan, making chart history there as the first international debut album ever to reach the summit.

Universal Music Russia has significant forthcoming releases from Russia's most successful female solo artist, Alsou, and a new male pop duo, Smash.

Junk, a native of Ohio, USA, in 1996 joined PolyGram (now Universal Music) Russia, the first western record company to establish a subsidiary in the country. He was promoted to Managing Director in April 1999.

"It has been a great joy and personal achievement to bring pop music from the former Soviet Union to the rest of the world," said Junk, "and I eagerly look forward to helping create other musical bridges for the former Eastern Bloc countries. I truly believe that Eastern Europe is one of the most exciting and progressive repertoire centres in the music business today."

UNIVERSAL MUSIC PRESS RELEASE ANNOUNCING NEW VICE PRESIDENT OF EASTERN EUROPE

MY WIFE NATALIA AND ELTON JOHN BACKSTAGE AT THE KREMLIN PALACE

BORIS ZOSIMOV AND THOMAS HEDSTRÖM

PAINTING BY ALINA ZANGIEVA, SURVIVOR OF THE 2004
BELSAN SCHOOL SEIGE

UKRAINIAN WINNERS OF *AMERICAN CHANCE* TV SHOW WITH PRODUCERS WAX LTD. IN HOLLYWOOD

IN SOCHI, RUSSIA, AT THE 2014 WINTER OLYMPICS

OLYMPIC STADIUM, HOME OF THE GIBSON GUITAR SHOWROOM IN MOSCOW

DIANA ARBENINA AND DMITRI KONOV, MY SUCCESSOR AT UNIVERSAL MUSIC RUSSIA

AWARDING PRIZE WINNERS A GIBSON ACOUSTIC AT THE INTERNATIONAL DELPHIC GAMES IN VOLGOGRAD, RUSSIA

GIBSON MILLION DOLLAR GUITAR

PART 5

THE BUILDING PROJECT

14

PIRATE BATTLE

The largest outdoor market in Europe for counterfeit CDs and DVDs, according to the IFPI, was called Gorbushka. It was located in downtown Moscow, next to a drama theater and concert hall, in full view of the Moscow city authorities. I was curious and saw for myself how much this market was stealing from the music industry. It was hugely popular, with thousands of Russians coming from all over the country to buy illegal products.

Piracy was so widespread that Russians could buy counterfeit CDs at kiosks throughout the city—on sidewalks, in train stations, and at the airport—anywhere with enough square footage of floor space.

It was impossible to tell if these kiosks were selling products that had fallen off the back of a truck or if something more sinister was involved. These stands were selling everything—cigarettes, gin and tonic in a can, and candy bars, so why not Elton John CDs?

These black market CDs were selling for the equivalent of two dollars. Legitimate CDs manufactured by companies like PolyGram and Universal sold for twenty dollars. Universal paid royalties to artists and songwriters; the pirates did not. There was no way we could compete in such a market.

The counterfeit CDs were easy to spot because the pirates weren't interested in making replicas of a particular album. They would cherry-pick an artist's greatest hits and maybe include a couple of other songs. Instead of making counterfeit versions of a particular Beatles album, the pirates would make CDs of the biggest hits from the group's entire catalog and throw in "Imagine" by John Lennon as the final track.

I could understand why people bought them. They had the songs every-one wanted, you could get them anywhere, and they cost 10 percent of what we were charging for the official versions. We were also limited by having to sell our products exclusively at legal record stores, and Moscow only had six of those. In the rest of the country, from St. Petersburg to Vladivostok, there were none.

The situation was costing Universal and its artists money, but that wasn't the only problem. An IFPI investigation revealed that the pirate factories were controlled by organized crime groups who used the money from coun-terfeit CD sales to support international drug trafficking, sex trafficking, weapons trafficking, and terrorism.

There were two approaches to putting the pirates out of business. One was my attempt to get the laws changed. Then there was the approach fa-vored by my colleague Chris Abel-Smith, the president of Premier Video.

Chris had worked for the London-based major record label and chief ri-val to Universal, the EMI Group in the Middle East, then he joined the film industry, where he'd helped major studios like Warner Bros. move into Rus-sia. He also had connections to the security services, and Queen Elizabeth II was his godmother. He reminded me of the Most Interesting Man in the World from the Dos Equis commercials.

Chris was my closest friend during my time in Russia and the only other expatriate I socialized with. I invited him to all of our record-company par-ties as well as concerts by everyone from Sting to Rammstein. We bonded because we were both warriors in the fight against Russian pirates, with me on the music side and him on the film side.

Chris liked to be on the front lines with the security types. He had personal bodyguards and retired KGB agents working for him, as well as well-placed sources at intelligence agencies to tip him off. If the pirates were transporting counterfeit DVDs from Russia to Eastern Europe by train, Chris and his team would coordinate with Interpol and stop the trains to confiscate them. They weren't afraid of anybody.

I wanted to confront this problem in a different way. I wanted Russia and the international community to put effective laws into place. That would take the backing of other multinational record labels.

My timing was good because IFPI chairman Jay Berman, who had been one of the toughest lobbyists in America when he'd been with the RIAA, was now focused on Russia alongside me. Jay thought the best way to combat the pirates was to give local law enforcement assistance through Interpol. That organization tracked the pirate factories and kept tabs on them whenever they moved.

Moving a factory was easy. Most of them were on army bases because the military was in cahoots with the criminals. The pirates would just load the CD duplication machines onto a truck and move them to a different army base if they had to.

Jay brought two retired Interpol agents to Moscow to accompany local law enforcement on a raid of one of the factories, and some colleagues and I went along with them early one morning. They handed us all bulletproof vests to put on, which was a first for me. I had never even been in a situation where I thought I might need one. I had never considered the possibility that I might die in a hail of bullets all in the name of helping an artist retain more of their royalties. I'm certain no other Universal record executive was risking their life for an artist's income.

We were loaded into vans and given a police escort to the factory. This was a special police division created for the express purpose of fighting piracy, and one of the officers told me what to expect. "What we're going to do is enter the factory," he said. "Once we're in, we'll take photos of everything and get fingerprints."

He said it was important to identify where the duplication machines had come from. They were snuck in from other parts of Europe, and we needed to learn where. We also needed to review the counterfeit discs themselves and sort out which artists were from Universal and which ones were from BMG, Sony, EMI, Warner, or from a small independent label. Every confiscated counterfeit CD had to be carefully analyzed to determine who owned the copyright. All of that evidence would be presented in court. My job was to confirm that the pirate factory was violating international copyright laws, which would be the cornerstone of our legal case.

Moscow is surrounded by forests, so when we drove half an hour from the city to the factory, we were really in the middle of nowhere. The factory itself was surrounded by fences, and the only way in was through an automated parking gate.

Just past the gate were a couple of guys whom I would describe as thugs. They weren't wearing military uniforms or badges, just baseball caps, pullovers, and oversized jackets to keep them warm while they stood around, smoking cigarettes.

The members of our Moscow police escort went over to talk to them while the former Interpol agents stayed behind with me. The police spoke to the guards for a while, but they were far enough away that I couldn't hear what they were saying.

One of the ex-agents looked at me and said, "I haven't seen an American record executive on a pirate raid before, and I've been doing this all over the world for years. How the hell did you get here?"

"I came to Russia through PolyGram," I replied. "Now I'm with Universal, and I'm here to make sure Mariah Carey gets her royalties."

That got a laugh out of everybody. Then they asked Chris how he got his job. "I got my job when Thomas Topadze was murdered," he said.

The laughing stopped. Thomas Topadze had been director general of Varus Video, a distributor based in Moscow, and he had been Chris's boss early on in Russia. Chris had been hired by Varus because they figured if he could handle working in a hotspot like the Middle East, he could handle working in Russia.

Until that point American studios wouldn't work in Russia because of the piracy. Through Varus Video's distribution network, American studios saw a way to get back into the Russian film market. They signed deals with Warner Bros. and were ready to move in, full speed ahead.

Varus had a big party at the Slavyanskaya Hotel in Moscow in 1994 to celebrate those deals. At one point Thomas stood up and made a speech worthy of Winston Churchill in which he described the many ways in which the war against piracy would be fought. Less than a week later, he was shot and killed at the door of his Moscow apartment.

"So that's how I got promoted," Chris explained. He moved over to Premier Video two years later.

As we continued to wait in the van, he regaled us with tales of trying to shut down pirate factories. His approach was risky, to put it mildly. "I was on a raid a couple of weeks ago," he said. "A police officer brought me in. I hid in the trunk of his car, and when he parked, I snuck out, found a ladder, and climbed up to the factory window. I could see the machines printing DVDs, but while I was up there, the police officer I was with heard that military police were coming, over his radio. They had caught me on their security cameras."

Chris said they just barely escaped. These factories were guarded by the military and the Kremlin's property department, and it's entirely possible that they would have killed him if they'd caught him. I could tell the tough agents were impressed with Chris's heroics.

It was taking a while for our police escort to get us through the gate. It was evident something was wrong. Then Chris said something that worried us all: "I bet this one is a military installation."

I looked out the window and saw two army vehicles that were guarding the territory suddenly pull up to the gate. Chris recognized the markings on their car and said, "It's the military police [MPs]." So Chris was right about this being a miliary base. At that moment the thugs stepped aside, and our police escort was talking directly with the MPs. "We're not getting inside here today," one of our escorts told us. "This is government property."

The ex-Interpol agents were shocked we were turned away and were looking at me and Chris for answers. Chris explained that the Moscow police don't have authority to enter secret government property. "The military police are in charge, and they don't have to let us in." The ex-agent replied, "This place is worse than I thought. You'll never be able to shut down pirate factories here if the damn Russian military is protecting them."

I was depressed that the raid had failed. As chairman of our music industry group, I had to report back to our members, and I was worried it was going to cause us to fall apart. We were losing the war on piracy.

When we got back to Moscow, I told Jay what had happened, and he was livid. I explained that if we wanted to shut down these factories, it would be a game of whack-a-mole because even if you closed one down, another one would just pop up at a different military installation. I told Jay that now that we knew the Russian military was working with organized criminals to protect pirate factories, the situation had become too dangerous for more raids.

We agreed that the tougher approach taken by my buddy Chris and the film and video companies was not the best way. A diplomatic push at the highest levels of government was needed. Jay lobbied the Kremlin to shut down the factories. To illustrate that the pirates were a threat to the Russian music market, he awarded t.A.T.u. a platinum disc from the IFPI, the first of its kind for a Russian artist. It was a gesture that seemed to say, "If you like when Russian acts get international attention, you should help us shut down these factories."

While Jay was meeting with Kremlin officials, I had the opportunity to take our concerns about music piracy to the most important US government official in Russia, Ambassador Alexander Vershbow. The ambassador's love of jazz gave me the chance I needed. Because I represented the only American music company in Russia, I was sometimes invited to plan cultural events at the ambassador's mansion, Spaso House. These events would include a musical performance for VIPs and other world dignitaries. I had just signed a record contract with Russia's top jazz saxophonist, Igor Butman, and I asked Igor to perform for the ambassador. Igor was accustomed to high-profile events like this; he had previously been invited to perform in the White House for President Clinton.

"I'm so glad you're enjoying Igor Butman," I said. "A big part of my job here in Russia is to find artists and develop them and promote them internationally."

"I didn't know that," the ambassador replied. "But I do know about t.A.T.u. That's probably the biggest project ever in Russian music history."

"It definitely is," I told him. "We're really proud of it."

Chris was there, too, and I introduced him to the ambassador. Then I told the ambassador my tale of woe. "Our business is hurting really badly. I'm lucky that I found a group like t.A.T.u., who can sell records internationally, but that's rare. The small Russian record labels who can't sell records internationally are dying."

I explained that Universal would survive whatever happened since it was a huge label that could weather the problem. My concern, I explained to him, wasn't about that.

"Russia needs its own music industry," I said. "It's crucial for tax revenue and for jobs, and it's great for the economy." Then I gave him an example I had referred to many times with other people: "Look at what ABBA did for Sweden."

After the party Vershbow started very publicly going after the Kremlin. He went to the top of the food chain in the United States, asking then president George W. Bush to keep Russia out of the World Trade Organization until the pirate factories were shut down. This had to have pissed off the Kremlin.

We kept the pressure on. Chris and I were interviewed by the *New York Times*; I wrote an editorial for the *Wall Street Journal* and an article for the American Chamber of Commerce, all supporting keeping pressure on Russia until it closed the factories.

The Kremlin eventually yielded, and the factories were closed. Rumors were flying in our local group that one of the factories had belonged to the wife of a prominent politician. It wasn't surprising to hear. Piracy controlled by organized crime and protected by a corrupt military had nearly killed off the nascent Russian music industry. But it managed to survive and, eventually, thrive.

What really mattered was that by pushing the issue, legislation was passed that helped the music and film industries in Russia. They signed all the intellectual property treaties that the United States and Europe demanded, and they required factories to prove they were manufacturing legitimate albums. They recognized that their music was an important industry and started to protect it. Closing pirate factories was a necessary step to my biggest achievement in building a modern music industry in Russia. But after spending so much time fighting the pirates, I was eager to get back to signing artists and making records.

I WANT MY MTV
ON RED SQUARE

One of the main building blocks in creating the modern Russian music industry was the introduction of MTV, which would become an extremely valuable tool to promote Universal's artists on Russian television.

The man responsible for bringing MTV to Russia was the executive who interviewed me for my first job at PolyGram, media mogul Boris Zosimov. When I met Boris, he had his own broadcasting company, BIZ TV, which was also known as Zosimov TV. Boris had a background in concert promotion, which was his jumping ground into music television.

Boris was politically connected to the Kremlin, having helped Boris Yeltsin win a tough reelection with his Rock the Vote campaign targeted at Russian youth. The Communist Party was trying to make a comeback after the fall of the Soviet Union, and Yeltsin needed Boris's help to get the youth to vote for him. It worked brilliantly and saved Yeltsin. It wasn't a surprise to anyone when MTV's Bill Roedy asked Boris to head up the Russian version of the music network. That gave Boris access to all of their music videos as well as to shows like *Beavis and Butt-Head*.

MTV signed on in Russia on September 25, 1998, as a broadcast channel, but it was August 1999 when the music channel had its coming-out party in Moscow for which Boris relied on his concert promoter skills to stage the largest live-rock concert in Russia's history. Boris already had experience in this field.

On September 28, 1991, Boris staged the Monsters of Rock concert on the Tushino Airfield in Moscow. The headliners were AC/DC and

Metallica, and it was reported that 1.6 million people attended. Russia had never seen anything like it before.

In 1999 Boris topped himself by bringing Red Hot Chili Peppers to Moscow for a live performance in Red Square, with the sacred site of St. Basil's Cathedral in the background and the embalmed corpse of Lenin lying in a mausoleum nearby. Boris used his Kremlin connections to get permission to stage this event in Red Square. It didn't hurt that the Red Hot Chili Peppers were already very popular in Russia, with their album *Californication* selling massive amounts and the lead single, "Scar Tissue," in heavy rotation on MTV.

The Red Hot Chili Peppers playing live in Moscow was a victory for the United States, for this Los Angeles–based funk rock band had brought American pop culture to the very heart of what Ronald Reagan once called the evil empire. Watching the Chili Peppers perform their song "Give It Away" to several hundred thousand Muscovites gathered in the Square (and beyond, to the riverbanks and even farther) for this free concert was totally surreal. Backstage, I watched Boris operate like he did at the MTV channel—barking out orders to his young staff and managing all the details behind the scenes.

Right before it was time to introduce the band, while the thousands of people in the crowd were waiting in anticipation, Boris pulled aside the concert emcee, MTV's VJ Alexander Anatolovich, and sternly said, "Before you go out there and introduce the Chili Peppers, thank President Yeltsin for letting us put on this free concert here in Red Square. They'll kill me if I don't say something."

Boris turned to me and gave me a wink. I loved watching him in action and learned so much from him. Boris had more charisma than a Hollywood actor and more political savvy than an American politician. And that night in Moscow was his greatest achievement.

■

Before MTV began broadcasting in Russia, the only twenty-four-hour music video channel was Muz-TV. They played Russian music videos exclusively, and they were terrible. Without competition from better Western videos, Russian videos lagged in production values, story, and quality. They were amateurish. Muz-TV required payment for video rotation, a type of video payola that's been illegal in the West but, in the world of Russian show business, was transparent and official. This allowed vanity projects to flood Muz-TV's airwaves, lowering the quality. It was well-known that oligarchs would often buy their wives a song and a music video and let them pretend they were a real pop star for an anniversary gift. This was disastrous for real artists. MTV was the desperately needed antidote to Muz-TV, and young Russians were hungry for it.

No one knew that better than Boris, who was happy to roll out the red carpet for us. That built up Universal to be the dominant force in the Russian market. The Universal brand was considered cool because we were releasing all this cutting-edge music from Nine Inch Nails, Eminem, and No Doubt.

Having our own MTV channel in Russia meant that local Russians were making programming choices and producing locally made shows, so they were no longer licensing content from New York headquarters. Most countries didn't have their own dedicated MTV channel; we were the first in Eastern Europe. That gave us direct access to America's MTV. I took full advantage of that and had a whole team dedicated to providing the channel with Universal's music videos. We would receive them via courier from the United States from all of our labels, including Def Jam, Geffen, A&M Records, Republic, Interscope, and more. We would run them over to the MTV offices once or twice a day. That was how we developed sales for our international artists, by getting their videos on MTV so quickly.

We had our priorities, and we learned to barter our new and developing artists onto the MTV platform. We'd promise MTV the new Bon Jovi video—but only if they would play a video from our newest signing, the boy band Smash!! By leveraging the artists from the West, we were able to develop our Russian acts, and we did that better than anyone else. It wasn't that difficult to pull off, because Russians were hungry for Western music.

One of MTV's highest priorities was hip hop. They wanted Snoop Dogg. They wanted 2Pac. We'd bring them the latest video from the Irish boy band Boyzone with Ronan Keating and their response would be, "We don't want that. Our kids want to hear Dr. Dre." The combination of American hip hop music coming from Universal and the videos on MTV led to the birth of a huge and important Russian hip hop community that still exists today.

MTV was always open to American music but skeptical about European pop, with the exception of Sweden. They loved Ace of Base and the Cardigans and just one German band—Rammstein.

I delegated the responsibility for deciding which videos went to MTV to my staff. But over at the network, Boris was extremely hands-on. Nothing went on the air unless he saw it first and approved it. He'd assemble a dozen young people from his staff in his big, elegant office at a long oak table, and they would screen videos. If Boris didn't like something, he'd exclaim, "I hate it! That one sucks! That one is stupid."

He was like a Roman Emperor giving a thumbs-up or -down to the gladiator before he made the final cut. If he liked your video, you were golden. Heavy rotation on MTV could mean an artist would no longer have to perform in small clubs and private parties but could progress to large arenas and stadiums. If Boris hated your video, you were invisible. For an artist, that's a fate worse than death. But Boris ruthlessly guarded MTV Russia's quality control and maintained that cutting edge on every program and in every music video allowed on air.

MTV Russia had its own original series as well, and they would push boundaries much more than MTV programming did in the West. They didn't follow the rules. They were young and brave, and they took chances. One show that was especially controversial was *Shit Parade*, hosted by my marketing director, Asya. I was the only record label CEO in the Universal Music Group whose head of marketing had her own weekly MTV show making fun of pop stars. I loved what she was doing.

The point of the show was to review new music videos on MTV, but Asya quickly turned to scandalizing the artists, poking fun at their poorly made videos and/or their mediocre singing abilities. She was cruel and sarcastic. I thought it was a million times funnier than *Beavis and Butt-Head*. I couldn't believe she was getting away with some of things she was saying. Unfortunately, too many complaints came in from artists and their managers, and Boris had to cancel the show after a famous pop artist, dressed in a long fur coat, marched into his office and screamed at the top of her lungs that Boris needed to fire Asya after she'd called the pop legend "a talentless wife of a bored oligarch who pays for her shitty music videos." For Boris, that was the final straw.

The series was replaced by *12 Angry Viewers*, where ordinary people did the same thing Asya had been doing. Celebrities would be invited to join in, and once, I was invited as a guest to comment on videos and say outrageous things.

■

It was a golden era of music for Russians. At last young Russians were watching the same music videos the rest of the world was enjoying. That affected video directors in Russia, who had to make better music videos so their own artists could match their Western counterparts. They stepped up and made higher-quality videos, which were very Russian but with influences from the heavy metal, pop, and hip hop videos they were seeing from the West. A prime example of that new form was the proliferation of locally made hip hop videos by Russian rap artists, such as Detsl, Ligalize, and Bad Balance, whose videos were inspired by American rap videos.

Boris was not only my first boss in the music business, he was a larger-than-life mogul, fascinating to watch and learn from. I stayed close to Boris after he left PolyGram to run MTV, and my relationship with him brought huge benefits for Universal artists and helped us become the no. 1 record label in Russia. The American pop culture invasion of Russia was in full force.

MARIAH MAKES IT HAPPEN IN MOSCOW

One of the biggest, loudest, and wildest bands in America is KISS, the foursome that boldly introduces itself at each concert with the opening "You wanted the best, you got the best. The hottest band in the world."

My childhood friends and I, growing up in the 1970s, worshipped KISS. Universal Music was promoting their album *Psycho Circus*, a hot seller that featured all four original members of the band, who had reunited for the first time since the 1970s. So, in 1999, with KISS going out on tour in Europe, I lobbied hard to get them to play dates in Russia. They booked the Olympic Stadium in Moscow for two nights in April and the Sport Stadium in St. Petersburg for one night. The Moscow dates were sold out, and it was going to be the biggest show ever for an American band in the new Russia.

But KISS canceled at the last minute, when the North Atlantic Treaty Organization (NATO) started bombing Yugoslavia in late March during the Kosovo War. The band was under the impression that the action was near Moscow, and they were worried about getting caught up in the armed conflict. I received many phone calls from KISS's management and spent hours on the phone trying to assure them Yugoslavia was nowhere near Moscow or St. Petersburg. The war zone was over a thousand miles away.

But the decision was made, and it was a huge defeat for us. I didn't get the hottest band in the world to Moscow, and I was devastated. The Russian music business was never going to develop into a modern industry without big-time artists touring here. I felt defeated. Perhaps I really was working at some faraway outpost of the music industry that no major act was ever going to visit.

2222122222221112

111

Some bands, like Ace of Base, would come in just for a promotional appearance but without playing a live date. Then our fortunes changed, and in 2000, we got our first big international star: Enrique Iglesias, the first Universal solo megastar to perform live in Moscow during my tenure with the label. It was important to him to prove that he was a bigger draw than his father Julio, and he was. His live show was extremely successful, and because of his presence, we sold thousands of his albums. We thought that would inspire other artists on the roster to come to Russia to play live shows.

For my young marketing department and me, it was important psychologically to be part of a campaign to promote an international artist on tour. But Russia had such a bad reputation at this point that very few were brave enough to tour. Throughout the chaotic 1990s, Russia was deemed a risky bet by promoters and insurers. It only got worse in 2001, when American media reported, "Magician David Copperfield is trying to recoup $500,000 he spent to free his show equipment from a company he believes may have links to the Russian mafia."

Copperfield's production had required multiple semitrucks full of equipment. But apparently, they didn't bribe the right people, because they had problems getting their property out of the country. That sent shockwaves through the live-music industry. As if that wasn't enough to keep artists away, there were the gangland killings and rumors of bears running wild in the streets. I did my best to persuade our American colleagues to send us their biggest artists, but it was to no avail.

■

Then Mariah Carey signed with Universal after her long tenure with Columbia Records and a brief time with EMI. Doug Morris and Lyor Cohen were personally involved in bringing her to the company, and she was the highest priority. At the time, Universal was a music group without a major female diva; we didn't have Celine Dion or Kylie Minogue or Whitney Houston. Mariah filled a major hole in our roster, and Doug had a lot riding on her success.

There is a myth in the music business that labels push a "button" for a specific artist, which means every affiliate in the world must commit to focusing all energy and time on this person. I can tell you it is not a myth; it's true. I was in the meeting where Doug presented Mariah's first album for us,

Charmbracelet. We were given very specific orders that it was mandatory to make her no. 1 in each of our territories.

Never in my wildest dreams did I imagine the phone call I would receive one day from Faisel Durrani, then senior VP of international marketing for Island/Def Jam. Faisel told me, "Guess what? Mariah has added a show in Moscow to her European tour, and we need you to guarantee she gets in and out of the country safely."

Mariah was a precious asset for Universal, and I knew how important it was that her journey to Russia go without incident.

We were already promoting the heck out of Mariah's new album—her videos were in heavy rotation on MTV, and her album and singles were selling, all reaching no. 1 on our charts. The first thing I did after talking to Faisel was to ask Asya to marshal her team. We had all done such a great job with Enrique that I knew we could do this.

But I was more nervous about Mariah than Asya was. I told her, "Faisel says she's bringing nine trailers full of props and lighting. She's got dancers, backing vocalists, and her own jet. It's the biggest international entourage coming to Moscow ever. We've never had an artist put on this big of a show."

She confidently replied, "Are you kidding me, David? This is going to be easy."

I asked, "How can you be so sure?"

And she simply replied, "The promoter is Nadia Solovieva."

Some promoters were easy to work with, and some were difficult. Nadia was the toughest businesswoman I had ever met in my entire career, but she was friendly and a dream to work with. She ran the biggest concert agency in Russia—when Boris Zosimov moved on from concert promotion to MTV, Nadia was the top person in her field. She made a deal with Alpha Bank, an institution connected to the Kremlin, to sponsor all of her tours, and so she was able to promote some of the world's biggest artists.

Nadia worked really well with Universal. It was perfect synergy. She wanted to know what we needed—and the answer was lots of free tickets to give to deejays and our friends. And she let us know what she needed—to have Mariah all over the media.

I met with Nadia in her office to discuss cooperation. Hanging on the walls were concert posters of every show she'd produced. I saw photos of her with well-known Russian artists and a few European stars she had brought to Moscow. But Mariah Carey was going to be her biggest show to date, and it was important to her that everything run smoothly. We had a mutual interest in Mariah's success in Moscow. "You know David, if I fuck up, you may get in trouble with your bosses at Universal, but if you fuck up, I will lose clients, and that would make me very angry. I don't want to promote little rock bands. I want to bring Sir Paul McCartney to Red Square after Mariah, so don't fuck this up for me!"

We were there from the moment Mariah arrived at Sheremetyevo International Airport with the largest entourage I have ever seen for any artist. I later joked to the staff at the US Embassy that her entourage was bigger than the group that traveled with the president of the United States, and it was much more glamorous. Mariah took over several floors in her hotel with the stylists, dieticians, dancers, and backing vocalists. I was just part of a big welcoming party at the airport, and I was introduced to her as the head of Universal in Russia. She greeted everyone warmly, and next on the agenda was a press conference organized by Nadia.

I was seated next to Mariah, and she was sweet, polite, and pleasant. The Moscow press, especially the music media, usually asked rude or overly personal questions of visiting international stars, but they seemed to be as starstruck by Mariah as I was. The usually tough journalists asked softball questions, and Mariah had fun engaging with them. It went like this:

Press: "Would you like to live in Russia?"
Mariah: "Yes, I'd like to buy a mansion in St. Petersburg."
Press: "Do you have future plans in Russia?"
Mariah: "Yes, I want to make a movie with a Russian director."
Press: "Are you single?"
Mariah: "Yes, I'm single and would consider a Russian boyfriend."

The only question I got was "How are her records selling?" I said, "Great!" and talked about how Universal was honored to have Mariah on our roster and that Mariah's duet with Busta Rhymes was no. 1 on MTV Russia. That night I showed up on the network news silently sitting next to Mariah, with everything I'd said sitting on some figurative cutting room floor.

Like most artists who visit Russia, Mariah took a walk through Red Square. It was always a mind-blowing experience, like seeing the Grand Canyon or the Eiffel Tower for the first time, and the wonderment was reflected on her face.

It was fun to watch local citizens be surprised when she walked by them. I felt a sense of pride as we escorted Mariah around, as she was a more popular icon in Russia than the president of the country, who was sitting in his nearby office at this very moment.

After Red Square, Mariah had lunch at a famous Moscow restaurant, Osteria Mario, right near the Kremlin. I was there with Faisel and Mariah's tour manager, who mentioned that Mariah wanted to be in a musical in London's West End.

Faisel protested, "No, no, no, she has to focus on recording more music."

The manager replied, "I agree. We know this. We want to talk her into staying focused on making music. Acting should come later."

Faisel countered, "*Charmbracelet* is setting records around the world. She is back and we need to keep her on top, where she belongs."

I saw the tension between them. Watching Mariah and how Faisel interacted with her, I understood that despite my successes with Alsou and t.A.T.u., working with an artist of Mariah's stature is a whole other level—the Clive Davis or Berry Gordy level—and it was fascinating to experience. Faisel was one of the best executives I'd ever seen working with world-famous divas, developing their international careers. He understood the delicate balance of representing the record label's interests while looking out for what's best for the artist. Another diva, Beyoncé, would later hire him to run her management company.

Moscow was abuzz with Mariah Carey fever. No visiting pop star had dominated the city's culture like Mariah, with her sold-out shows in the Kremlin Palace. Tickets were the hottest commodity in town. She was the biggest diva to ever perform in Moscow, and we made sure everyone knew it.

People have paid thousands of dollars to sit in the front rows for her performances. Many artists who come to Russia are frustrated because the people sitting down front are wealthy oligarchs, corrupt generals, or rotten people who are obscenely wealthy. These are usually people who do not show their excitement or appreciation. Sure enough, Mariah received polite applause from those down front, but there were enough younger fans in the back rows to move the love forward. The folks in the $5,000 seats were not up and dancing like the people in the back.

Mariah sang many of her hits, and the moving set pieces, lighting, and huge number of dancers onstage made for a perfectly working machine. It was a carnival-themed set with some of the largest props ever used onstage in Moscow. Watching this spectacular, I understood why it took nine big rigs to haul all of her equipment. The massive set production alone ensured that it was one of the best shows ever staged in the Kremlin Palace.

I was rarely in my seat, as I ran all over the place while she was performing—sometimes backstage, sometimes at the mixing board, and sometimes avoiding the people who came up to me and asked if I could get them backstage to meet Mariah.

Standing with Faisel backstage behind the curtain, watching the crowd erupt with applause after Mariah had belted out her first hit, "Vision of Love," I said to him, "I'm so proud of Mariah."

"Why?" he asked, surprised.

I replied, "You don't understand why the Russians love her so much. She's giving them a live performance with real vocals and real backing vocalists. She has a real band. Pop stars in Russia usually lip sync. Mariah is real. That's why they love her."

For the lucky invited guests, there was an official meet and greet after the show. It was in an elegantly staged area, separate from the venue. Against a backdrop of beautiful purple curtains, Mariah was seated on what looked like a throne, facing a long line of oligarchs, VIPs, business executives, government officials, and billionaires who wanted to have their picture taken with her.

I was impressed how efficiently this after-concert photo op was managed by Mariah's team. I hadn't seen anything like it when Enrique was in Moscow. It reminded me of subjects paying tribute to their queen. Russia's rich and powerful lined up without any priority given to who was the wealthiest or who was a gangster or a Kremlin bureaucrat. They all waited to have their moment.

Most of them had gifts for her—diamonds, Fabergé eggs, watches, earrings, and flowers. But it was Mariah who was generous with her time following the show. A two-hour performance with costume changes between songs and multiple dance numbers must have been exhausting, but there she was for her fans.

After about forty-five minutes, we said our goodbyes. Mariah took her limo back to the hotel. I went out for drinks—lots of drinks—with Faisel, and later, the tour manager met up with us.

They told me that Mariah was extremely pleased with the turnout but not thrilled with the people in the front rows being so reserved and quiet. Faisel was just happy that nothing went wrong—which he knew was a big deal in Russia. To me, Faisel is another of my American angels, as he made sure Mariah didn't change her mind about coming to Russia like KISS had.

Mariah left a lot of new fans behind, including the Russian media. Her reviews were amazing. Critics wrote that her concert was a lesson in how real show business is done. Mariah remarked on how beautiful Moscow is, and the Russians absolutely loved her.

Even though my time with Mariah was short, I didn't let our partner Def Jam or Universal CEO Doug Morris down. Mariah's visit to Moscow as part of her 2003 comeback tour was an unequivocal success.

■

Like with MTV and the industry trade group, establishing that Russia was a safe place for artists to perform was another building block in creating the modern Russian music industry. Mariah may not have realized it, but her appearance at the Kremlin Palace went a long way to establishing that it was safe to travel to Russia. You would not get eaten by a bear or get caught in the middle of gang violence. Following her live show, other artists made Russia a stop in their tour itineraries, including Diana Ross, Herbie Hancock, Bryan Adams, Shaggy, Def Leppard, Diana Krall, Moby, and Eurythmics.

Over the next six months, Mariah's record sales kept increasing, lifting her album to double Platinum in Russia. Mariah's success didn't just impact us at Universal. EMI, BMG, and Russian labels were learning how to manage a megaevent like a Mariah Carey concert. They watched us do it, and they followed our moves when their artists performed live in Russia.

The opportunity to work with one of the most iconic performers in the world is one of the reasons why I was always desperate to keep the company alive and not lose my job. This was the most glamorous industry on earth, and Moscow was one of the most exciting cities in the world, and I was a part of it all.

PART 6

THE GOLDEN YEARS

17

THE RUSSIAN WHAM!

Because of our success with promoting Russian artists internationally, the Universal label was very well-known by the Russian public—and musicians. By 2002 Alsou's and t.A.T.u.'s major breakthroughs made us the hottest label in town, and everyone wanted to sign with us. People would line up at the front door of our four-story building, so much so that I started using the side entrance. Veteran artists, some of them icons, would show up at the office, hoping to meet with me. I didn't have any interest in signing them, because I knew they wouldn't sell outside of Russia, but out of respect, I always met with them.

Other labels were signing lots of artists. My strategy was to sign one act at a time and give them our complete attention. At this moment in time, boy bands were dominating the charts around the world—acts like Backstreet Boys, *NSync, 98 Degrees, Boyzone, Westlife, and East 17. We had already made magic with a female duo, so I thought it was the right time for me to find a male duo.

■

On a flight from Los Angeles to Moscow, I started a conversation with a gentleman sitting across the aisle from me in Aeroflot's business class. He was an entrepreneur involved in the restaurant business. I gave him my card and didn't think anything more about it.

A short time later, he called me, asking if I would do him a huge favor and meet with a friend of his who had a family singing group made up of his two children and a friend. I thought, "Family act? We are way past the Partridge Family."

I politely tried to decline. "We're not looking for that kind of new band at the moment, but you should talk to Sony, they're looking for new artists," I said.

But he was persistent. "Please, if you could just meet my friend, I would be really grateful. He's a good guy and he loves his children, and by the way, he has a great idea how Universal could have the rights to the first song recorded in space."

That caught my attention.

I agreed to take a meeting with the father, Mikhail Topalov, who was famous in Russia for building commercial satellites. His plan to record in space involved sending his family to the International Space Station to produce a pop song high above the Earth.

I did some research and discovered he was actually serious. He owned a company that had a contract with NASA and the Russian space agency. Russia couldn't make good cars or mobile phones, but they had a space program that was very competitive with the United States, going all the way back to their 1957 launch of the first artificial satellite to orbit the Earth, Sputnik. That event surprised the world and launched the space race between the two superpowers. Thanks to the creation of NASA and President Kennedy's 1962 declaration that America would put a man on the moon by the end of the decade, the United States surged ahead with a lunar landing in 1969, with Neil Armstrong becoming the first human being to set foot on the moon.

Mikhail Topalov invited me to meet him at the Havana Club, a famous and exclusive cigar club in Moscow. He ordered me a Scotch and a Cuban cigar (legal in Russia, one of Cuba's allies) and presented me with a homemade CD, a recording his kids and their friend had made in a garage. There were photos of his son Vlad, his daughter Alina, and Vlad's best friend, Sergey Lazarev, posing in a cheerleader-style pyramid with Alina on top.

Mikhail was a tall man wearing round, shaded sunglasses. He was hard-drinking and hard-smoking. His English was flawless. And he was fun.

His family's band was called Troika (not too original for a trio), and the lead track on the CD was "Belle," a cover of a song from the popular French musical *Notre-Dame de Paris*. Although they were Russian, they recorded it in the original French. I assumed it was going to be terrible and did not listen to it right there. I went back to my office and asked Asya to listen with me.

It was a bit hokey, and we were laughing at it, but then Asya said, "The boys are really cute."

We listened some more, and they did have a nice sound. Even though it was raw and not well produced, and the sister was messing it up a bit, the boys sang well. Asya and I looked at each other, and I said to her, "Simon!" (as in Wham! manager Simon Napier-Bell).

And she said, "Yes!"

I had stayed in touch with Simon after Valeriy, Alsou's manager, fired him. Simon was a music legend in the United Kingdom, especially for turning Wham! into a pop sensation. I loved his stories about working with music industry icons like Clive Davis and Walter Yetnikoff, about taking an Italian song and writing English lyrics to create the hit "You Don't Have to Say You Love Me," and about his interactions with Beatles manager Brian Epstein. Simon believed that buddy groups would always be successful, like buddy movies (think of *Butch Cassidy and the Sundance Kid*). I figured that Vlad and Sergey were buddies.

I told Simon I would fly him to Moscow and put him up in a hotel if he would come and listen to Troika. He trusted me enough to say yes. Mikhail wanted us to come to his house and listen to the group play in his living room, but I declined. I wanted to do this right, so I rented a small nightclub with a stage. Simon arrived in the morning, and that afternoon we were in the club—just Simon, Asya, some of our Universal staff, Mikhail, and the band onstage. I explained to Mikhail who Simon was and that we needed to hire him if we were going to turn his family group into stars. Mikhail was a huge fan of British rock, especially bands from the 1970s. He had an encyclopedic mind for the genre and never missed a show when legends like Deep Purple, Status Quo, or Uriah Heep came to Moscow. Mikhail was obsessed with all things related to British music, and once he realized who Simon was, he panicked.

"I don't know if we're ready. What do we do?"

I calmed him down, and the audition proceeded.

When Sergey and Vlad sang, they were magnetic. And then Alina vocalized, and I looked over at Simon, who had this incredible frown on his face, as if he had eaten some bad food. I knew where this was going, and I winked at him. We let them finish, and Mikhail ran over.

"What did you think?" he asked. "It could have been better. Maybe we should do it again?"

Simon, who never held back, was about to tell him we had to get rid of the girl, but I stopped him because the three kids were coming over to join us. I didn't want him tearing down Alina in front of everyone.

Simon spoke to Vlad first: "You are amazing. You are so fantastic."

Then he addressed Sergey: "I love your approach, and I really like the sound of your voice."

And then he looked at Alina, and before he could say anything, I spoke up: "And you were wonderful, dear. You really did a good job. Good for you."

But I could tell that Mikhail knew what Simon was thinking. So Simon and I pulled Mikhail aside while Asya engaged the three kids in conversation.

Simon was blunt. "You've got to lose the girl. She can't be in the group. This is a boy band. They are a duo."

And Mikhail protested, "But she's part of the band. They've been singing together for months. They worked on the songs."

Simon continued to be brutally honest. "I cannot work with a band like this. I can make Vlad and Sergey the biggest duo in the country."

That's when I interjected, "Wham! Remember Wham!?"

We saw that Mikhail was torn. I felt bad for him—we were asking a father to tell his daughter she can't be in the family group. Mikhail next asked Simon, "Will you help manage them?"

And Simon responded, "I'll go back to London, and I'll send you a contract."

███

Before we left the club, Sergey invited us to see his performance of *Romeo and Juliet* that evening in the most prestigious theater in the city. Simon and I were in the audience to see Sergey in the lead role of Romeo, and it was confirmed: we had a superstar in the making.

That very day, Simon came up with a new name for the duo: Smash!! (with two exclamation marks, one more than Wham!). And there were echoes of Wham!: Sergey was brunette and Vlad, a blond, was supporting him. It was the George Michael / Andrew Ridgely relationship all over again. The only difference was that Mikhail was Vlad's father, not Sergey's. That would eventually become a problem, as Sergey was the real star, and Vlad was more like Ridgely. But Vlad's dad was paying the bills.

Between the afternoon audition and the evening theater performance, Mikhail informed Alina that she couldn't be a part of the act. I saw her at the theater and tried to console her: "I really thought you were fantastic, and I hope you are not too upset."

She said she was fine. I believe she knew the two boys had something special and didn't want to get in their way. It was never spoken out loud, but I had the distinct feeling her father had been forcing her to be in the group and that it wasn't something she really wanted.

18

SMASHED!!

We did it! Simon and I re-created Wham! in Russia in the form of Smash!! George Michael and Andrew Ridgeley were our role models for Sergei Lazarev and Vlad Topolov. With the genius management of Simon, I knew we had every chance to make Smash!! as big as Wham! It seemed like nothing could stop us. Our guys were handsome, and they could sing, but more importantly, they were true friends, just like George and Andrew. It was a formula for success, and we were determined to make them superstars. But first, we needed songs. Simon leveraged his years of working in the UK music industry and approached some top songwriters.

Simon Napier-Bell: We were looking for songs and met with a top publisher in London, someone who was a little bit arrogant. He said, "Two Russian boys. What can you do?" Vlad, who spoke perfect English, said, "We can sing pretty well, actually." And the guy was a bit shocked, because he thought he was going to hear this Russian accent. And he said, "Really? You think so? Well, why don't you sing for me?" Vlad was silent for a couple of seconds, and then he whispered to Sergey. They stood up. He started clapping his hands, and they sang "We Will Rock You" like they were a major rock act. What they both knew is that when you're a singer, you always give your all. You never give a half-hearted performance. They sang as if they were on stage at Wembley Stadium with one hundred thousand people in the audience. The publisher was completely overwhelmed. He felt embarrassed he had such a wrong impression of them, so he tried to recover. "I see. You want a rock song." I said, "No, we don't want a rock song. You just asked what they could sing. They sang for you what they can sing. We want a ballad."

Whenever I flew to Los Angeles on business, I met with songwriters to see what they might have for the boys. Between Simon and me, we came up with material for an album we called *Freeway*. We recorded a better (and more professional) version of "Belle" without Vlad's sister. But when it came time to choose the first single, I think we misfired.

We picked a song called "Should Have Loved You More." It had a good up-tempo beat, and Simon suggested we shoot the video in Thailand, where he was living. We flew Sergey, Vlad, and Mikhail to Bangkok and had some wild experiences. Simon brought Mikhail and the boys to their first ever drag show, and it was amazing, as good as any Las Vegas spectacular. During the final number, when the drag queens sang the Three Degrees' hit "When Will I See You Again," Mikhail was shocked to realize he was looking at men dressed as women. Bangkok opened his eyes.

For the video, we recorded Sergey and Vlad sailing down the famous canals in the south of Thailand, then we returned to Bangkok and put them on top of a skyscraper, with a helicopter filming them. The final shot was of Sergey and Vlad on a beautiful sandy beach at sunset. It was breathtaking.

Simon had a clear vision for the video and insisted that it showcase the strong bond between Sergey and Vlad, using similar imagery he had used in making videos for Wham! Even though we created a cool video, it just didn't grab anyone's attention—maybe it looked more like a video produced by a tourist bureau, showing off Thailand rather than our artist.

Simon Napier-Bell: I live in Thailand, so making the video there was a natural thing to do. I'm fluent in Thai. You can hire top photographers and production crew, and it's much more inexpensive to produce there than in the United States or Europe. But the father ruined it, because our stylist had two or three different things for them to wear, and the father said, "Oh, you've got to wear different clothes in every shot." So he went out and bought them fifty outfits, and every shot, they're wearing something different. There was no cohesion. There was no continuity at all. It was the father's interference.

The video didn't work, but we didn't panic. Simon assured me, "David, you shouldn't worry about the first single tanking. Wham!'s first single

'Young Guns (Go for It)' didn't even crack the top forty. Not until they got their lucky break."

"What was that?" I asked.

"Live TV. That's what made Wham! A big star suddenly canceled their appearance on *Top of the Pops*, so the BBC invited Wham! at the last minute, and that changed everything for the boys."

I realized that's what we had to do for Smash!!

We booked them on the live TV competition *New Wave*, filmed in Jūrmala, a seaside resort town in Latvia, where the Russian elite liked to holiday. The contest was very popular during Soviet times but was canceled after the breakup of the USSR. It was being relaunched with an expected TV audience of several hundred million viewers in fifteen countries and with Russians watching from America. No bigger platform existed in Russia for new artists to launch their careers. The idea was for a jury of artists and music executives to find a superstar. Thomas Hedström, who had left Universal for EMI by this time, was on the jury. He was the only foreigner on the jury of Russian celebrities and music professionals. We knew Thomas would support Smash!!, but he would do so much more.

The boys performed "Belle," and Thomas told the other jury members, "We know they're the best. We know they are going to win. They could be the biggest thing since t.A.T.u. Why don't we unanimously give them our support, and this will be the launching pad for their career."

When it came time for the jury to announce their decision, they held up cards, á la the Olympics. And each jury member gave them a ten. It was a rocket launch into stardom. They became an overnight sensation in Russia.

We filmed a music video for "Belle," which was directed by Fyodor Bondarchuk, the son of one of Russia's most honored directors, Sergei Bondarchuk (*War and Peace*). After "Belle" Fyodor went on to have his own distinguished career as a director. The video, inspired by Madonna's video for "Rain," was beautiful and stylish and was played in heavy rotation on MTV.

With the success of "Belle," Simon was able to get Universal's offices in Taiwan, Thailand, and South Korea interested in promoting Smash!! in their countries, giving them some international success. Sergey and Vlad never reached the global level of t.A.T.u., but they were much more fun to work with. They were good, innocent boys, and they'd genuinely been best friends since childhood. Vlad's family was wealthy beyond belief, and he'd had everything handed to him; Sergey was poor and had to work his butt off to get anywhere. But that did not affect their friendship.

After "Belle" Smash!! had another hit single in Russia with "Talk to Me." And then, following in the footsteps of Wham!, we filmed a video in China, a cover of George Michael's "Faith," which was also a huge hit for Smash!! in Russia.

Simon was employing his China strategy to launch Smash!! onto the international stage. It was the same tactic he'd employed to make Wham! one of the biggest bands in the world. In 1985 there was great interest in China, with Communist society opening for the first time since the revolution. At this point in time, music acts from the West were not welcome to perform in the country. Simon saw a public relations opportunity for Wham!; he made multiple visits to Beijing to lobby high-level bureaucrats, finally persuading the Communist Ministry of Culture to allow Wham! to be the first Western pop band to perform in China. But Simon's real target was not the Communist nation. It was America, and sure enough, Wham! became huge in the United States after their time in China was covered on the nightly news in America. Being the first Western band to perform in Communist China was a massive publicity coup. Soon after, Wham! became one of the biggest touring acts in the United States, thanks to Simon's clever China strategy.

■

After their French-language recording of "Belle," all of the other Smash!! songs were recorded in English. They insisted on not recording in Russian. That should have helped them become successful in America.

To get the attention of record executives in the United States, we needed to bring Sergey and Vlad to America. Simon wanted Smash!! to be in the top rung of boy bands, and Sergey and Vlad (as well as Mikhail) listened to what Simon had to say (and they loved hearing stories of his rock 'n' roll life). But the thing about duos is they don't always last forever. Fame comes between the two individuals. It happened with Wham! when George Michael gained more of the spotlight. It wasn't a shock that it happened with Smash!!, as Sergey grabbed more attention than Vlad.

But what was surprising was that it was Vlad's father, Mikhail, who was the jealous one. Mikhail was becoming increasingly envious of Sergey's popularity over Vlad. Their cover of George Michael's song "Faith" was a breaking point for Mikhail. Sergey was featured in the video much more than Vlad, and Mikhail thought it was not only a reminder that George went solo but that it was foreshadowing how the same thing would happen to Sergey.

Mikhail was turning into a show business dad. His son and his best friend were no. 1 on the charts, but it was Mikhail who was enjoying the spotlight and being interviewed on TV. He was turning into a Valeriy, but Simon was still in control and wanted to put a band together so that Smash!! could go on tour for the first time.

Mikhail suggested making his college buddies the backing band for Smash!! He knew a pianist, a drummer, and a couple of guitarists, along with a backing vocalist who had a jazz background. They might have made a fine lounge band for someone singing Sinatra songs. Then Mikhail said we should rearrange the duo's dance songs and give them a hard rock edge. He told us, "I studied Deep Purple, and this is how they did it."

We responded, "We've been following the Wham! model all this time. Why are we switching to Deep Purple?"

When they were in Ukraine doing a live show, Sergey told Mikhail it was all wrong and refused to go out on stage. Mikhail shouted at him, "Get out there! I own you!" Sergey still refused, and Mikhail punched him in the face, so Sergey walked away. Vlad went out and performed alone. With Sergey gone and the duo over, Mikhail took control of Vlad's career. Simon was fired and Smash!! was done. I thought it was a tragedy. We were on the cusp of an American breakthrough.

Sergey never performed with Vlad again. I begged him to come back. I asked him to come to my office and sit down with Vlad. Sergey was always kind to me and respectful of what I had done for him, but he said he could never go back. He signed a solo deal with Sony. Mikhail tried to turn Vlad into a solo artist and go out on tour. Vlad hated that and missed his best friend, Sergey. This beautiful thing the boys had was blown apart by a father trying to live vicariously through his son. I really liked Mikhail and appreciated his passion for classic rock music. Had Smash!! stayed together, they might have made history by being the first pop act to perform on the space station. Mikhail could have made that happen.

To this day, Sergey is one of Russia's biggest musical stars. He is one of the most talented male pop singers to come out of Russia, and I'm eternally happy that I discovered him.

Smash!! had many fans in Ukraine, and in 2014, Sergey spoke out against the invasion of Crimea. The Kremlin was not pleased, and he was quickly taken off the airwaves. Since then he has been quiet and is back on TV. He has been cowered into silence, like so many other Russian artists.

Even though Smash!! broke up before they could enjoy success in America, which was heartbreaking for me, I still consider myself very fortunate to have worked with Simon to develop two Russian acts, Alsou and Smash!!, and observe his brilliant management practices. It was important for me to learn from these skills, especially his knowledge on how to use publicity. But my fondest memories with Simon are the times I'd sat with him in Moscow restaurants, drinking ample amounts of red wine, and listening to his wild stories about famous characters from the UK music industry, ranging from Brian Epstein and Marc Bolan to Jimmy Page and Dusty Springfield. He'd had so many personal experiences with legendary figures that were mostly hilarious and always entertaining.

19

MEETING THE MAESTRO

My launching of three Russian acts (Alsou, t.A.T.u., and Smash!!) beyond the country's borders caught the attention of a lot of people, including Moscow-born Valery Gergiev, who was so famous a conductor of classical music that he was the subject of an in-depth article in the July 20, 1992, issue of *Time* magazine, which focused on the state of the arts in post-Soviet Russia. I found it fascinating that someone of Gergiev's stature was aware of me. Gergiev was based in St. Petersburg, where he was the general director of the famed and historic Mariinsky Theatre.

One day I was holding a marketing meeting in my office to discuss upcoming classical releases, including a new album from Bond, an all-female electric string quartet signed to Universal's Decca label. The head of our classics and jazz department, Boris Ivashkevich, was there. Boris looked like Rowan Atkinson's Mr. Bean character, but he was very smart and shrewd. I was always grateful to Boris, one of my most valued employees at Universal. He was older, wiser, and calmer, especially as compared to my wild and free-thinking marketing department on the pop side. An expert in the classical music field, he had been with the company since the PolyGram days. Album sales of classical music were not as large as our pop product, and even though the pop side of the company was bringing in more money, I kept Boris's classics and jazz department on equal footing. He was always respected by the younger marketing staff.

During the meeting Boris informed me, "Decca's favorite conductor, Maestro Gergiev, is hosting his White Nights Festival in St. Petersburg."

I replied, "I really miss St. Petersburg. I was a broke student from San Francisco studying Russian there long before I made it to Moscow." Boris asked if I wanted to attend the festival because our classical labels were long-time supporters of Gergiev.

I responded, "Sure, why not. It would be cool, and you will come with me!" Boris came back to me later in the day and confirmed that we had tickets. But there was a catch, according to Boris.

"The Maestro wants to meet you."

Boris was excited, but I was intimidated. Valery Gergiev was a force of nature and would go on to make numerous live recordings with the London Symphony Orchestra, where he was principal conductor. He is still considered one of the greatest conductors of all time, as well as one of the most talented Russians in history.

Gergiev was signed to Universal's Decca imprint, so before heading to the Festival, I called my colleague, Costa Pilavachi, president of the Decca Music Group in London, and asked him about Gergiev. "Good luck and have fun," he told me. "He's a great guy, and you will love him. But we're not interested in making a new record with him."

I asked why, and Costa replied, "Sales are not happening. We're cutting back on the number of new albums we're making each year and focusing on our catalog." Then he asked, "Have you seen Bond? They are the future of classical music." Costa was one of the most respected record executives in the world of classical music and knew what he was talking about.

Boris was in my office during the call, and when it ended, I asked him, "What are we going to do if Valery Gergiev asks about recording a new album?"

He replied, "Don't worry about it. Maybe he won't even bring it up." That calmed me down because I trusted Boris implicitly with everything.

The White Nights Festival was the most important annual event for the city of St. Petersburg, and Gergiev was director of the week-long happening. Classical music performances and operas were held in the major concert halls throughout the city. International tourists flooded in. And because it was summer, the sky never turned dark; it remained full of light even at twilight, when St. Petersburg's famous drawbridges on the Neva River were raised for ships to pass through. It is always a stunning sight to see.

After we arrived it quickly became apparent to us what a powerful man Gergiev was in the city. His staunch ally, President Putin, was there. Boris and I checked into the Grand Hotel Europe, the most beautiful hotel in St. Petersburg. We unpacked and headed to the grand Mariinsky Theatre. It's even more impressive than the Bolshoi in Moscow. Opened in 1860, it is where the Russian royal family would watch Tchaikovsky's works from their royal box. For the last three hundred years, St. Petersburg has been the cultural center of Russia, and the Mariinsky is the most treasured institution in the city. And this was Gergiev's headquarters.

Boris, who was very familiar with the place, was waved past all the lines of people, and we headed to Gergiev's private dressing room backstage. Boris said to him, "Mr. Gergiev, Maestro, this is David Junk, the CEO of Universal Music Russia. As you know, he signed t.A.T.u., and they have been successful all over the world."

I could see that Gergiev was sizing me up. I told him it was an honor to meet him and that I was looking forward to the riverboat cruise after the concert. And the last thing Gergiev said to me before heading to the stage was "There's something I need to talk to you about. We'll meet afterward."

And I realized I'd been invited here only for one reason—not to enjoy the show. Gergiev had taken care of the limo and the hotel because he wanted to ask me something. Now I was really nervous, but Boris told me to relax. We went to our seats located right in the center of the theater and watched the performance, and then we were off to the river cruise. I noticed that Gergiev had groupies—wealthy New York socialites with money to burn. They were known as the Friends of Gergiev, and they told me how they'd followed him around the world and that they were already planning their next trip to Japan for his concert in Tokyo. They would pay Gergiev's way, and I realized he didn't have to sell CDs, but he needed to keep releasing new recordings to keep these women happy. He was not selling a lot of music, and so his royalties were very low, but these women were subsidizing him. In the marketplace, he was competing with younger, hotter classical musicians like Vanessa-Mae, the Bond quartet, Anna Netrebko, and Andrea Bocelli. Gergiev was amazing and fantastic, but he wasn't sexy, and he wanted to remain relevant.

It was getting late on the boat, and finally Gergiev called me over to talk. Boris was nowhere to be found, so I faced the maestro alone. Speaking excellent English, he got right to the point: "When are you guys going to let me record another album?"

I told him I had talked to Costa, and he immediately said, "I know Costa doesn't want me to record anything new. But I want you to tell him I am his best artist and I need a new album."

Unexpectedly, I found it to be a very poignant moment, and I responded honestly: "I will definitely pass that on, sir."

I don't know if Gergiev really thought I could persuade Costa to change his mind, but he thanked me and let me go back to my table to enjoy my filet mignon as we sailed under the drawbridges in a very magical setting.

I went back to Moscow and called Costa and told him about my encounter with the maestro. He listened politely. He thanked me and said he would call Gergiev, but I don't think he changed his mind.

I did have one more interaction with Gergiev. On September 1, 2004, there was a terrorist attack instigated by a Chechen warlord at a school in Beslan in North Ossetia in the Russian Caucasus. More than 1,100 people were taken hostage in the three-day siege, which ended when Russian security forces stormed the building, resulting in the deaths of 333 people, including 186 children and 31 of the attackers.

We produced a charity concert to aid the survivors, and Gergiev sent us a video message in support. I appreciated what he did, but we did not meet in person then or ever again. In 2010 *Time* magazine named Gergiev to its list of the one hundred most influential cultural figures in the world. Then the man who'd once conducted the World Orchestra for Peace became an ardent supporter of sending Russian soldiers to war. Gergiev's unwavering support for Vladimir Putin has been the cause of his downfall. From the Metropolitan Opera House and Carnegie Hall to symphony halls around Europe and Asia, Gergiev is no longer welcome. It is a spectacular fall from grace, like in a Shakespearean tragedy, and the perfect symbol for the corrosive effects Putin's war is having on Russia and individual Russians, even the most talented and gifted ones.

AT THE BALLET/
JAZZMAN

As Universal's CEO in Russia, I knew it was my job to import music and promote artists from the massive roster of more than a hundred labels and subsidiary labels in the worldwide Universal Music Group. The biggest genres were pop, rock, and hip hop from top labels Interscope and Def Jam, but my favorite labels to work with were the classics imprints, such as Decca and Deutsche Grammophon.

Even though my first foray into classical music with Valery Gergiev didn't work out, I was still fascinated with the rich tradition of classical music in Russia, arguably the country that produces the most talented classical musicians in the world.

Boris Ivashkevich could get me tickets to the Bolshoi Theatre or the Moscow Conservatory, and I took my wife to many classical music concerts. I felt like I was expanding my cultural horizons and was no longer all about pop and rock music, which I still loved.

My next natural step was to explore the world of ballet. While there were recordings of music from ballets, like Gergiev's *Swan Lake*, ballet itself is a visual medium, not something that would normally involve a record label. But the rise of DVD technology was expanding opportunities for record companies like Universal to market and sell ballet and symphony performances on DVD.

Boris was still invested in finding a classical artist for me to sign, and one day, he walked into my office and asked, "What do you think about producing a movie?" My reaction was that we were a record label and our bosses were not going to finance a film. Boris replied, "We don't have to pay for it. It's already produced. All we have to do is distribute it and sell it."

He explained that it was a performance of one of the most famous Russian ballets, *The Return of the Firebird* by Igor Stravinsky, one of Russia's greatest composers. I asked Boris what it was about. More than jazz or the symphony, Boris loved Russian ballet. He excitedly described the story to me as though he were a college literature professor: "It's based on a Russian folk tale about the defeat of an evil sorcerer who is holding thirteen beautiful princesses hostage. They are rescued by a courageous Prince Ivan, son of the tsar, who kills the sorcerer with the help of a beautiful, magical firebird."

Boris paused in order to emphasize this last part. "The firebird symbolizes renewal and rebirth in Russian folk tales, like modern Russia after the Soviet Union."

That got my attention, and I asked him who the star was. "Andris Liepa," said Boris.

I had no idea who that was. I did my research and discovered he was an accomplished dancer for the Kirov and Bolshoi and was from the most famous family in Russian ballet. His father, Maris Liepa, was considered one of the greatest dancers in Soviet history, and his sister Ilze was awarded the People's Artist of the Russian Federation award for her dancing.

I met with Andris at the Bolshoi in 2002. He and his father and sister had performed on the Bolshoi stage. It was an honor to meet him there. He was tall and blond and walked with the assured stature of a ballet dancer. He wanted to tell me more about *The Return of the Firebird* so I could understand why Stravinsky wrote the ballet for the legendary impresario Sergei Diaghilev's Ballet Russe touring company, which staged the world premiere in 1910 at the Opéra de Paris.

Andris explained to me why the ballet was so important: "Diaghilev wanted to show the world that Russian art was at the cutting edge of sophistication. And I want to bring Diaghilev's beautiful message to the world again about the new Russia after the fall of the USSR." He was very emotional. "With your help, and Universal's, we can take the ballet on tour worldwide."

Then Andris told me, "We will put the film on DVD, and then we will have a major screening here in Moscow at the Bolshoi. No, let's do it at the

Kremlin! I'll ask the president; he'll let me do it. We'll announce to the world that we have joined forces with the great international record company, Universal."

I imagined the possibilities—we would be at the Kremlin with the head of the country, and I would be making the presentation onstage. I was in! But first, I had to call our London office to get approval, and we all know how that went when I wanted to record a new album with Gergiev.

Boris made a great suggestion: instead of talking to Costa Pilavachi, who didn't want to record a new album with the maestro, we would approach a different executive in the classical music division, Chris Roberts, who was well-known in the industry as the PolyGram executive who released the Scorpions' song "Wind of Change" and had brought the band to meet President Gorbachev in the Kremlin. He was one of the reasons PolyGram opened an office in Moscow, so I thought he might be more sympathetic to my request.

Boris and I flew to London to present our idea to Chris. The first thing he told us is that he loves Russian culture and the Russian people. He was happy to meet Boris, and he knew all about my success with t.A.T.u. He agreed to produce the DVD of Andris's film and release it all over the world on the Decca imprint.

We returned to Moscow to give Andris the good news, and he told us he already had a date for the Moscow premiere of *The Return of the Firebird*. It was going to be screened for a star-studded audience in the Kremlin Palace. Andris was one of the most politically connected artists I'd ever worked with; he had a network of support inside the Kremlin and across the ballet world.

The night of the premiere, I was backstage at the Kremlin with Andris. I'd been there many times, including when Enrique Iglesias, Elton John, and Bryan Adams had performed. I was familiar with the underground tunnels and secret entrances to the backstage area where the artists wait before going out onstage. It was like any other concert arena. But when I came from behind the curtain with Andris and walked to the front of the stage with a hot white spotlight on me to introduce the film to the three thousand people gathered there in this famous hall, I became overwhelmed with the sense that, on this same stage, Joseph Stalin, Nikita Khruschev, and Mikhail Gorbachev had given speeches to the Communist Party congresses. Putin did not attend the ballet, but the prime minister, Mikhail Kasyanov, did, along with many other important government officials and members of the Russian elite.

It was another moment where I could savor a win for the United States. What would Stalin have thought about an American record executive standing on this stage? I don't think any of the Communist Party leaders in the Soviet Union, even Gorbachev, could have foreseen an American record executive promoting a Russian ballet from the Kremlin stage.

Andris followed in the footsteps of his hero Diaghilev, and he premiered *The Return of the Firebird* in Paris. It was such a huge success that he later took the show to London. He has produced it many times on stages throughout Russia and the former Soviet Union. Throughout his distinguished career, Andris produced and performed in many ballets in Russia and around the world, but *The Return of the Firebird* is his crowning achievement. Like his hero Diaghilev, he wanted to present a new Russia to the world with ballet, and the best way to bring this ballet to the world was through the promotion and distribution power of an American record label like Universal.

More than any other Russian artist I knew, Andris symbolized the rising of Russia in the new century. He remains one of the leading cultural figures in his country and is currently the director of the Kremlin Ballet. There is something else for which I will be eternally grateful to Andris: he created a company that worked with businesses in the West to plan their corporate events. Citibank hired Andris to stage a Diana Ross concert for their customers.

Thanks to Andris, I met Diana backstage at a Moscow opera house in 2003. While the Soviet Union did not release most American rhythm and blues (R&B) music in the USSR, they did embrace Motown, and as a result, Diana was extremely famous in Russia.

Soviet propagandists had used music like Marvin Gaye's "What's Going On" to shine a spotlight on inner-city strife in America in order to distract from the problems at home in the USSR. But even after the breakup of the Soviet Union, very few Motown artists had ever performed in Russia, and Diana was one of the first.

I am convinced Motown is one of America's greatest contributions to world culture. I was excited to meet Diana because Motown was now part of Universal and I was selling her records in Russia. But also, as a kid growing up in Ohio, I heard a lot of her music because my mother adored her. She'd played the first Supremes and Temptations team-up album so often that I think she wore out the vinyl. I was able to tell Diana about my mother when we had our photo taken together. That's when I made a faux pas. I told her I had just purchased a home in Los Angeles and asked her, "Where do you live?" She smiled and said, "I usually don't give out that information." I quickly apologized and explained I just meant in general—I wasn't asking for her home address. I'll never forget my gaffe, and I will never forget meeting Diana Ross.

I felt pretty good about the success we had with Andris. Boris and I teamed up again when I focused on our jazz roster. When Rock & Roll Hall of Famer Herbie Hancock came to Russia to perform in the city's shiny and new modern concert hall, the Moscow International House of Music on Bolotny Island on the Moscow River, I was there to welcome him, and after his show, I was even more inspired to find a Russian jazz artist I could add to the pantheon of great Universal jazz artists.

Things fell into place when Diana Krall came to Moscow in 2003 to perform at the Moscow Conservatory, a prestigious venue where Rachmaninoff studied and from which he graduated in 1892. Tchaikovsky also performed there in the nineteenth century. Just four blocks from the Kremlin, it was like a Mecca for musicians. Diana was well respected by the Russians and was invited to play there rather than at a pop concert venue.

Her album was selling well for us, especially in Moscow, making her one of our best-selling artists—bigger than Pavarotti or Bocelli. I met her before the show backstage—except there was no backstage at the conservatory, just a prep room that served as her dressing room. I mentioned to her that I was looking to sign a local jazz artist, and she offered, "I studied with Igor Butman at the Berklee School of Music in Boston. You should check him out."

Boris and I had already been discussing that we should sign a legendary jazz artist rather than a new, up-and-coming musician. Butman was a virtuoso saxophonist who was so revered that President Bill Clinton, who knows something about the sax, invited him to perform at the White House. He checked the "legend" box for us.

Boris knew how to find Butman—he owned a place called Le Club in Taganskaya, a cool cultural region of Moscow where many famous jazz musicians have played. I didn't know if Igor would be interested in joining Universal, but I was willing to do my best to persuade him. He had been releasing his albums on his own small label in Russia. He pushed back on my offer and said, "t.A.T.u. was great. You can sell pop records. But jazz is different. If I sign with you, how do I know I will sell records in America, because that is what I want to do."

It's true that Universal was not the strongest jazz label. We were no. 1 in the classical world, but EMI had a much stronger jazz roster than we did, and when they found out I wanted to sign Butman, they went after him too.

◼

As an American CEO in Russia, I had a relationship with three different US ambassadors to Russia during my stay in the country. The ambassadors were always trying to bring American and Russian business people together during this great era of cooperation between the two superpowers. The US government had a deep desire to help Russia right its economy and learn market principles and capitalism.

The ambassador I had the best relationship with was Alexander Vershbow. I was on his radar for all kinds of events, and one day, I received a call from the cultural attaché at the US Embassy. He said the ambassador wanted to know if I would be interested in inviting some of my artists to perform at his residence, Spaso House. It is a fantastic estate and has an entire wing dedicated to presenting entertainment events in a gigantic glass ballroom. I said I would be happy to do so.

Thanks to the ambassador's request, I was able to tell Igor, "If you sign with me, I can promote you in the United States. I could even organize a concert for you at the American Embassy."

That piqued his interest. "I could play at Spaso?" he asked.

Every Muscovite knows about Spaso House, but few have ever been inside. Built in 1913, the neoclassical-style mansion became the official residence of the US ambassador in 1933, when America recognized the Soviet Union. Russians have always been fascinated by Spaso House, including author Mikhail Bulgakov, who wrote about the famous ballroom inside the mansion in his novel *The Master and Margarita*. Igor got his invite to play there, and I signed him to Universal.

The ambassador's residence is gated. It is a massive mansion with a residence. We were the first to enter, and it was post 9/11, so security was extremely tight. Guests were screened before they arrived. We passed through a gigantic rotunda into the glass ballroom. There were about two hundred guests, including my marketing team. I also invited everyone who worked in our warehouse, and everyone accepted because it was probably the only time in their lives they would be inside Spaso House.

I introduced Igor to the ambassador in the coat check room, and then we adjourned to the ballroom and mingled with the minister of culture, the chairman of Exxon, and ambassadors from France and South Korea, as well as many powerful Russians and Americans.

I went up onstage to introduce Igor, and he performed a brilliant one-hour set. He was on top of the world, and I had won his trust, arranging for him to play at this event and signing him with a major American label. The evening was a perfect preamble to getting him quickly into the studio to record his first album for us.

That night at the residence, the ambassador suggested that Igor play at Birdland in Manhattan. "When I lived in New York City, I would see a lot of great jazz at Birdland; you should book a show there," the ambassador said. Igor smiled, "Do you play any instruments, Mr. Ambassador?" The ambassador was happy to respond, "Yes, I was playing the drums when I studied at Columbia." The ambassador's Birdland suggestion was so popular with Igor that I wanted to make that happen.

Chris Roberts had been elevated to president of the classics and jazz division, and he helped organize an album release party at Birdland. It was a spectacular evening: Igor invited his friend, jazz vibraphonist Joe Locke, to perform with him onstage, and after the show, we went to my favorite restaurant in the city for dinner. The Russian Samovar in Midtown Manhattan, co-owned by Mikhail Baryshnikov, has twenty different flavors of vodka and the best chicken Kiev in the world.

In the end we did not sell a lot of Igor's albums, but at the time, no one was selling a lot of jazz records in the United States. Still, Igor was able to go back to Russia and tell everyone his album was on sale in America and he had played the legendary Birdland. It was good for his prestige at home.

Igor came to me with more projects. He wanted to record an album where Russian jazz vocalists would sing in English over his saxophone playing. I heard some of the demos, and they were not very good. I didn't think the album was going to work, so I passed.

Igor never recorded a second album for us. He returned to recording on his own independent label in Russia. He got what he wanted—an album released in America. I got what I wanted—I launched a Russian jazz artist in the United States. I liked working with Igor and being in the jazz world, but my responsibility was to make more money for Universal. If I was going to keep my job, I needed to be concentrating not on classical or jazz artists but best-selling pop stars like Elton John.

FIFTY-FOUR AND ABOVE

In the Soviet era, Moscow was a dull, gray city. But in the 1990s and early 2000s, everything changed a decade after perestroika, glasnost, and the presidency of Mikhail Gorbachev. A major factor in this transformation was money—Russia suddenly became flush with cash because the price of oil went through the roof, and Russia had a lot of oil to sell.

In the Soviet Union, there were no night clubs or discotheques. Russians love to party, but under the watchful eye of the KGB, they could only do so in underground venues and events in basements and cellars, as well as in dachas (second homes in the country for the wealthy). It was all in secret, but Communists had the wildest parties.

In the new economy, those brave Russians who organized the secret parties were now operating discotheques in Moscow. One of the most famous was Titanic, the first club to embrace the dance culture and feature deejays. In those early days, it did not have fancy lighting or state-of-the-art sound, and it was in an old bunker, so you could dance all night *and* survive a nuclear attack.

As basic as it was, Titanic made it possible to dance in public without being harassed by the police. But you could feel that better things were coming. In the early 2000s, Yeltsin left the stage, and Putin ascended to the presidency. Still, relations with the West were at their highest point since the Cold War. American companies were moving in, as were businesses from France, Germany, the United Kingdom, South Korea, and Brazil. Moscow was the first destination for these foreign companies, and their money flowed into the city. St. Petersburg was a second choice for these newcomers, but it was far outshadowed by Moscow.

With billions of dollars pouring into the capital, real estate, construction, and the automobile industry all benefited, but there was also enough money to fund these restaurants and night clubs. Massive dance clubs proliferated, and all of them had unlimited funds to create beautiful, luxurious environments with state-of-the-art lighting and sound. They were centered along the banks of the Moskva River. By 2002 Moscow had become one of the main destinations for clubbers from Europe.

Driving the development of these venues was the gay culture in Moscow—club owners who were not shy about their sexuality. Inspired by Studio 54 in New York City, gay promoters were bringing in the best gay deejays. Boy George, the Pet Shop Boys, and Mark Almond were coming to Moscow on weekends to deejay in these clubs. The first gay clubs opened in Moscow after homosexuality was officially decriminalized in 1993. Strongly influenced by the culture in the West, Russia's gay clubs were some of the first to invest in state-of-the-art sound and lighting systems. For a brief interval in time, gay culture in Russia was not under the constant repressive threat it had been during the Soviet Union, and this coincided with electronic dance music and club culture bursting onto the scene.

It was all allowed, and it was all just steps away from the Kremlin. In Moscow the closer a club was located to an institution of authority, the more rebellious or outlandish the club was. My favorite disco, Club XIII, was just across the street from KGB headquarters. Located in a historic mansion built in 1898, it had a beautiful interior that featured marble statues, large paintings, a winding staircase, and a fountain. It was the most decadent of all the clubs. There were multiple floors of go-go dancers and the hottest dance tracks from Europe blaring loudly through speakers.

Celebrities loved it and so did the oligarchs and powerful government officials. Even Russia's firebrand politicians from the State Duma would visit it, like when Vladimir Zhironovsky, who would rail against the LGBTQ community every day, dressed up in costume at one of Club XIII's wildest parties. The tradition of celebrating Halloween in Moscow started in the club, and one of their coolest events was a performance by the electronic dance music (EDM) duo Deep Dish, based in Washington, DC. They released a live album from the show. Club XIII helped make Moscow one of the coolest cities in the world.

During this exhilarating time, I noticed something strange about my young staff at Universal. They were brilliant at marketing our music and artists, and the company was doing very well. But they were no longer listening to our own artists. When I would visit with them or ride in their cars, they were never playing our music. Asya had assembled a team of the coolest twenty-year-olds in the city. They were smart, hardworking, and very good at promoting our artists. But they were listening to EDM. I jokingly confronted them: "Why aren't you listening to Smash!!? Don't you like t.A.T.u. anymore?"

The 1990s were the early days of the EDM culture in Moscow, and it was difficult to gauge who the most popular artists were. It wasn't just me—all of the major record companies were late to the EDM game. The genre was ruled by independent labels led by Ministry of Sound, based in London. There were others, like Café del Mar in Ibiza and Buddha-Bar in France.

By the early 2000s, hardly any major labels were releasing dance music compilations. They were not keeping up with the EDM movement, which was growing fast. Maybe because I was based in Moscow, where this new dance culture had taken over the city, I was a little ahead of my European colleagues. It helped that I recognized my own limitations in figuring out who were the best artists and relied on my clued-in marketing team to tell me. Inside of our marketing department was a special projects division that created music compilations for corporate clients to give away to staff. The biggest client was Absolut Vodka; the company had bought a special compilation of Swedish tracks to give to five thousand guests at their corporate Christmas party. Incredibly, the CD was shaped like an Absolut bottle; the women running special projects found technology to produce that unique configuration. It was one of the coolest gifts a corporation gave out that year, and it made us some money.

So I turned to this same division of entrepreneurial young women to create a new division for dance music compilations to license EDM music from Europe, mostly from small independent labels in places like Milan and Amsterdam. The independents were excited that Universal wanted their music. Of course, it wasn't worldwide Universal; it was Universal Russia, but it was still cool.

I met with the folks from Ministry of Sound at Marché International du Disque et de l'Édition Musicale (MIDEM), the annual international conference and trade show held in Cannes every January. We had lunch at the Hôtel Martinez on the Croisette, and I could tell they were worried about being seen in the company of a major label—they considered it flirting with the enemy.

I had to convince them that we were just "little ol' Universal Russia" and that we loved their music and wanted to license their tracks for our own domestic compilations. I said, "If you license your dance music to us, we'll make it popular in Moscow's dance clubs, and that will lead to paid gigs for your artists. It can be lucrative for your deejays to go on tour in Russia." This was a convincing argument. I managed to persuade them, and we built up trust and licensed their tracks, which led to other independent labels (like Hedkandi in the United Kingdom) that would not normally work with the majors getting in touch with us to see if we wanted to license their music.

Our new dance division's most popular series was a line of EDM compilations themed to different cities, including Paris, Berlin, and London. These were the days before Spotify and iTunes, so these collections gave Russian deejays access to music from all over Europe. The artists on these compilations loved it because it helped them get paying gigs in Russia. Most importantly, we were giving them exposure in our market.

The young women in the special projects division had created this successful new dance division that was producing some of the best dance compilations on the market. I didn't wait for my bosses to catch up with the dance music phenomenon. I knew, from listening to my young staff, we needed to ride that wave. Importing European EDM music led to domestic Russian artists recording their own dance music.

The biggest success was a duo known as PPK. Their track "Resu-Rection," which featured the voice of the first human being in space, Yuri Gagarin, on the remixes, was an international hit, peaking at no. 3 on the UK singles chart. That made them the first Russian act to appear on that British chart (just shortly before t.A.T.u.). I wish I had been able to sign PPK, but they made a deal with Paul Oakenfold's label. They never approached me, because they also didn't want to be associated with a major. Still, we were very supportive of them and were happy for their success.

My team and I promoted many different genres during my tenure at Universal Russia, but being involved in the EDM movement was one of the coolest things we ever did.

22

COMEBACKS

A versatile record executive—for example, Clive Davis or David Geffen—
is able to build the careers of new artists and legends alike. One of the
most satisfying things a record executive can do is resurrect the career of an
artist who was once at the top of his or her game and then fell on hard times.
I admired what Geffen had done to revive John Lennon's career after signing
him to his new eponymous label (shortly before the former Beatle's death).
Davis helped many artists, but my favorite story is how he rescued Carlos
Santana's career after he was dropped from his original label. Clive signed
him to Arista and gave him the biggest-selling album of his career.

After I turned three new Russian artists—Alsou, t.A.T.u., and Smash!!—
into superstars, I wanted to see if I could revive the fortunes of some former
stars who'd enjoyed a period of success and then found their careers stalled.

First, there was Kirill Tolmatsky, also known as Detsl. He'd been a young
boy in his early teens when his father, a media mogul and nightclub owner,
decided to make his son a pop star. The youngster's name was Kirill, but he
was given the stage name Detsl, which means "a little, not much." Detsl's
father lavished money on his son's career and produced videos to go along
with his songs. One video had the fifteen-year-old driving up in a Hummer
full of bikini-clad girls. Signed to an independent Russian label, young Detsl
had a couple of hit albums (*Who Are You?* in 2000 and *Street Fighter* in
2001), and his videos got some play on television.

Unfortunately, he was miserable. Kirill loved to write poetry and
wanted to compose his own music, but his father, Alexander Tolmatsky, a

Soviet-era deejay turned shrewd media mogul and nightclub owner in modern Russia, insisted on looking for songs from Russia's best pop songwriters.

A smart kid, he attended the British International School in Moscow and learned all about Europe right from childhood. Then he studied in Switzerland, where his roommate introduced him to hip hop music. When he turned eighteen, Kirill approached us at Universal to get a record deal. Some of us were skeptical because of his teen pop persona, and we didn't know if he would be taken seriously. Asya believed in him and was his champion at the label. She convinced me that we could produce an album that would make people forget about his past. She was right. His debut album for us turned out to be the biggest selling Russian reggae/hip hop album of all time.

He wrote all the songs and invited guest artists from the local hip hop community to be featured on some of the tracks. His songs were very spiritual, like his biggest hit, "God Does Exist." We filmed a video for it on the sand dunes of Morocco.

His father wanted to manage his son, but I was able to prevent that by sending artists to his club Infiniti (the first venue in the city to exclusively play hip hop music) to perform, including Akon, when he was in Moscow. That made the father happy and distracted him from wanting to be in charge of his son's career.

His album was so powerful that I wanted to get him signed to an American label. It never happened. But Asya reached out to the folks at Def Jam in the United States and arranged for Detsl to record a duet with Lyor Cohen's big new signing, Christina Milian. Meanwhile, the success of his album led to a massive tour of large venues in Russia; it was the biggest tour of his career.

But then he started to get in trouble for speaking out against Putin, the police, and the security forces. Rap music became the most popular music in Russia, and Detsl was one of the bravest voices speaking truth to corrupt authorities. He was my first artist to be boycotted. He was on the Kremlin's blacklist and couldn't get airplay or live gigs, and that effectively wrote the finish to his revived career.

Tragically, Detsl died of a heart attack in 2019 at the age of thirty-five. He had just given a performance near Moscow. His father, Alexander, was devastated by his son's untimely death. He had come to fully support Detsl's career in reggae and rap. Although he had envisioned a pop career for his son, after the album Detsl recorded for Universal, Alexander recognized his son's undeniable talent.

A year before Detsl's death, President Putin denounced rap music in a speech in St. Petersburg, claiming it would lead to the degradation of Russia and that it rested on the pillars of "sex, drugs, and protest." According to the Associated Press, Putin said that if it is "impossible" to stop rap music and its growing popularity, then government officials "must lead it and direct it."

I regret that I was unable to break Detsl in the West. His reggae/hip hop music was truly cutting edge, and he was a special talent gone too soon.

■

My next signing was an artist who went by the name of Dolphin (born Andrey Vyacheslavovich Lysikov). He was probably the most talented artist I signed to Universal. He had been a founding member of a Soviet-era boy band called Malchishnik. They were supposed to be a Russian answer to New Kids on the Block but turned out to be more in the brash and raunchy style of 2 Live Crew. Andrey was the driving force; he wrote their biggest hit, "Nonstop Sex." He pushed boundaries and took advantage of Gorbachev's opening of the Soviet Union by being one of the first artists to include explicit lyrics in his songwriting.

Dolphin left the boy band to pursue a solo career and was making beautiful, amazing music, but he wasn't marketed properly, and no one was paying attention to his career development. Asya bumped into him at a club and found out he had recorded a new album. She wanted me to hear it. I thought it was outstanding, in the same vibe as Moby and Radiohead, and I offered him a deal.

The album was a masterpiece, but I didn't hear a hit single. It was risky to launch the album without a powerful first song for radio. For the lack of a hit, the album might not take off, and it was too good to take a chance. When Jimmy Iovine received the master for Eminem's album *The Marshall Mathers LP*, he loved it but didn't hear a song that could be a huge radio hit. He asked Eminem and Dr. Dre to come up with one more track that could be a hit song. Eminem was pissed but came back with the biggest hit of his career at that point: "The Real Slim Shady." *The Marshall Mathers LP* album went on to sell more than fifteen million copies. Jimmy Iovine had been right, as he'd cared about the success of Eminem's masterpiece. I was in the same situation.

Further, Dolphin's entire album was in Russian, which limited my ability to make him a star in Europe. So I insisted he record a duet with a young woman from Los Angeles who was recommended to me by our office staff in London, where they were working on her new album. She was a terrific singer named Stella Kastsoudas. We flew Stella to Moscow to record the song "Eyes" and to make a video. Dolphin sang in Russian, while Stella sang in English. Russian radio loved it, and the song went to no. 1 on our alternative rock station and on another station that only played Russian rock.

"This is history in the making!" announced Mikhail Kozyrev, legendary deejay for Nashe Radio. "We've never played a song in Russian and English on this station before, this is the first time it has been good enough." Mikhail was one of the most influential persons on the radio in Russia; he had learned his radio skills in Los Angeles and applied them in Russia. His support for Dolphin helped launch the album.

We knew Dolphin's album was going to be special when Russia's leading music critic, Artemy Troitsky, wrote a positive review. Troitsky was an important antiestablishment figure and a prolific writer whose articles inspired Russian artists to adapt and progress to compete with the West. Dolphin was this kind of artist.

Despite the song's hit status, Dolphin never forgave me for pushing that idea on him, because it didn't line up with his vision. *Star* was the best-selling album of his career, and it returned him to the top of the charts, where he belonged. So I'd been right as far as improving the album but wrong about going against his own vision.

To make it up to Dolphin, Asya and her marketing team made a music video for his second single, "Vesna," which means "Spring." It's an emotional song that Dolphin had wanted to release as the lead single for the album. The video was made entirely from stock footage of the opening and closing ceremonies for the 1980 Summer Olympics in Moscow. President Jimmy Carter had ordered a US boycott of the Olympics that year because of the Soviet invasion of Afghanistan.

To see these images was a big revelation for me. They showed an Olympics that were hidden from us in the West. But Asya's team chose not to use any footage of the sports competitions, opting instead for the footage of the ceremonies. The video was all about international friendship and peace. In the final moments, as the Olympic flame was about to be extinguished and the ceremonies were coming to a close, a gigantic inflatable balloon shaped like a Russian bear and named Mishka was released into the air; it flew above Olympic Stadium into the Moscow evening as the crowd waved goodbye. It brought a tear to my eye to see the finished product Asya's team had made for this beautiful song. It's one of the most emotional songs and videos I've ever seen.

■

In 2003 Björk came to Moscow for a sold-out concert at Olympic Stadium. The promoter was my old friend, Nadia Solovieva. We were working together to publicize Björk's show when Nadia told me that a banker friend of hers, Lev Isakovich Geiman, the father of one of Russia's legendary artists, had reached out to her with a request. His daughter wanted to meet Björk.

I asked who the artist was, and though Nadia only told me it was Linda, I knew exactly who Linda was. She was very successful in the 1990s, when I was a student in Leningrad. She had a great run of hits, including one of Russia's first antidrug songs—"Marijuana," released in 1996. But she had been controlled by an evil Phil Spector–type producer. There had been allegations of the producer being violent with her, and she had to stop working with him, which hurt her career very badly.

In the early 2000s, BMG signed Linda. They released an album titled *Zrenie*, and it was just OK, nothing great. But they didn't do any promotion, and the album failed. Linda, a very sweet, sensitive, and fragile soul, was understandably depressed. I'd seen what Doug Morris and Lyor Cohen had done for Mariah Carey after she left Columbia Records, and I thought I could do the same for Linda. So I cleared it with Björk's manager for Linda and her father to attend the show and meet Björk afterward.

The show was amazing. Lev, Linda, and I were in a VIP zone just to the side of the stage. The after-party was wilder than the concert. We were in a huge green room usually used by athletes during sporting events at the stadium. Björk had her entire band there, playing acoustic instruments while she danced in the center of the room. The guests were all dancing, too, and singing along, and Linda couldn't help herself—suddenly, she moved into the center of the room and was dancing with Björk. I looked over at Lev, and he had the hugest smile on his face. His daughter's depression had lifted, and she was the happiest she had been in months.

I was a hero in Lev's eyes, and I was invited to their home on the top floor of a building Lev owned in downtown Moscow. They had prepared a tremendous Russian buffet for me, and they couldn't stop thanking me.

I knew this was an opportunity for me, but I wasn't sure if I should take it. Linda was still signed to BMG, and while the people running the label were my competitors, they were also my colleagues in our industry trade organization. I was enjoying the feast when Lev invited me downstairs to his recording studio on the first floor. It was a state-of-the-art, modern facility built by German engineers who'd been specially flown in to construct it.

Waiting there to meet me was Linda's producer, Mikhail Kuvshinov. He'd produced only the one album for her: *AtakA*. I had seen Mikhail's name in multiple places; at the time, he was a young kid who was just starting out in the business. And that's when I realized I was not the only person in the room with an agenda.

They played the first four tracks of an album they were working on. I was sitting at the recording console, and I had no idea what all the dials and needles meant, but I knew a hit song when I heard one—and I heard four of them in a row.

I asked Lev what their plan was for these new recordings, and he said that BMG wouldn't know what to do with them. "They will mess it all up," he insisted. "Only you can help us, David."

I couldn't believe this was working out exactly the way I wanted it to. I told Lev I wanted to play the four tracks for my team. The next morning, I invited Asya and our radio plugger, Sasha Rodmanich, to sit in my Audi and listen to the songs on the car's fantastic sound system. I always tested new demos from artists on my car radio to see if the song sounded like a radio hit. They agreed with me: we were hearing hit after hit. We immediately signed Linda, stealing her from BMG.

At the time, she was fascinated with Japanese culture, so we decided to introduce her as a Universal artist by hiring a production company in Japan to create an anime video for her first single. It went straight to no. 1 on MTV. The next three singles also topped the chart, and the album was Linda's best-selling release of her entire career.

With incredible lighting and sound in her live stage shows, Linda became one of the most avant-garde artists working in the Russian music business. Her show was like a Kabuki rock opera. It was always exciting to see her perform. Linda was one of the first artists to include strange and interesting visuals and unique percussion instruments in her show.

She was a consummate artist, like her idol Björk. I enjoyed my friendship with her father Lev. He was a strong man, an Ashkenazi Jew who had survived many struggles and was brought from Tolyatti to Moscow by Boris Yeltsin, then a Communist Party boss, to run a refrigerator factory. I was fascinated listening to his stories about the old Soviet Union; we sometimes sat for hours in the famous Sandunovksy Bathhouse, where the tsars had their sauna and steam baths and where one of the last scenes of the Hollywood film *Gorky Park* took place.

So I'd made my vision come true, reviving the careers of three well-known artists whose fortunes had dimmed. My achievement was recognized by *Molotok*, which was like a Russian version of *Spin* or *New Musical Express*. The editors ran a cover story with the headline, "They're Back." Although Detsl, Dolphin, and Linda never managed to break through internationally like my pop signings Alsou, t.A.T.u., and Smash!! had, they were very important to my development as a record executive. I wanted to be a versatile leader like Clive Davis, able to bring both new and veteran artists to their peak performance. When Quentin Tarantino cast John Travolta in the film *Pulp Fiction*, it had resurrected the career of one of cinema's most popular actors. I did my best to make the same thing happen for my three Russian comeback artists.

23

PEAK PERFORMANCE IN EASTERN EUROPE

My career as an American music executive had a definite trajectory that could be easily plotted, and the peak moment arrived when *Billboard* published an article about me upon my promotion to Universal's VP of Eastern Europe. Every recording artist would love to be written up in *Rolling Stone*, and every person in the music business would like to be featured in *Billboard*, the music industry's leading trade publication.

You can find print copies of the magazine on executives' desks all over the world, so having a feature story with your photograph registers in the consciousness of many industry leaders. Appearing in *Billboard* was the affirmation that I had finally made it after leaving the farm in Ohio. My mother bought dozens of copies and shared them with her friends.

My boss and friend for many years at Universal was London-based Thomas Hedström, who was in charge of all of Eastern Europe. As the CEO of Universal Music Russia, I reported to him until he was poached by one of our competitors, EMI. They put Thomas in charge of Eastern Europe and Scandinavia, which was a natural fit, since he was from Sweden. EMI wanted him mainly because of his success in developing t.A.T.u. into a multimillion-dollar enterprise for Universal. When Thomas moved to EMI, Universal Music International president and chief operating officer (COO) John Kennedy asked me if I wanted Thomas's job, and I said yes.

I moved into this new role on April 23, 2003, and it was a great opportunity for me to remain in charge of the office in Russia while looking after our labels in Bulgaria, Estonia, Latvia, Lithuania, Ukraine, Romania, Serbia,

Slovenia, and Croatia. I also handled Iceland, Malta, and Gibraltar, beyond the borders of Eastern Europe.

As *Billboard* pointed out in the article, I was the first person to take on this portfolio while based in Moscow. This position had always been filled by a London-based executive or someone in Berlin or Vienna. I thought it was more important to remain on the front lines and be closer to the offices in my charge than to sit in a top-floor corporate office in the United Kingdom.

A VP job is corporate by nature and filled with bureaucratic responsibilities, especially with overseeing a large region like Eastern Europe. But I didn't want to stop working directly with artists; being based in London or Berlin would have done that.

Of course, I had another reason for wanting to remain in my Moscow office: I didn't want to leave Russia. Natalia and I had just purchased our first apartment together in the Moscow suburb of Tushino. With two sons, our family was growing, and Max, our oldest son, was becoming completely bilingual while attending a great Russian kindergarten. My wife's father, Yuri, an award-winning nuclear scientist at the famous Kyrchatov Institute, lived nearby. We wanted to stay close to him. I had learned so much from Yuri. His father was a Soviet admiral and lifelong Communist Party member, but Yuri didn't join the party; he took a different path and was there in downtown Moscow when Yeltsin stood on a tank, calling for an end to Communist Party rule. Watching him love his daughter Natalia and our sons, Max and Nick, I can confirm to Sting that the Russians do love their children too.

On weekends and during summers, we lived at our country home, a log cabin in a pine forest on the famous Volga River. We'd invite family, friends, and neighbors from the small village nearby to play Russian billiards, a much harder game than American billiards. I would cut wood in the day and stack the logs in the fire oven that heated our old-fashioned Russian sauna to two hundred degrees Fahrenheit for a traditional Russian *banya* in the evening. Our summer home in the Russian countryside was a sanctuary from the chaos and pollution in Moscow. It was my favorite place to be in Russia. It was a life I did not want to give up.

I did fly to London once a month to meet with Kennedy about my territories, and I paid regular visits to all of the countries that reported to me.

When I was in the Moscow office, I spent half my day on business in Russia and the other half on all of the other countries. The main reason I could spend time away from the office is that Asya and her team were handling things so well while I was visiting Universal affiliates in Eastern Europe, such as Andrey Dakhovsky, who was in our Universal office in Ukraine, or Stanislava Armoutlivea in Sofia, Bulgaria, or Ioana Fesnic in Bucharest, Romania, or Boris Horvat in Zagreb, Croatia, or Rodoljub Stojanovic in Belgrade, Serbia. My role model for doing all this traveling was Thomas. He's the person who built up all these territories.

He and I were the first foreign record executives to set foot in Belarus, which was somewhat scary because Alexander Lukashenko was the president even then; his reign in office began in 1994. He has maintained a highly authoritarian government ever since, and I don't think he has ever appreciated Western pop music.

Thomas and I were also the first Western music executives to make a business trip to Kazakhstan, where I ate horse meat for the first time. I didn't know exactly what was on my plate until after I'd eaten it.

On these trips we were usually greeted at the airport by a small delegation on the tarmac, where, by custom, we would be offered a little piece of bread. Then we'd enter the country through a VIP area, and police escorts would accompany us to our hotel, where the local television news reporters would interview us. Thomas and I felt like Butch Cassidy and the Sundance Kid. Later we found out our colleagues in these countries were secretly calling us Beavis and Butt-Head.

When I was making these trips on my own, the Eastern European music executives wanted to know how they could create the next t.A.T.u., how to build their industry, how to install protections for songwriters and intellectual property, and how to run a label like we were doing in Moscow. I felt like a cultural ambassador for the United States of America. I was teaching young Eastern Europeans who were new to the music business how we were going to sell the new Black Eyed Peas album and promote the next Jay-Z release. I explained how they could work with radio and their local MTV, as well as the press.

This is why I left Ohio and moved to Russia in the first place: to bring American know-how to the former Soviet Union. Now I was expanding it to Eastern Europe. My success in Russia made me a credible voice.

I was a frequent visitor to the Baltic countries because we were making a hard push to sell our music there, which they were very open to after breaking away from the Soviet Union. Estonia had the most advanced music industry, probably due to their proximity to Finland, and they were poised for big success. Sven Aabreldaal, the record label head for Universal there, was one of the smartest executives in the Eastern European music business.

Even back then, they were warning me about Russia. Most people in the Baltics never believed Russia would become democratic. Under Soviet rule and repression, the people of the Baltics had suffered more than the Hungarians, Czechs, and Poles. They had a long, dark history with Russia, which left them no illusions about a "new Russia." In November 2002 they were invited to join NATO, along with Bulgaria, Romania, Slovakia, and Slovenia, and they were officially admitted in March 2004. They understood the Russians and knew they would be coming for them one day. They warned the United States, Britain, and Germany about this in the early 2000s.

During this time my new position meant I was becoming very well-known in all of the territories I visited. I was receiving all kinds of invitations, including requests to participate on expert juries at music festivals and song contests.

Eastern Europeans love their song contests. They have been a tradition for decades, long before *American Idol* and *The X Factor* appeared on the scene. It is why the annual Eurovision Song Contest is so important for all Europeans. I was once invited to participate in a prestigious song contest in Ukraine's western city of Lviv, an ancient city close to the Polish border. We had just opened a Universal Music office in the capital, Kyiv, and I wanted to do more to help Ukraine build its own music industry independent from Russia, which had overshadowed Ukrainian culture for centuries.

The wildest invitation to a song contest I ever received was to chair a jury in Transylvania. Romania's legendary song competition was the Golden Stag Festival, which ran from 1968 to 1971, when it was shut down by the Communist authorities. After the fall of the Berlin Wall and the end of Communist rule, the festival resumed in 1992.

The Golden Stag was a big deal, and every year, performers from all over the world were invited to perform. Artists who traveled to Romania include Diana Ross, UB40, Christina Aguilera, Tom Jones, Dionne Warwick, INXS, Cyndi Lauper, and many more.

In 2004 I was invited along with Thomas Hedström to be cochairs of the jury. It was great to be with him, even though he was now a competitor with rival EMI. The festival is held every year in the small town of Brasov in the middle of summer. When we were there, it was a beautiful night, and the sky was filled with stars.

The festival site in Brasov is only a few minutes' drive from Dracula's castle in Transylvania. Another police escort arrived, and we were loaded onto buses to take a VIP tour of the castle. Bram Stoker's Dracula was fictional, but the castle had actually been inhabited by Vlad the Impaler, who was so named because he impaled a lot of invading forces on behalf of the Ottoman Empire. He was eventually imprisoned in his own castle. Sensing a cash cow, the Romanians later turned the place into a tourist attraction.

After the tour it was back to the festival, where one hundred thousand people were gathered in the main square, surrounded by sixteenth- and seventeenth-century architecture. Thomas and I chaired the jury made up of Romanian celebrities. While the jury was deliberating in a building on the square, the headliner for the evening was performing. P!nk blew the crowds away in Transylvania that night.

As we cast our ballots, from the open balcony we could hear P!nk singing her latest hit "God Is a DJ," which was dominating music charts in Europe. It was another reminder that American pop music had won the hearts of Eastern Europeans. After the show Thomas and I went onstage to announce the winner of the song contest, Eleanor Cassar from Malta.

It was a thrill for me to be in Transylvania, onstage in front of thousands of Romanians, giving away the prize. It was the moments like this that made me realize I had one of the greatest jobs in the world.

The days I spent as VP of Eastern Europe were the best of my career. But dark days were ahead, with some dangerous, difficult experiences that would eventually drive me out of Russia.

PART 7

DARK DAYS

BAND TROUBLES

There were times during my years at Universal Music when I had to deal with some of the most controversial artists in the world who were making their first visit to Russia. It comes with the territory of running a label—you have a wide variety of musicians who require special handling. When one of Interscope Records' top artists, Marilyn Manson, announced a European leg of his new tour, "Guns, God, and Government," with a February 2001 stop in St. Petersburg and Moscow, I was immediately fearful this was going to the hardest test of my career as a record executive.

Marilyn's stage was full of satanic-themed props, and he had already caused trouble in the United States while on tour, getting arrested for physically harassing a police officer on stage. I was certain the Russian Orthodox Church would try to block the concert and picket in front of our record company office. I expected Marilyn Manson would be an easy target, and there was a reasonable possibility I would be visiting him in the Federal Security Service's Lefortovo prison. Fortunately for us, the church was in disarray in 2001.

It was rebuilding after decades of neglect and persecution under Communist rule, and it hadn't yet assumed its powerful role in everyday Russia. The church stayed largely silent on Marilyn's 2001 show. Only years later, in 2014, after the church had fully regained its power, was it able to block Marilyn Manson's planned tour of Russia on moral grounds. But on this first visit to Russia in February 2001, the main thing that stood in the way of his live, sold-out show at Moscow's Olympic arena was Mother Nature, which caused an incident on the road from St. Petersburg to Moscow.

It was a typical Russian winter, and there was a massive snowstorm. Russian snowstorms stopped Napoleon and Hitler, and this one stopped Marilyn Manson because the bus ran off the road and was stuck for hours before help arrived to dig the vehicle out.

When I heard the news, I was worried but not surprised. The Leningrad Highway was the most important highway in the country, connecting the two largest cities, St. Petersburg and Moscow. But it was one of the worst-maintained roads in the country. Crater-sized potholes would open up from the heavy traffic and the harsh winter weather conditions. Russian maintenance crews would throw salt to make it less slippery, but that only led to further deterioration. Repairs were haphazard, and government funds meant to upkeep the highway were siphoned off by corrupt local officials.

If the holes didn't get you, corrupt traffic police officers would. One of the scariest traffic stops I'd ever experienced happened when a corrupt traffic cop accused me of drinking and driving. I wasn't, but he ordered me to walk over to a rusty old ambulance parked nearby, where a nurse was prepared to draw blood to test my alcohol level. The bribe paid to that corrupt traffic cop saved me not from a DUI but from a rusty needle.

But the tour bus crash on the side of the notorious Leningrad Highway wasn't enough to stop Marilyn Manson; it only forced a one-day delay in the sold-out Moscow performance.

The upside of all of this was that I proved I could work with a controversial artist; I delivered for Interscope, and Marilyn Manson didn't get arrested in Russia.

■

A few years later saw another controversial act that was even more potentially dangerous for me than Marilyn Manson. Rammstein was East Germany's answer to West Germany's beloved Scorpions. That band's 1991 hit "Wind of Change," a song about hope and optimism, became one of the most consequential songs of the twentieth century and contributed in part to the end of the Cold War. The Scorpions were so popular in the Soviet Union, Mikhail Gorbachev invited the band to the Kremlin. Fast forward a decade, and Rammstein had replaced the Scorpions as the most popular German rock band in Russia, and their apocalyptic view of the world couldn't be more opposite.

The six members of Rammstein grew up in East Germany under Communist rule. Their fathers were intellectuals, and one was a professor who taught at Moscow State University, so the band had a deep connection to Russia. East Germany suffered badly during World War II and never really recovered under the postwar grip of the Soviet Union. The members of Rammstein were inspired by the East German punk rock scene that had blossomed at the end of perestroika.

The Scorpions sang about peace and freedom. Rammstein sang about cannibalism, sadomasochism, and murder, all typical topics for death metal music.

Rammstein's use of fascist imagery was controversial, especially set against their militaristic music and onstage pyrotechnics. The truth is that the six members are not Nazis or fascists. They are actually soft-spoken, left-wing liberals. It was all a performance. They weren't dangerous, but I couldn't help but worry about what Russians would think of them.

The band's third album, *Mutter*, was released in 2001 and was their first album with Universal. It was their best-selling release to date, and it topped the charts in Germany, Austria, and Switzerland. It was huge in Russia as well, so they decided to play a live gig in Moscow. We were excited about that because it was going to be a massive show. It was their fifth date on their winter European tour, set at the Dvorets Sporta Luzhniki arena, a thirteen thousand-seat venue that was built in 1956.

Tim Renner, CEO and chairman of Universal Music Germany, called me about Rammstein's upcoming Moscow show because the group was the label's number one priority and because their goal was to be a huge success in Russia. Tim wanted to make sure I would meet the guys and take them to dinner.

I assured him that we wanted everyone to be talking about Rammstein coming to Russia, that we would make certain MTV was playing their videos (they were), and that Russian radio was playing their songs (they were, which was rare, as they did not get a lot of airplay in other countries). We also mapped out plans for press interviews, which were easy to arrange because Rammstein was so popular in Russia. Every media outlet wanted to talk to them.

Tim had one main concern: "As you know, they use a lot of fire and pyrotechnics in their show. They can't do their act without them. It's already preset and synchronized to the band's music, and we are worried about the Russians because they're famous for extracting bribes."

I explained to Tim that this was the responsibility of the promoter, and I would talk to him to make sure everything was in place.

Rammstein's person in Russia was Ed Ratnikov, the second-best promoter in the country following Nadia Solovieva, and she only worked with the pop divas, leaving the rowdy rock bands to Ed's agency. Ed got his start with my old boss Boris Zosimov on the 1991 Monsters of Rock festival that featured Metallica and AC/DC. He was used to dealing with rock bands and Russian bureaucracy.

I promised Tim we wouldn't let the Russian fire marshal put Rammstein in jail. My first meeting with Rammstein was at the dinner Tim had asked me to arrange. Along with key members of my staff, I took them to Café Pushkin, one of Moscow's most iconic restaurants, set inside an eighteenth-century aristocrat's mansion. I was expecting to meet six heavily tattooed, motorcycle-driving, mean, rowdy, and muscled Hells Angels types. I was wrong. They showed up wearing jackets and dress shirts.

We were in a private room to keep us away from their fans, who were waiting outside the restaurant since they'd heard Rammstein was going to be dining there. Asya talked to the band about marketing and media, but I went in a different direction, asking them personal questions. That's when I discovered one of their fathers was a German-language professor who had taught at Moscow State University. They all had relatives in Russia, as well as many friends, because there were always a lot of Soviets in East Germany (Putin's career had been launched there, in Dresden).

We talked about Russian culture and Russian authors and Russian art. The evening felt like an intellectual cocktail party. The band had questions for me about the Russian music industry and the problem of piracy. I explained how their music was released on pirated CDs and they found that laughable since their main source of income was their sold-out concerts.

The night of the show, I asked Asya to find Ed and confirm everything had been worked out. But Ed wasn't answering his phone. I'm sure he was getting a million calls before the show from people asking for free tickets and things like that, but we needed to confirm that the fire marshal was satisfied with all the arrangements.

The Berlin office, which was nervous that it hadn't been worked out with the fire marshal, kept calling Asya. I was with Asya when I heard her yell into the phone to the label reps in Germany: "I'm not going to let them get arrested."

We both were starting to panic. It could be a disaster for us.

Asya noticed the fire marshal standing around backstage. It was thirty minutes before the show. We still couldn't find Ed. We had to make a decision.

I told Asya I was ready to pay the bribe. That was so common in Russia; it was done everywhere. Teachers were bribed in schools, doctors took bribes to provide better medical care, and almost all traffic police stops involved a bribe. Every year the fire marshal would visit our office building, finding infractions and demanding a payment of a few thousand dollars from our landlord, who then billed us. It was a fact of life in Russia, and so it would be no surprise if it were happening at a rock concert. I called my secretary and asked her to request the accounting department to give her $5,000 that she could immediately bring to the arena so I could take care of this if Ed hadn't.

I stepped outside the arena to meet my secretary and grab the cash, and then I ran back inside and heard loud music and drums—the band was already playing on stage. I was too late.

I hurried to the backstage area and saw fire raining down everywhere, as well as a barrage of pyrotechnics shooting out into the arena. I'd never seen so much fire. Richard Kruspe, the charming lead guitarist I'd talked culture with the previous night, was now a demon on stage, spewing a stream of fire from his guitar that reached far out into the audience. The arena was rocking. There were no troublemakers, just young girls and guys singing the German lyrics to "Du Hast" in unison with lead vocalist Till Lindemann. I noticed the fire marshal was watching; he wasn't making a move. I had the $5,000 in an envelope in my pocket, but it seemed he wasn't going to arrest anybody.

Then someone tapped me on the shoulder. I turned around. It was Ed Ratnikov. He gave me a big hug. I yelled, "Ed, the fire marshal, is he OK?"

Ed looked at me and winked. Then he moved on to take care of something else. I was so relieved. He never told me what he did to satisfy the fire marshal, but Rammstein was lucky to have a well-connected, unafraid promoter like Ed.

As for the $5,000, I returned it to the office safe the next day, though for one brief moment, I was tempted to take Rammstein out on the town after the show for the grandest night of their lives.

Their Moscow concert was a huge success and gave my team a lot of credibility. Tim was delighted. Rammstein returned to Russia many times; it was their second-biggest market after their home country. The band made a lot of money in Russia, but when the invasion of Ukraine started in 2022, the members immediately condemned Putin's war and were blacklisted. They sacrificed a lot of income because of their political stance, which I admire. They will never tour Russia again.

25

NOT *GUILTY*

After six successes in a row, three with new artists (Alsou, t.A.T.u., and Smash!!) and three with the revived careers of established artists (Detsl, Dolphin, and Linda), I was brimming with confidence and ready to take on a new challenge. I knew exactly what I wanted to do and was certain it would be another triumph in my career.

Alla Pugacheva was Russia's no. 1 female diva. Since her first-recorded song, "Robot" (1965), she'd released over a hundred records and sold more than 250 million copies. She is considered a living legend, with the same status we award to Barbra Streisand in the United States, and has been dubbed the Czarina of Russian Pop. She was part of the Estrada, a collection of artists acceptable to the Kremlin. This group of performers sing about patriotism and the ideals that Communist authorities want the masses to hear. They were the only artists allowed on Russian television, with their songs written by Moscow's Union of Russian Composers—like our Tin Pan Alley but with rigid censorship.

After being part of the Estrada for many years, Alla started to deviate from the party line and sing about forbidden topics, like the problems women have in Russian society. This new direction made her not only more popular but untouchable, because people appreciated her honesty. Her fan base included many elements of Russian society from housewives to workers to young people to grandparents.

One song that granted her superstar status was "Kings Can Do Anything," a song about a king who can never marry for love, and it was actually her brazen critique of male bureaucrats who steal and think they can get away with their crimes. She was told she could record the song but not perform it live in concert, because Communist leaders and VIPs would be in her audiences. She sang it anyway, never addressing a person by name; she would simply say, "This is for you, my dear governor" or "Communist Party boss."

Not only didn't she get in trouble, she kept winning more awards, like the Medal of the Order "For Merit to the Fatherland." A running joke during Leonid Brezhnev's reign was "Who is Brezhnev? He is a minor figure in the Alla Pugacheva era."

From 1969 to 1993, Alla had three marriages, and in 1994, she married her fourth husband, Russian pop star Philipp Kirkorov, a six-foot-four, outrageously dressed Bulgarian with a huge personality. It was a union of the two biggest pop stars in Russia. I met Philipp one year after he'd married Alla, when he was signed to PolyGram. Later, he was a huge supporter of Smash!! and was often seen at our office parties.

In 2005 I was reading a biography of one of my role models, David Geffen. After heading up Asylum Records, he started his own eponymous label, and his first three signings were John Lennon, Elton John, and Donna Summer. I thought about how he'd brought Lennon back to the top of the charts with *Double Fantasy* and how the first single, "Just Like Starting Over," was one of the biggest of Lennon's solo career. If it were not for his assassination in 1980, Lennon's comeback would have given him a long career with Geffen as his record label. This inspired me to consider doing the same thing by bringing to Universal a Russian icon who was no longer at the top of the charts. Asya and her team tried to discourage me, saying I shouldn't get involved with any artist who was part of the Estrada.

"They are the Kremlin's people," she told me. "Leave them alone."

But I had become a little arrogant; I didn't want to be told who we could and could not work with in Russia, and I was naïve about the Estrada. "What are you worried about?" I asked her.

So certain of my success rate and that I could not fail, I had a lot of conversations with Philipp, and then one day, inspiration struck. My mother was a huge fan of female vocalists. Her record collection included many albums by Carole King, Dionne Warwick, Gladys Knight, Cher, Helen Reddy, Carly Simon, Olivia Newton-John, and Barbra Streisand.

One of my mother's favorite albums was Streisand's LP record with Barry Gibb, *Guilty*. It was a great work for both artists—two giants coming together on a fantastic collaboration. Inspired by my mother's love of this album, I thought we could do Russia's answer to *Guilty* by recording a duet album with Alla and Philipp.

It would be even better than the Barbra and Barry team-up because Alla and Philipp were husband and wife. Nothing approaching this had ever been tried in Russia before. I talked to one of America's most successful producers about my idea; Walter Afanasieff had helmed no. 1 singles for Mariah Carey and Celine Dion. I knew it would be easy to fly Alla and Philipp to Los Angeles to record the album. Finding songs would also be easy—composers would love coming up with new material for Russia's top two stars. I envisioned the album cover. Alla loved being seen in the company of younger men, and Philipp was eighteen years her junior. Philipp loved to be seen with Alla. So the LP cover would be the two of them embracing.

■

I wanted to set up a meeting with Alla, but before I could, fate intervened. A year after Smash!! won the *New Wave* song contest in Latvia, I was invited back to be on the jury, and the chairperson was Alla. So I met her for the first time during the three-day event. In my career I've worked one-on-one with Sting, Elton John, Mariah Carey, and Bryan Adams, among many others, and I was never nervous.

But I was starstruck with Alla.

I truly wasn't ready to pitch her the idea yet—I needed more things to fall into place first, so I figured while we were both in Latvia, I would just get to know her better. During our jury meetings, the conversation was limited to talking about the competing artists and their songs. And although the jury was filled with celebrities, I was the only label executive on the panel, and I noticed Alla paying attention to the things I had to say.

I knew that the Russian authorities always wanted a Russian singer to win the contest, but I thought the singer from Ukraine, Tina Karol, deserved first place. I persuaded the jury, entirely made up of Russians, to vote for Tina, and ultimately, I had to persuade Alla, as the top prize was named the Alla Pugacheva Award. If Alla hadn't supported Tina (who then became the best-selling female pop artist in Ukraine and a cultural ambassador for her country), I don't think she would have won.

That told me a lot about Alla—she was sincere, authentic, and did not stick to the party line. As a result, I knew she was going to agree to my team-up idea once I pitched to her. My staff warned me one last time not to proceed with the project, but I didn't listen. I arranged to have a big, fancy dinner with Alla and Philipp.

Mikhail Topalov, the father of Smash!!'s Vlad, joined us. He had become good friends with Philipp after Smash!! was invited to be the opening act on Philipp's tour of the United States that included a sold-out show at the Kodak Theater in Hollywood. Mikhail knew all the best private clubs and restaurants, and since we needed to impress Alla but not in a public setting, I asked him if we could have dinner at his private club. Private clubs in Moscow were popular with celebrities and gangsters because of the tight security to get in, but they also featured some of the best dining in city.

I asked Mikhail and Philipp to meet me ahead of time so we could rehearse the presentation to Alla. Philipp was immediately all in when I explained my idea. "This is going to happen," he told me. "Barbra Streisand and Barry Gibb—yes!"

Mikhail was excited because he was helping me to bring together two Russian legends. I was just as thrilled because this was going to be bigger than t.A.T.u.—probably the crowning achievement of my career. I was certain people would call me the Clive Davis of Russia after the success of this album.

Alla walked into the restaurant with her bodyguards, and it was like a queen was arriving. There were a few powerful people dining that evening but none of them more important than Alla. The patrons and staff in the restaurant all stood, frozen in place, watching her walk toward us.

Alla gave me a short glance. She flashed a brief smile, and that was it. But I knew we were colleagues from the jury in Latvia and everything was going to be OK.

I found out later that her cold exterior was a cover for being nervous. The last time she was associated with an international label was when she'd recorded an English album titled *Alla Pugacheva in Stockholm*, produced in Sweden. Alla wanted an international audience, knowing she could be as big as Streisand on the world stage. But her Swedish album did not do well.

We all sat down at the table, and before the food arrived, I told her about my mother's love for *Guilty*. Mikhail and Philipp were all smiles, but Alla had a strange look on her face. I continued and told her, "So I was thinking how amazing it would be—and what an honor it would be for Universal and me personally—if we produced an album of duets with you."

She looked up suddenly and said, "Duets? With who?"

I replied, "With Philipp—your husband!"

And she looked at him and said, "I'm not singing with him. Ever."

It was the first time that evening that she made direct eye contact with me. Mikhail and Philipp were staring down at the table. With laser-like focus on me, she said, "You must not understand. I don't sing with him. I don't even think he has that much talent."

I apologized and said, "Maybe I'm out of line, but I thought it was such a great idea and I was hoping you would—"

She cut me off and said, "I'm not interested in that, and if you can come up with a better idea, let me know." She looked over at her people and stood up and left. The food hadn't even arrived yet.

It was earth-shattering for me. My winning streak ended right at that moment. I asked Philipp why Alla acted so surprised at my idea—he had already told me how much she was going to love it. But it was clear that he'd never brought up the concept to her. Oddly, he wasn't as upset as I was. I thought he was going to feel humiliated, but he just said, "That's Alla! What are you going to do?"

In November 2005 an announcement of Alla's divorce from Philipp was made. In 2011 she married comedian/singer/TV presenter Maxim Galkin, who was twenty-seven years younger than his wife. Maxim has been a vocal critic of Russia's war in Ukraine, as well as of the country's anti-LGBTQ laws. One month after the invasion of Ukraine began, the couple left Russia for Israel. Alla returned to her homeland in August 2022, and one month later, her husband was declared a foreign agent. Alla condemned the war and made a public statement saying that if Maxim was a foreign agent, then she must also be declared one. In October 2022 Alla left Russia again and returned to Israel.

Philipp continued to adhere to the party line after the invasion of Ukraine, which has cost him in terms of working internationally. I find that sad because, despite his bold bluster, he is a decent person. Alla can work around the world now but not in Russia.

In 2022 Russian journalist Ivan Yakovina wrote about Alla on his Facebook page: "Now the average Russian must make an uncomfortable choice. Who is the hero and who is the villain?"

Alla is more powerful than ever. I am very proud of the brave stand she has taken.

After my failure to produce an album of Alla and Philipp singing together, I paid more attention to what my staff would tell me. I stopped being a maverick who thought he had a genius idea. Every project needs a champion, but it also needs support from an entire team. It's difficult to go it alone, even with great ideas. To this day I think an album of Alla and Philipp would have been tremendously successful and one of the best-selling Russian recordings of all time. With Alla refusing to record with Philipp, my luck had run out in Russia. I had gotten too confident, and this duet project falling apart was a wake-up call. I wasn't going to be the kind of invincible record executive I wanted to be. To this day I regret that it didn't happen.

26

THE UNDERWORLD

Being the CEO of a record label in Russia is riskier than working in any other country in the world because you have to deal with the Russian criminal underworld.

I had read Fredric Dannen's legendary book *Hit Men*, which is about corruption and organized crime's influence in the American music industry, including radio deejay payola scandals and other criminal activity. But I recognized that Russian organized crime groups were bigger and more powerful than what the book had described, and their entanglement into the Russian music industry grew each year. I had my first experience with the Russian Mafia when Sting came to Moscow to perform.

He kicked off his "Brand New Day" tour on October 14, 1999, at the Hard Rock Hotel in Las Vegas. He spanned the world and finally arrived in Ukraine on May 31, 2001. After two nights in Kyiv, he traveled to St. Petersburg, and then appeared at Moscow's Olimpiyskiy National *Sports Complex* on June 4.

Sting was one of the first artists to play all three cities, and I hoped others would follow his lead. He was already a regular visitor to Moscow, having played live in the country more than almost any other artist (except for the Scorpions and Rammstein).

This was his first large stadium gig, and the show was sold-out. He was a Universal artist, and we were excited to work with him, even though his *Brand New Day* album was not selling well. It was like a red alert for us— record labels prepare their budgets based on the number of albums they expect to sell, and with this one falling short, panic was spreading throughout the company.

The first single from the album was the title track, and it was only a mild hit in the United Kingdom and Italy and did not help album sales. Then in early 2000, the second single, "Desert Rose," had a video that received a lot of play on television. It featured Sting in the back seat of a Jaguar S-Type while a masked female chauffeur drove him through the Mojave Desert. Now that the album featured a hit song, sales picked up.

The Universal office in London sent one of their executives, Lee Ellen Newman, to look after Sting while he was in Russia. She was in charge of international promotions and artist relations at Universal Music Group. She oversaw media campaigns, working closely with our labels around the world, and traveled extensively with our artists to implement those campaigns.

It was her first time in Russia. She had been all over the world with our artists but never in such a dangerous place.

I met Lee Ellen at the airport and brought her to our office and assured her that Sting was with a promoter, tough-as-nails Nadia Solovieva, who would take great care of him. Lee Ellen asked if I was going to give Sting a gift when I met him backstage, and truthfully, I hadn't thought about it, but I realized at that moment that I had to come up with something unique to give him.

I asked our special projects managers to come to my office so we could discuss what kind of gift we should procure for Sting. On this particular day, one of them was experimenting with her hairstyle, and she was sporting a punk look with twig-like structures of hair sticking out all over her scalp. Lee Ellen was taken aback and thought she was meeting someone from a band. I assured her our special projects staff would come up with the perfect gift. Lee Ellen was asked if Sting enjoyed vodka, and she answered affirmatively. My staff said they would meet me backstage, gift in hand.

Lee Ellen and I headed over to the Olympic Stadium, and everything was calm. Crowds were starting to arrive. Sting was backstage. The police were in attendance to ensure security. Lee Ellen asked me how I could live in Russia. "There are criminals, bombs, and gangsters everywhere," she said.

I told her that everything was going to be fine.

As we stood there, a huge crate was delivered. I looked inside, and it was an old Soviet mortar—a weapon capable of disabling a tank. I thought it was an unusual gift, and then I opened the mortar, and it was filled with vodka. It was a brilliant present, but it was gigantic. The only way Sting could get it out of the country would be on a private jet, which was fortunately his mode of transportation.

I met Sting backstage. We shook hands, and I gave him the mortar. He was quite surprised to receive it.

"Seriously," he asked, "there's vodka in there and not something else?"

"It's vodka, I promise."

He wasn't sure what to do with it at first. He politely said, "I'm sorry, I can't drink it right now, but I will try it on the plane."

I told him, "No problem. You have a show to do. We just wanted to give you something to remember us in Moscow."

That's when I knew it was time to leave him alone. Before I departed the backstage area, I mentioned that "Desert Rose" was climbing the charts and the video was on its way to no. 1 on MTV. It felt great to be able to give him good news about his music in Russia before the show.

I left Lee Ellen with Sting, and as I did, she said something that has stayed with me for years.

She told me she was amazed at how calm and collected I was around a worldwide celebrity and that she had never seen that from a new record label head. She was impressed how easy it was for me to chat with Sting, like I had known him for years. I was always calm around famous rock stars. My friendly midwestern roots worked to my advantage. Visiting artists treated me as a peer, and maybe that was a good thing. This calmness around celebrities is a character trait I would never have known I have had I not worked for a record label.

Lee Ellen Newman: When I think back to my time in Russia, I am reminded of three things: working with the American head of Universal Music Russia, David Junk; experiencing the former Soviet Union for the first time; and accompanying one of our label's major artists, Sting.

David worked in a very challenging country, which was rampant with piracy. He spent money and devised marketing campaigns with his team, only to see the pirates stealing a living from his efforts. That would have infuriated me, and I was taken by how much he took it in his stride. He understood that selling records legitimately would take time and patience.

David was also a lot of fun. He had an ironic sense of humor, able to navigate the customs in the country, and he pulled together a very good team at Universal Russia. He worked through a difficult time and maintained that sense of humor and was very welcoming and hospitable.

When we had a little time, he took me on a quick drive around Moscow, he pointed out the Stalinesque buildings and a market, and he made me feel very relaxed. He was a fan of Sting, so it was great to go to the show with him.

Since Sting was performing in Moscow and St. Petersburg, I traveled to those two cities and was excited to be in both places. St. Petersburg was beautiful—Venice meets Vienna. And I was in awe of Red Square, which was more stunning than I ever imagined it would be. I was able to easily converse with a number of David's Universal staff members, as they spoke English, but for the most part, it was difficult to communicate with Russian people.

It was a privilege to work with Sting. He commanded every stage he was on, and his set showcased the breadth of his award-winning catalogue. He was deeply interested in all cultures and loved to travel. He once told me that he always had a suitcase packed and ready for his next trip.

I took my leave of Lee Ellen so I could check in with Nadia to see how things were going. That's when I learned it was pure chaos outside. The Russian mafia and the police had colluded to sell counterfeit tickets. The show was sold-out, but hundreds of people showed up with phony tickets that had been sold for hundreds of dollars each. The police were letting the mobsters run the ticket scanners. There was a shouting match in the VIP section between the oligarchs who had legitimate tickets and the people streaming in with counterfeits. Nadia was there with Moscow's police chief, and she was arguing with him—actually, threatening him. "I know the prime minister, and I'm going to have him call you," she told him.

He was trying to act naïve, but she was having none of it. He patronizingly told her, "Dear, I don't know what you're talking about, we're here providing security."

Nadia loudly interjected, talking over him, "Don't give me that, I know you control your officers, and I saw them selling counterfeit tickets."

I started to approach Nadia but turned away, not wanting to get involved in this fight. But Nadia noticed me and calmly turned to say, "Hello David. I hope you enjoy the show."

Then she turned back to the police chief. "Do I need to call my friends at Alfa?"

Even I was taken aback by that threat. The owners of Alfa Bank, Nadia's financial backers and the main sponsor of Sting's concert, were two oligarchs closely associated with Putin. "I understand," the chief said, and he walked away. Nadia had successfully diffused the situation, and the oligarchs, bankers, and Kremlin officials were able to take their seats.

■

My first up-close experience working directly with a gangster came during the height of the Russian music industry's fight against piracy. Eirat Sharibov was the CEO of one of Russia's largest pirate factories, which manufactured hundreds of millions of counterfeit DVDs and CDs. His uncle was a high-ranking officer in the Russian security services, so his protection was deep and wide. But Eirat was not a typical gangster. He was smooth-talking and confident. He didn't show off or speak in criminal slang like his gangster rivals, and he was a big thinker.

But what really made Eirat unique from most gangsters was that he wanted to bring his business out of the dark shadows of the criminal world and into the light. He wanted to pursue a legal path for his company. He opened a record label called Mystery of Sound and tried to go legitimate. He did everything he could to project an image of an aboveboard business. His plan was to beat his rival gangsters by working with the major record labels and helping them close down other pirate factories. It would be a "fox guarding the henhouse" situation.

He visited my office and made me the following offer: to stop stealing Universal artists' copyrights in exchange for becoming an official distributor, thereby legitimatizing his company. He said to me, "I always try to negotiate a deal for the copyrights before I have to steal them."

I knew what he was capable of. He had famously manufactured and distributed across Russia two million pirated DVDs of a blockbuster Harry Potter movie. But Eirat put the DVD on sale even before the movie was in the theaters. His connections in the Hollywood movie studios were able to get him an early cut. It wasn't even the final print.

The long arm of the Russian Mafia into Hollywood was a great connection for his business. It was risky talking to him. I knew that a deal with

Universal would give him credibility, but I didn't trust him. I did want to promote a new Bon Jovi album, so I gave him a test case to produce legitimate copies and not counterfeit versions. It worked and was a huge success. Sales were through the roof, and no pirated Bon Jovi CDs could be found anywhere. I told my bosses in London that this could be a template for the future. We could bring pirates out of the shadows and into the light of the legitimate music industry. I warned them that Eriat was a gangster, but at least there was a possibility that the pirates would leave us alone with him on our side.

Then one day, I got a call.

Eirat was shot three times in the head and died outside of his Moscow office. His murder was never solved.

It was speculated that his Mafia bosses didn't like his plans to go legit. It may have been revenge from a competitor in the criminal world. Eirat had been secretly working with law enforcement and given them information leading to a raid on one of his rival's factories, resulting in millions in lost revenue. His murder could have been part of a turf war involving the security services. It might have also been a message to his uncle. With Eirat's death, the deal with Universal was off, and it was back to 90 percent piracy levels and criminal control of the music market—business as usual in Russia.

The most dangerous encounter I ever had with the Russian criminal underworld was not directly targeted at me, but I came very close. It happened in 2005, when the fight with piracy was getting increasingly dangerous, especially after we revealed the Russian military's connection with organized crime, protecting the pirate factories. My second-in-command, our general manager Olya, had been receiving anonymous threats, but that was not unusual.

At the end of one workday, she found a grenade with its pin intact lying on the front passenger seat of her car in our back parking lot. Her parking spot was next to mine. I wanted to call the Moscow police, but she was wiser in how these things operated and didn't want to involve corrupt police officers.

She called a private security firm to immediately come over to our office. "This is how you do it in Moscow," she told me and then continued, insisting, "It was directed at me, and this is how I want to handle it." The security agents determined the grenade was live, but it would be impossible to track its source.

Olya hired them to start protecting our building, including the outside perimeter. We didn't have any trouble after that. It was never determined if the grenade was intended for me or not, but the message was clear. Living and working in Moscow was getting increasingly dangerous, and I better watch my back.

My last experience with the Russian Mafia was in 2005, when Shaggy performed in Moscow for the first time, five years after he'd had a worldwide hit with "It Wasn't Me." He was the first superstar reggae act from Jamaica to play a major venue; he was booked into the Luzhniki Palace of Sports, with a seating capacity of 13,000.

But he made a bad mistake. He made a deal with the local Jamaican community to sell tickets to his show. Mobsters controlled ticket sales in Russia, but the Jamaicans told him it would be no problem; they would simply print their own tickets and sell them. People were asking us why they couldn't find any tickets to Shaggy's show for sale. There was an explanation—the Russian Mafia had told all of the kiosks and agents not to sell the tickets, or else. The Jamaican promoters were forced into selling their tickets one at a time to individuals.

The Russians weren't going to let that happen either, so they put out the word that it was going to be very dangerous to be in the stadium that night. That scared off a lot of people. Less than a thousand brave people showed up, and many of those had received free promotional tickets.

I had never seen such an empty venue for a major act. I was worried about how Shaggy would react. The Jamaican promoters didn't tell him, because they were nowhere to be found on that night.

Shaggy did show up, with his twelve-piece band. When he arrived, I knew it was up to me to explain why there were only less than a thousand people in the vast stadium.

I told him, "I'm really sorry. Your promoters let you down."

He shrugged it off and just said, "It's going to be alright, man. Don't worry about it."

He went out onstage and performed like he was playing to a full house. Only the front rows were occupied, and the rest of the stadium was empty, but he gave it his all, which is why he will always be one of my favorite artists.

It was a fantastic show in spite of everything. During his performance I walked to the back of the arena, and I thought about how much he was going to hate this place and that he would never return. But he did come back, and he even did a major show with Sting a few years later. I guarantee you he never used the Jamaican promoters again.

27

ON DANGEROUS GROUND

Between 1996 and 2005, there were five escalations into the dark side of Russia, and each one led me closer to leaving the country.

The first inkling that there might be trouble came at the beginning of my music industry career, when I was interviewed for the position of financial controller at PolyGram. I was flown to London and spent the entire day in the St. James's Square offices, visiting the various departments and getting to know the British-based staff. The final meeting of the day was on the first floor of the beautiful headquarters building.

Dr. Jonathan Smilansky from HR was there so I could sign my contract. The first thing he did was congratulate me, and then he said, "No one really wanted this job. We've been trying to fill this position forever. Thank God that headhunter found you in Europe. I couldn't get anyone to transfer to Moscow. The guy [who had the job] before you was from Poland and didn't know his butt from a hole in the ground. You're a blessing for us, an American with an accounting degree. We need you because we don't know what Boris [Zosimov] is doing there in Moscow. We're counting on you to turn things around, and we appreciate you understand the danger of the situation, and your salary will reflect that."

When Jonathan told me my annual salary would be $100,000, I nearly fell out of my chair. At that point I had never earned more than $40,000 a year. If I were going to work the same job in the London office, the salary would have been $65,000. The rest was hazard pay.

Before I signed the contract, Jonathan gave me more information. "You get health care. We'll fly you out for emergencies, including evacuation in case of war." I heard what he was saying, but I was just trying to keep my cool, and of course, I was going to sign. I put my pen to paper, and after the deal was sealed, Jonathan added, "Here is the company insurance policy. Your wife will get one million dollars in event of your violent death. Poly-Gram is taking out an insurance policy on you so if you are kidnapped, we guarantee up to a $5 million ransom. This is standard for anyone working in a high-risk zone, according to the underwriters. Russia is right up there with North Korea." I was just thinking about my $100,000 salary, and I agreed to it all. I raced back to Moscow to celebrate my good fortune with my wife.

At that time, Chechnya meant nothing to me. That would change. Chechnya is a republic in the North Caucasus of Eastern Europe. Conflict between Russia and Chechnya dates back to the eighteenth century, when Catherine the Great conquered the republic. By 1864 Chechnya was a part of the Imperial Russian Empire. As they have done throughout the years, Russia did an ethnic cleansing, sending many Chechens to the Middle East. When the Bolsheviks took control of Russia in 1917, Chechnya tried to gain independence, but the Bolsheviks rejected that bid.

After World War II, Joseph Stalin sent troops into Chechnya and deported five hundred thousand citizens to Siberia, claiming they were colluding with the Nazis. With the collapse of the Soviet Union in 1991, Ukraine, Belarus, and Kazakhstan went their separate ways. The new president of Russia, Boris Yeltsin, had to bring the remaining eighty-eight republics together, and eighty-six of them signed a treaty. Chechnya said it would never ever sign that agreement, declaring itself an independent country in 1991. Three years later, the Russian army had invaded, subduing the local government. Chechen fighters humiliated the Russian forces, killing over one hundred thousand troops. Yeltsin, perceived as weak, had to sign a peace treaty with Chechnya.

In 1999 the Chechen army invaded the neighboring republic of Dagestan. That triggered Russia to go back into Chechnya in what has been called the Second Chechen War. Yeltsin continued to be weak, but the same couldn't be said for his prime minister, Vladimir Putin.

Chechnya initiated a terrorism campaign. Four apartment buildings in Russia were blown up. Bombs were placed in their basements, and the buildings collapsed, killing hundreds of people. Putin blamed Chechnyan terrorists, and that became the justification to send more Russian troops in and carry out a massive aerial bombardment. The city of Grozny was brutally destroyed, and thousands more died. The fighting continued constantly, but by 2000, Russia had regained control of Chechnya, installing Akhmad Kadyrov as a puppet leader.

The insurgency kept growing, and there were more terrorist acts. One night during this period, while I was busy with a new Bon Jovi album and was excited about a new U2 release, I came home from my office and turned on the TV. What I saw was gruesome, but I didn't understand what was happening. My wife explained, "Four workers from a British company called Grainger have gone missing in Grozny." The men were victims of a medieval torture method that kept them in a three-meter-deep pit called a *zindan*. The word *zindan* is Persian for "prison" or "dungeon" and was first used in Central Asia around a thousand years ago.

The next thing we saw on the Russian broadcast were four decapitated heads on the side of the road in Chechnya. It was the four electrical workers. There had been a raid to rescue them, and it didn't go well. Grainger executives thought negotiations were underway, but Russian security forces had decided to conduct a rescue and botched the job.

I figured I was safe. I wasn't ever going to Chechnya. I was busy in Moscow with show business. Everything would be fine. In other words, I turned a blind eye to this horrible act of violence. I did some research to find out how much money the kidnappers were demanding for their victims, and it was around $4 million each, so I knew I was under the $5 million threshold of my company insurance policy.

There were more kidnappings: a physician from the organization Doctors Without Borders and some Red Cross workers. But I was still far away from any abductions. In August 2000 I had a visitor from our London office, Universal Music's head of international marketing, Max Hole. I thought Max was a great guy although we'd had some run-ins over business matters. I had my opinions and made them known. At the same time, I was delivering big results for the company, so we got along well.

Max came to Moscow because he had never been there before, and he wanted to see what was going on in our office. Normally, I had a lot of advance notice when a UK executive was coming to visit. Max gave me a heads-up just one week before his arrival. He was only going to be with us for a couple of days, so I quickly put together a short tour of Moscow for him.

. It was summer, a beautiful time of the year in the city. We walked down Moscow's main thoroughfare, Tverskaya Street, which leads directly to the Kremlin. We were on our way to his hotel in Red Square, and we were talking business.

"Lucian [Grainge] thinks you should be selling more S Club 7," he said. "You did really well with Eminem, but you need to toe the line. When we say push Ronan Keating, we mean push Ronan Keating."

I got it; he wanted me to be more of a team player, and he thought in this post, which was so far from London, I might have been too detached from company priorities.

Lucian, who was rising quickly through the corporate ranks, was putting pressure on Max to get us on board. It was amazing to witness his advancement and experience his competitiveness. Once when I'd been in a meeting of Universal's European CEOs in Hamburg, Lucian was speaking to the group like he was rallying the troops. He said, "I wake up thinking how I am going to fuck over EMI today."

"Welcome to the cutthroat record industry," I'd thought to myself. But that edge was what made him successful. Having started as a song plugger at Polydor, he was inevitably headed to the top of the company. Years later he was appointed as chairman of Universal, the first Brit in the job, leapfrogging my friend Zach Horowitz as well as Jimmy Iovine and Lyor Cohen. Lucian would eventually buy EMI and merge it with Universal, making the largest record company in the world even larger.

Max and I were passing by the famous Pushkin Square, halfway to Red Square, and I was explaining the significance of Alexander Pushkin, one of Russia's most famous literary figures. Max was fascinated with Russian history. Suddenly, our conversation was interrupted by a loud explosion. We didn't know what it was. Alarms were blaring everywhere, and then we saw smoke pouring out of an underground Metro station just a hundred yards away. There'd been an explosion in the pedestrian underpass to the Moscow Metro Pushkin Station, one of the busiest stations on the underground.

Max was shocked and asked me what we should do. I was hardly an expert on emergency procedures, but I told him we needed to get him back to his hotel. I don't know how I did it, but somehow, I remained calm, and as we walked, Max asked what I thought was the cause of the blast. I told him that while we had terrorist attacks in the country, they were hardly ever in the heart of Moscow. I thought it might have been a fire.

We walked briskly as police cars and fire trucks raced by us, heading back to the disaster scene. It took fifteen minutes to get to his hotel. Max was still shaken and asked if I would come up to his suite. We turned on CNN, and the news banner read, "Terror Attack in Moscow." Max didn't see the screen, as he was on the phone to his wife in London. She had been watching the news on BBC and was panicked. I called for a taxi, and Max headed immediately to the airport.

"I'm really sorry, David," he said. "My wife is very nervous, and I need to get right back."

I escorted him to the taxi, which had to take the long way around to the airport because the main route was clogged with emergency vehicles. It did not occur to me that I should flee Moscow. I was still blinded by the size of my annual salary and didn't think I would personally be caught in any terrorist action.

It wasn't until the third escalation that I started to think about my exit from Russia.

My job interview with PolyGram, where I was told the company would pay my wife $1 million in the event of my violent death and would pay up to $5 million ransom if I were kidnapped, did not deter me from living in Russia. Walking by an underground station as a bomb exploded did not change my mind about living in Russia. So what would it take to disturb me enough to start thinking about my exit from the country? I was eventually going to find out.

On the evening of October 23, 2002, I was sitting in El Dorado, a famous restaurant on the banks of the Moscow River, owned by the husband of an artist I wanted to sign. Her name was Jasmin, and she was from Dagestan, a Russian republic that borders Azerbaijan, Georgia, and Chechnya. El Dorado was popular with Chechens living in Moscow. Jasmin and her husband as well as a music producer who had worked with Alsou were sitting with me at the table; we were talking about song ideas when we heard pandemonium in the kitchen. Suddenly, someone rolled out a television, and we watched the startling news: the police and the military had surrounded the Dubrovka Theater, just five minutes away. The Dubrovka was one of Moscow's premier venues. A musical called *Nord-Ost*, a sort of *Les Misérables* with Russian soldiers, was currently playing.

The news anchor explained that the 850 people in the audience were being held hostage by forty Chechen terrorists. I first thought, "My wife Natalia is seeing the play tonight!" I frantically called her phone, and she picked up, calm as anything. She was home—in my panic, I forgot that she had seen the play a few days earlier. She hadn't heard about the hostage situation yet, so I asked her to turn on the news.

Sitting in the restaurant, we were all frozen in place, not sure what to do. Someone changed the channel from Russian TV to CNN, and US Ambassador Alexander Vershbow, who was new to the position at this point, was on screen, talking about the situation. He was at the site because several of the hostages were Americans.

The dinner had started with great promise; I was hopeful that I would sign Jasmin to Universal. She was eager to work with me and my team. Shortly after we tuned in to CNN, I thanked Jasmin and her husband for the evening but said I had to return home. I told them we would stay in touch, but we never spoke again. Jasmin ended up becoming part of the Estrada and never pursued an international career, something I really wanted for her.

For the next three days, we were all glued to the TV, watching the horrible situation unfold. Each day became more chaotic. On the first day, I watched an interview with the police captain in charge of the hostage rescue. He was slurring his words and cussing on camera—so inebriated that he was removed after that TV interview. It was frightening to think he was in charge.

At 1:30 a.m. on day two, a twenty-six-year-old woman who lived near the theater entered the building on her own, confronting the captors while urging the hostages to stand up for themselves. The terrorists believed that she was a Federal Security Service agent and immediately killed her. The media claimed that she managed to enter the crime scene because the Moscow police had failed to perform basic functions like securing the perimeter.

On day three, at the terrorists' request, singer Iosif Kobzon, who was a member of Parliament, was brought in to negotiate. Risking his life, he managed to secure the freedom of a mother and her three children as well as a male British citizen.

The terrorists were demanding independence for Chechnya. On day four, the Russian military decided they'd had enough. They stormed the theater and pumped gases into the ventilation system to render everyone inside unconscious.

Some of the terrorists were wearing gas masks, and some were in parts of the building unaffected by the gas. Over the next two hours, a battle raged in the theater, resulting in the deaths of many of the terrorists. The hostages were pulled out of the theater, with many dying on the spot because there was no one there to offer medical aid or an antidote to the gases.

It was horrifying to watch this botched hostage rescue on live TV. The Russian Federal Security Services response was brutal and unprofessional, with complete disregard for the life of the hostages. I was shaken by the thought that it easily could have been my family in that theater.

And yet there was more darkness to come. In 2003 Moscow was under siege by women who'd been widowed at the hands of the Russians fighting against Chechnya. Dubbed the "black widows," they were pumped full of drugs and turned into suicide bombers.

On December 9, 2003, a Chechen woman detonated herself outside the National Hotel on Manezhnaya Square. The hotel was one of Moscow's most popular spots, and I had spent a lot of time there. It was widely believed that her bomb detonated prematurely, and her actual target had been the State Duma, the lower house of Parliament building across the street from the hotel.

Terrorism hit the Russian live music industry hard when two black widows went to a rock concert at Tushino Airfield and exploded their devices around the ticket line, killing fifteen.

Concert attendance across the country was affected. Russians were afraid of going to public places. Everyone in my office was worried for the safety of our artists touring around Russia, especially in the Caucasus and nearby Sochi. There was another bombing in the Metro that killed forty people.

The worst was still to come. September 1, 2004, was the first day of the school year, and per a tradition dating back to Soviet times, parents would escort their children to school and participate in a parade and other ceremonies on the schoolyard grounds to celebrate the new school year. On that day terrorists hijacked a police van and arrived at a school in Beslan, a village in North Ossetia, near the Caucasus. They took 1,100 people hostage, including 777 children. They were all taken inside the school building and were threatened with bombs and detonators. A few men were executed immediately. It was a hot day, and there was no water, so the hostages were forced to drink their own urine.

Again the hostage situation played out over several days on live TV. But this time, the Russian State TV channels were playing down the seriousness of the situation and hiding the truth, while CNN and the foreign press were showing the chaos on the scene in real time.

Russian security forces brought in tanks and attack helicopters with thermobaric rockets. It was obvious that this was going to be another hostage rescue gone terribly wrong. As journalist/military analyst Pavel Felgenhauer would report later, it was not a hostage rescue but an army operation to kill the terrorists. The result was 333 people dead, including 186 children. Watching the carnage unfold on live TV, I sat in my office at the record label and cried.

The Beslan school massacre proved to be my breaking point. The heartlessness, incompetence, and unprofessionalism of Russia's security services and their inability to protect its citizens from terrorists was too much for me to make my family endure. I finally realized I had to leave Russia. The first step was to send my wife and two sons to the United States. I let Universal know I would not renew my contract at the end of the following year and would leave Russia in 2005. It was a difficult year, as fear and anxiety took a toll on my mental health. I often stayed awake in bed at night, paranoid that terrorists would capture me and throw me in a *zindan* pit or cut my head off and leave me on the side of the road.

Every day that I remained in Moscow, I worried about getting kidnapped. During all my years in Russia, I wasn't intimidated by gangsters and pirates. But terrorists and Russia's inability to deal with them made my anxiety and fears grow. I started drinking heavily and living an unhealthy lifestyle.

What kept me going was the chance to spend my final twelve months at Universal on a yearlong farewell tour. I visited every Eastern European office to say goodbye; I even made it to the furthest one from Moscow, which was in Malta. In London, at Universal's headquarters in St. James's Square, I said goodbye to executives I had known throughout my career, including

Adam White, the head of corporate publicity who had brilliantly featured t.A.T.u. in the press, and Richard Constant, the head legal counsel who had given me my marching orders years ago to fight piracy in Russia.

But the best meeting was with my boss John Kennedy, the head of international. He asked me, "How can you leave now? You have created an empire. You're Jimmy Ioviniski!"

We laughed, but I was incredibly humbled by his reference to Jimmy Iovine, a true legend of the music business. Kennedy told me, "You could be in my job someday."

It was the highest compliment I'd ever received in my professional career. I returned to Moscow feeling good about my meetings in Eastern Europe and London, but there was one more thing I needed to do before I could leave the country.

Talking with John Kennedy about his experiences producing Live Aid with Bob Geldof in 1985 gave me inspiration to do something similar in Russia. I decided to produce a charity concert for the children of the Beslan tragedy. It was the Christmas season, and our artists were on the road, touring, but they all cleared their schedules to participate. It was a somber affair, with Alsou, t.A.T.u., and Smash!! all headlining. My special projects team handled all of the logistics.

Ours was the first charity concert staged in Russia. Most Moscow theaters weren't interested in having an American record label produce such an event, but the Gorky Moscow Art Theatre on Pushkin Square was a willing partner. We brought in some of the children who'd survived the Beslan attack, and as I stood backstage, watching my artists perform and seeing the faces of the children in the audience, I realized the importance of what we were doing.

Peering from behind the curtain, I was overwhelmed with emotion. The concert should have been no different from the hundreds I'd attended, but it wasn't usual at all. It was the most special concert of my career. I was doing something really good, really meaningful, with the Russian artists who'd brought me to the place where I was that night, and they each gave the best performances of their careers onstage that evening; Alsou sang more beautifully than Celine Dion, and I knew I was right that she was the most talented vocalist in the country. The duo t.A.T.u., the obvious headliners and the most famous act performing, brought their touring band and gave the small theater a show worthy of one of their stadium performances. When they sang their cover version of the Smiths' "How Soon Is Now?" (which Morrissey proclaimed to be his favorite version), I finally saw Julia and Lena as true rock stars, not just pop icons. Andris Liepa produced the show like a Bolshoi Theatre production, including a shiny blue floor installed for a greater lighting effect for the TV cameras. MTV filmed the concert and aired it, the first time a charity concert had ever been broadcast on TV in Russia.

During my final difficult year, there was something that kept my spirits up. I produced a DVD of the Beslan concert to raise more funds for the charity. On the day of its release, I knew it was time for me to book a flight home to America and rejoin my family.

Before I flew home, people from the charity supporting the children in Beslan came by my office to thank me. They gave me a painting by a young girl named Alina Zangieva, who had survived the terrorist attack. It was a colorful painting of a large oak tree and birds flying free. I will never forget the tragedy of Beslan. I kept it with me the entire plane ride home.

PART 8

UKRAINE AND RUSSIA

28

AN AMERICAN
IN UKRAINE

In 1992 I was riding on a train from Leningrad to Budapest, and from the window of my passenger car, I saw Ukraine for the first time. I didn't get off the train, but I still fell in love with the country. It was summertime, and I was a student with very little funds. I had just finished a summer Russian-language program at Herzen University in Leningrad. I was headed to Budapest, Munich, and then home to America.

But it was on the journey through Ukraine that I saw the most magnificent landscapes. There were fields of wheat for miles and miles. As a midwestern farm boy, I identified with the agriculture of Ukraine; it felt like home. Ukraine was always known as the breadbasket of the Soviet Union because that was where all the food was grown.

The next time I saw Ukraine was in 1999. No longer destitute or enrolled in school, I was now a record executive. I was with my boss Thomas Hedström, Universal's then head of Eastern Europe, and we were determined to open a Universal Music office in Ukraine. Thomas had always been the most aggressive record executive for opening new labels in Eastern Europe, but with Ukraine, our mission was to separate the country's music industry from Russia. We didn't see it as one music market even though it had been that way during the rule of the Soviet Union. Why should the Russian music industry control the Ukrainian music industry? It didn't make sense to us; they were two different music markets. Ukraine needed to step out of the shadow of Russia, and the only way for them to do that was for Western record labels to move in.

Thomas and I went to Odesa and met a partner recommended to us, but having him in charge of a major record label felt wrong. His name was Oleg Filimonov, a popular Ukrainian comedian, who was like a Jonathan Winters type on TV. He ran a CD and DVD distribution company based in Odesa as a side project. Odesa was historically where people in show business lived, but Kyiv was the country's capital. Western companies needed to be in the capital city, but Oleg insisted on Odesa.

While we were there, we noticed a young guy named Andrey Dakhovskyy in the CD warehouse. His father was an important physicist who'd come up with a famous theory on semiconducting. Andrey was under pressure to follow in his father's footsteps but didn't really want to be a physicist. Music was his first love, and in order to be around music all the time, he sought employment in Oleg's warehouse.

Andrey Dakhovskyy: I loved international music, which I found in my dad's vinyl collection. In high school I discovered a wonderful world of rock music, which was not accessible if you were not listening to Western radio stations like Voice of America or Liberty or BBC or Deutsche Welle. They mainly spoke about politics, but in between, they had some half-hour musical programs. Soviets tried to make it impossible for anyone to listen to these radio stations. My ma once caught me listening to Voice of America, and she asked if I knew what I was doing. I knew that both my grandfathers were arrested during Stalin's time and accused of spying for the United States and Japan simultaneously. They threw millions of people in concentration camps at that time. So my ma was concerned because I was crossing a fine red line, and I told her, "Yes. I'm cautious. I'm not telling anyone. I'm just listening to this music because I need it. I love it." That was the start of my journey.

During Gorbachev's perestroika, forbidden vinyl suddenly appeared in record stores in the Soviet Union. Before that, I was hiding my collection. I had a box of classical organ works by Johann Bach, and I hid my Led Zeppelin albums in that box when I would leave my apartment, taking my forbidden vinyl to share with friends of mine. It was a real problem if someone was caught with Western vinyl. You could have been expelled from university and sent to Afghanistan at the time of Russian invasion.

Thomas and I tossed around the idea of Oleg being in charge of the Ukrainian office, but we both had doubts. I mentioned Andrey's impressive knowledge of music and that he would probably be good at understanding

Western music. He might also be good at promoting our international artists in Ukraine, and we could get him some help finding local artists. Thomas wanted someone who would not screw things up, and we'd trusted Andrey right away. But there was a glitch. When he'd first invited us to Kyiv, he tried to trick us. Andrey asked a friend to let him borrow his big, beautiful office with Italian furniture in a modern building in the city center. He was trying to convince us that he was a serious guy and could run Universal.

Andrey welcomed us: "I would be your great partner, and I hope you will trust me and give me a chance."

He said all the right things about Western music. "I love all of Universal's artists. I've always loved the Cranberries and am a huge fan of Pavarotti. Metallica is great."

But Thomas had experience with being deceived. When he'd opened PolyGram in Russia with Boris Zosimov, Boris had played tricks on him too. So Thomas decided to test Andrey and told him he needed to use the restroom. He walked out and stopped to talk to Andrey's secretary, making small talk. "How long have you been working for Andrey?"

She replied, "An hour and twenty minutes."

Thomas returned and didn't say a word to Andrey. Thomas and I agreed that he should be our guy in Ukraine. Years went by before Thomas told Andrey about the conversation with his "secretary." It wasn't unusual for people in Eastern Europe to fool people into thinking they were more prominent than they were, and we never held that against Andrey.

The next step was to open Universal Music's first office in Ukraine and appoint Andrey as CEO. Universal would become the first major Western record label in Ukraine; it was a big step in developing an independent Ukrainian music industry, helping it move away from a decades-long dependence on Russia.

When Thomas moved on to our rival EMI, I was promoted to his job as vice president of Eastern Europe; I became Andrey's boss. Andrey loved hip hop, and as I had done in Russia, he'd brought hip hop and rap music to Ukraine and done a fantastic job. I was feeding Andrey's team in Ukraine the latest videos and music from Def Jam and Interscope and providing them with anything needed to promote hip hop in Ukraine, which they did successfully. Andrey was most proud of his work with Eminem and 50 Cent. In 2006, 50 Cent came to Kyiv, the biggest rap artist ever to do so, and Andrey rolled out the red carpet for him. Andrey was killing it, importing Universal's roster of West Coast artists to Ukraine.

The duo t.A.T.u. had their first big international success in Ukraine. We made sure Andrey's brilliant marketing director, Dimitri Prikordonni, had received all of t.A.T.u.'s promotional materials at the same time as the Russian media had received it; we were working in synchronicity to make t.A.T.u.'s debut a big deal in Russia and Ukraine simultaneously. It worked. This early success eventually got the attention of my colleague Petr Riava, the Universal Music CEO of next-door Slovakia and Stanislava Armoutlivea, the CEO of Universal Music Bulgaria and then the rest of Eastern Europe. Western Europe, Asia, and America soon followed. Andrey and Dimitri helped establish t.A.T.u.'s worldwide success. When I left Russia in 2005, Andrey and Universal in Ukraine were rocking. I felt good about what we had accomplished together.

Andrey Dakhovskyy: We were very successful in promoting the Universal catalog. We signed contracts with some local artists, like Katya Chilly (folk electronic music), Stereoliza (hip hop artist, later released by Universal International, and she did well in neighboring Poland) and Verka Serduchka, who was the runner-up at the Eurovision Song Contest in 2007 with "Dancing Lasha Tumbai." Universal France called me the next day after the Eurovision final and asked if I could help them sign Serduchka. It was not easy but I did it, and his Eurovision song went top six in France, which was the biggest-ever success of a Ukrainian artist in a top music market like France.

When I returned to Ukraine in 2007, things had dramatically changed. Universal Music had closed Andrey's office and once again put the Ukrainian branch under Russian control. The work I had done to separate Ukraine from Russia was nullified by my successor, a Russian TV host who'd been appointed CEO. I was disappointed Universal made that move; it was a loss for Ukrainian independence from Russian control.

29

AN *AMERICAN CHANCE* IN UKRAINE

With Andrey out at Universal Music in Ukraine, I wanted to see what I could do to help him make his next move. I traveled to Kyiv in May 2007 to work with him on securing a new deal. We focused on the German-based major BMG.

But that wasn't my only reason to return. I had an ambitious idea for a reality TV project: create the Ukrainian version of the Spice Girls. The show would be filmed in Ukraine and Los Angeles. Andrey arranged a pitch meeting with executives from the leading Ukrainian TV network. More importantly, he enlisted a famous friend to produce the show and join us in the meeting.

I asked Andrey, "Who is our producer?"

He said, "My college roommate has the no. 1 TV show on Sunday nights. It's called *Karaoke on the Maidan*."

Andrey's roommate was Ihor Kondratiuk, the producer who'd created and hosted the show that featured average citizens singing karaoke in Maidan, the main square in Kyiv. Ihor was very famous in his home country, and I thought that was great because no one could say no to him. I met Ihor for the first time in the elevator to the penthouse as we were heading to a meeting with the network executives. I wanted to know what he thought of the idea.

He asked me, "You can do everything you say you can in Hollywood?"

I told him I could, and he continued, "This is a chance of a lifetime for Ukrainian singers. Let's call the show *American Chance*."

I thought it was a brilliant title. Ihor led the pitch meeting, and as I'd predicted, they couldn't say no to him. We made a deal, and they gave us a budget for eleven episodes to film in Ukraine and Los Angeles. And so the work began.

Ihor's production team held auditions in five Ukrainian cities each with a total population of no fewer than a million people. We started in Odesa, the entertainment capital of Ukraine. At the last minute, right before filming the first episode, Ihor decided to make me the host of the show. It was never my intention, and it was never written into the script.

I told Ihor, "I have zero experience; I've never hosted anything. I don't have the talent for this." Ihor looked me in the eyes and said, "You are going to be the host not because you have talent but because you are the only American on set. Ukrainians will want to see you."

After Odesa we went to Lviv, the biggest city in the west, very close to Poland. From there we went to Kharkiv, one of the biggest cities in the east, the closest to the Russian border. Dnipro was our fourth city. After that we invited one hundred semifinalists to Kyiv for the finale so we could pick the twelve who would go to Los Angeles. I brought two representatives of the Hollywood Pop Academy, a school that trained pop stars, to be members of the jury because I wanted to bring in some Hollywood professionals into the final event in Kyiv. Once we had our twelve finalists, it was off to Los Angeles for the next stage.

Ihor's production crew put the contestants in a beautiful multilevel mansion in the Hollywood Hills, along with the twenty-person Ukrainian TV crew. For a month nearly forty Ukrainians were living in this Hollywood mansion, where Bob Marley and Eric Clapton had once resided. American celebrities appeared throughout the show. In the first episode, the girls learned about fitness with Dennis Rodman at Gold's Gym in Hollywood. For the next episode, Grammy winner Brian McKnight met the girls at Sunset Sound Studios and taught them how to sing his hit song "Back at One." The girls also met Stevie Wonder at the Hollywood Pop Academy. Ihor filmed the girls doing a photo shoot in Malibu and performing on Hollywood Boulevard for tourists.

We got lucky when the Los Angeles Police Department closed the thoroughfare for an upcoming event at the Kodak Theater, the home of the Oscars. The girls were scheduled for choreography lessons, but Ihor quickly improvised and assembled them on Hollywood Boulevard to recreate *Karaoke on Maidan.*

I was surprised by his plan and asked him, "You'd rather film the girls singing on the street than taking choreography lessons?"

"Yes!" he exclaimed. "We're going to call it *Karaoke on Hollywood Boulevard.*" When the girls started singing, tourists gathered around. One little girl approached the Ukrainian girls and asked for an autograph. The girls were surprised how enthusiastic the applause was from the tourists for their performances.

There were many other activities around Los Angeles. The girls had the most fun at Universal Studios as well as the luxury shopping street Rodeo Drive (in Beverly Hills).

To choose the final five on the season finale, our celebrity juror was actor Eric Roberts, who'd starred in some films that were very popular in Ukraine, including Soviet director Andrei Konchalovsky's *Runaway Train.* When our contestant Nadya Dorofeeva from Crimea belted out "Lady Marmalade," Eric was blown away. "That's unbelievable vocal range," he said approvingly.

He turned to me and said, "These Ukrainian girls can really sing!"

It was time to pick the final five. Standing side by side, Eric and I delivered the news to the winners and losers. That was hard for both of us.

The winning girls came up with a group name, Glam, and we found a lot of songs for them; they picked a tune called "Thirsty" and recorded it in Hollywood with producers WAX LTD (Wally Gagel and Xandy Barry), who had been recommended to me by Universal Music. The season finale ended with the girls back in Ukraine, performing their first concert live on national TV.

American Chance was a ratings success. It went head-to-head with the popular HBO miniseries *Rome* during the 2007 Christmas TV season and beat it in the ratings.

Our series remains one of the most highly rated music reality shows on Ukrainian television. I was already somewhat famous in the Ukrainian music industry because of t.A.T.u., but after I became the host of this show, I was a real celebrity in Ukraine, at least for that TV season.

Andrey and I had hoped the successful TV show would lead to a record deal, but the financial crisis of 2008 suddenly hit the music industry hard, and our prospective label, BMG, pulled out of Eastern Europe. Without a record deal, we had nothing to offer the girls, and we couldn't keep them together.

It's one of the biggest regrets of my career that I couldn't get BMG to sign them. They were a supertalented group and could have been Ukraine's Spice Girls. They ultimately went their separate ways, but each of them ended up working as successful solo artists.

Yana Solomoko from Chutove became even more famous on TV when she won the Ukrainian version of the American show *The Bachelor*. Nadya Dorofeeva is currently one of the biggest pop stars in Ukraine and is well-known as the most fashionable. Her first-ever fashion shoot on the beach in Malibu had a lasting effect on her career.

Throughout my career I've done what I could to help Ukraine escape the shadows of Russia: rallying the Russian-leaning jury in Latvia to award the top prize to Ukrainian pop singer Tina Karol at the *New Wave* song contest, opening Universal's first office in Kyiv, and bringing Ukrainian pop singers to Los Angeles for a TV show, among other efforts. I always loved Ukraine and looked at its music industry as separate from Russia's, never buying the Kremlin line that Russia and Ukraine are one nation.

Since the fall of the USSR, Ukraine has been looking to the West. One of the things I'm proudest about is that the *American Chance* TV show brought the city of Los Angeles into the homes of millions of Ukrainian TV viewers, allowing them to see some amazing things about the United States through the eyes of these twelve Ukrainian girls. Although I started my career building bridges between Russia and America, this time, I'd built a bridge between America and Ukraine.

Andrey Dakhovskyy: As David would say, Ukrainian culture and Ukrainian artists were always overshadowed by Russian culture and Russian artists. And it was not about business. It was about politics. A long time ago, Ukraine signed a treaty with Russia to help each other defend their territories, and after a few years, that treaty from the seventeenth century was turned into occupation of Ukraine. Russia wanted to advance into new territories and make those people Russians. They were very serious about destroying local culture and replacing it with Russian culture. Local languages were not appreciated, even forbidden to be taught at school.

If someone wanted to succeed in making a career of writing in the Russian Empire, they had to write everything in Russian, and they had to pretend they were Russian.

There were writers who did not give up their nationality, like Taras Shevchenko, who is honored in Ukraine. He kept on writing in Ukrainian, and he was in the Russian Army for twenty-five years. He was promoted many times. He could become an officer. The only thing he should do for this is just stop writing in Ukrainian and start writing in Russian. He didn't give up, and for this he is remembered in Ukraine, and people remember his poems.

It was exactly the same in the Soviet Union. It works exactly the same in Russia now. The reason for this war is the empire wants to get their territory back, and they don't want anybody to be Ukrainian.

30

AN UNEXPECTED
RETURN

fter I left Russia and returned to the United States, I needed to figure out
what I was going to do for employment. The logical move was to get a
job in the American music industry, but it turned out to be a tough transition
from my work in Moscow. Thanks to a job referral from Zach Horowitz, the
president of Universal Music in America, I was hired by Machete Music, a
label based in Burbank, CA, that specialized in reggaeton music. Machete
was the hottest new label in the Universal Music Group. I reported to Machete's CEO, Gustavo Lopez, one of the most successful executives in the
Latin Music Industry. Zach was one of the angels who'd saved my career in
1999, when Universal swooped in and purchased PolyGram.

Machete's biggest star was the supertalented reggaeton rapper Don
Omar, from Puerto Rico. I worked on his number one album *King of Kings*
and even got the chance to executive produce a music video for his song
"Conteo," which was featured in the film *The Fast and the Furious: Tokyo
Drift*. After a year at Machete, I left to start a music consulting business.
Because t.A.T.u. was such a big success, I was receiving a lot of calls from
would-be pop singers in Russia who wanted to come to America to make
an album and launch their career. Heading up my own company, I advised
these Russian artists on what to do and who to work with in the United
States, but none of these projects went anywhere. I couldn't seem to repli-
cate the success I'd had at Universal Music Russia.

My music consulting business was going nowhere, and I needed a lucky
break. I had been away from Russia for seven years when an old friend and

colleague from Universal Germany, Boris Löhe, called to tell me about his new job as head of Gibson Guitars in Europe. I congratulated him on the excellent news, and then he dropped a bombshell on me.

"Gibson wants you to move to Moscow to open the first Gibson guitar showroom in Russia."

"Why me?" I asked.

He was honest. "No one else is brave enough to do it."

America has many iconic brands like Disney, Apple, and Harley-Davidson. But no brand is respected more among musicians worldwide than the legendary Gibson Guitars in Nashville. So I immediately jumped at the opportunity.

I was ready for the challenge of starting a second iconic American company in Russia. And Gibson was even more remarkable than Universal. I would be giving away guitars to rock stars; it would be the best job ever. But there were obstacles to overcome before I could take the job, including the objections of my wife, Natalia; my complete lack of knowledge about guitars; and Gibson's archaic aptitude test.

Natalia had mixed feelings. Our youngest son was still in school and relocating him to a high school in Moscow would be impossible. We didn't want to do that for several reasons, including our longtime fear that because of Natalia's Russian citizenship, our sons could be drafted into the Russian Army, despite being born and raised in America. That wasn't a risk we were willing to take.

But the Gibson job would be an excellent opportunity for her to visit Moscow and spend summers and holidays with me in the city or at our country home on the Volga river. She was willing to let me take the job. I still didn't know much about guitars, but Boris told me, "Don't worry about not knowing the difference between a Les Paul and an ES-335." He didn't know either. We are record industry guys. We were unaware if our artists played on Gibson or Fender and what the difference was anyway. What I knew as well as anyone was how to do business in Russia. Boris said I could hire someone who understood guitars when I arrived in Moscow.

But my most challenging obstacle to working for Gibson was an aptitude test created in the 1970s for employees working in the Nashville guitar factory. I was sitting in front of a computer screen for hours, struggling with the archaic questions: How many boxes are there? How many squares are in a box? What would you do in this situation? All of my life, I had consistently failed these types of exams. To make matters worse, Gibson's Human Resources Department hadn't updated it in decades; I couldn't even run this program on my Mac and had to borrow a PC. But I couldn't pass the damn thing. Then one day, I got a call from Gibson's HR director.

"You didn't pass, but we're passing you anyway," he told me. "We don't have anyone else willing to work in Russia."

This reminded me of the scene in *Skyfall* when James Bond failed to pass a round of tests to rejoin the service and was considered an "old dog"; M passed him anyway. His country needed him. The same choice confronted Gibson. I was the only one who could do the job.

■

I arrived in Moscow in the spring of 2013. I was nervous and excited about opening the Gibson showroom. Seven years ago, Moscow had been a dangerous and dirty city, but now it seemed safer and cleaner. There were no brutal terrorist attacks or high-profile kidnappings, and Russian troops were no longer in Chechnya. All the things I'd feared most while living in Russia in the early 2000s were no longer issues.

The flat I rented was in a popular neighborhood called Sretenka, in a nine-story building built by German prisoners of war after the end of World War II. My pleasant lady landlord was excited to have an American tenant. She had decorated the apartment in a New York City motif and was a fan of all things American. Around my neighborhood, the streets were not dilapidated, the kiosks that used to crowd the sidewalks had been removed, and what was a dark city at night was now full of light, even brighter than Paris, the City of Lights.

Walking along Tvetnoi Boulevard, I was amazed that cars were stopping for pedestrians in the crosswalk. This was new; I used to risk my life crossing the street in Moscow. Gorky Park, in the city center, where wild dogs used to run free, chasing kids and joggers, had been transformed into a Russian Disneyland. The Moscow air was cleaner because Muscovites had stopped buying dirty, polluting Russian-made vehicles and started buying foreign cars. Luxury European autos were everywhere; more Rolls-Royces were being sold in Moscow than in any other city.

I checked out a shopping mall next to the Kremlin, full of fancy restaurants and designer boutiques. I left the mall and walked along Moscow's main boulevard, past the Ritz-Carlton, where Donald Trump stayed when he'd brought his beauty pageant to Moscow in 2016. I was shocked to see that this luxury hotel had replaced the rundown old Soviet Intourist Hotel, infamous for having hidden cameras in the rooms and spying on tourists.

Russia was flush with cash. The price of oil had skyrocketed, and Russia was the world's leading exporter. An avalanche of foreign investment from around the world had come pouring in. Everyone wanted a piece of Russia, and Moscow was becoming more prosperous. Business was booming.

Moscow might have been safer and cleaner, but I could sense a darkness lurking beneath the surface, bubbling under, ready to reveal its ugly head. Previously, the Kremlin had made Chechens the enemy of the people, but Chechnya was now under Moscow's control and no longer an enemy. The Kremlin always needs an enemy to rally the people and keep them from overthrowing their leaders. In the past seven years, while I was away, the Russian Orthodox Church had become stronger, wealthier, and willing to help the Kremlin keep its power.

Both institutions teamed up and turned two groups into the enemy of the people in 2013: the LGBTQ community and Ukrainians. It was a deal. The Kremlin was able to get the Orthodox Church to support its anti-Ukrainian narrative, and the Orthodox Church was decisive in getting the Kremlin to push anti-homosexuality laws through the State Duma. Julia and Lena had broken up t.A.T.u. by the time these laws passed; they could have been thrown in jail under the new law, and I probably could have too.

The Kremlin's targeting of Ukrainians was new. I hadn't originally noticed a hatred of Ukrainians, but in 2013, that feeling was growing fast. I started hearing Russians saying dismissive remarks about Ukraine's Orange Revolution. They would accuse Ukrainians of betraying their Slavic brothers by wanting to move closer to the West.

These dark clouds coincided with an increasing militarization of the country. Billboards plastered the city, recruiting for the Russian Army, and the cinemas were full of a steady drumbeat of movies about the great World War II victory over the Nazis and the heroes of the Soviet Union. In seven years the Kremlin had militarized the whole country—almost hypnotized it.

Russians were reminiscing about the USSR, growing nostalgic for it and even glorifying Stalin's accomplishments, overlooking the evil he had committed. On TV talk shows, I heard Russians say, "Remember the good old days of the Soviet Union." That wasn't spoken out loud seven years earlier.

Some Russians who were self-called monarchists talked openly about bringing back the tsars and rebuilding the Russian Empire. This fit perfectly into the Kremlin's narrative of taking back Ukraine.

There were also significant changes in the music industry. I invited an old colleague, Alexei, to my apartment for an update. Alexei had been a music journalist before he'd worked in my marketing department at Universal. I hadn't seen him in seven years.

"Streaming is big, music is now online, and digital pirates have replaced those pirate factories we fought," he told me. "The overall music industry is growing, and it's safer and more legal now. Nobody gets killed."

We laughed. I was satisfied to see what I had started years ago was going strong. "You will be especially proud that the Russian hip hop community is alive and kicking," he said. "Russian hip hop artists are dominating the music scene."

I was thrilled to hear that my efforts to import American hip hop years ago had paid off. He told me all the major Western labels were here and that there were more Russian record labels and independent labels from Europe. The music industry had gotten stronger. Alexei was ecstatic about my news regarding Gibson Guitars. Talking with him convinced me that the reaction in the Russian music community to Gibson coming to Russia would be overwhelmingly positive.

31

PUTTING IT TOGETHER

My main challenge at Gibson was creating a company from scratch. I didn't have a corporate bank account or a legal agreement. I didn't have staff, and I needed to build a showroom. I knew how to start a business in Russia. I had done it when opening Universal essentially out of thin air. It was a merger, but still, we had to start a brand-new company. Gibson was not even a merger. There was nothing.

I procured the proper powers of attorney from Nashville and went to the appropriate offices in Moscow to register the company and create a bank account and a tax ID. All of the bureaucratic things you would do to open a company in America are at least a hundred times more complicated in Russia.

According to Transparency International, Russia is one of the most corrupt countries in the world. I already knew that at nearly every step of the registration process, a "special payment" to a high-placed bureaucrat is required to move things along; otherwise, opening a new business can sometimes be delayed for years. For a foreigner, it's difficult to determine who to make these payments to and what amounts the payments should be; it's one of the most complicated parts of opening a business, so I hired a Russian law firm to handle this part of it. As soon as I got Gibson registered as a business in Russia, I needed to build a local team.

■

The first person I hired was named Anastasia. I'd met her years earlier, when I was CEO at Universal. She had opened the first private school in Moscow to teach classes about the music business, and she would sometimes invite me to lecture there. Her connections in the music industry were vast. She was an art connoisseur and an expert on cuisine too. My timing was perfect; she was looking for a new job, but there was one problem: like me, she knew nothing about guitars.

"What's Gibson?" she asked.

"The most famous guitar manufacturer in the world," I responded.

"Why would I want to work for a guitar company? I'm trying to develop my art portfolio, my connections with galleries."

I explained why it would be cool to work for Gibson and promised her she could connect Gibson to the art community however she liked.

"Even in St. Petersburg?" she asked.

"Yes! Even inside the Hermitage, if you want."

Thankfully, she agreed.

I still needed someone with knowledge of guitars in the showroom. Boris had a man in his Berlin showroom who was very knowledgeable about guitars. Ulf Nadrowski, known as Herman the German, was a professional bodybuilder, stuntman, and a bodyguard for Rammstein. He was so popular with the band that they gave him a part in their live shows. He was deeply connected to the German heavy metal industry, and I needed someone like him.

I was attending the annual Moscow trade show for musical instruments at the Sokolniki exhibition grounds, and there I found a guitar tech, Petr. He was completely the opposite of Herman the German, but I was desperate to find someone. He was short, bald, funny, and cheerful. He was in his midtwenties and a little nerdy. It didn't require any persuading for me to hire Petr, as it was the dream job of his lifetime. He enthusiastically accepted my job offer. It reminded me of my lucky break with PolyGram years ago. Petr was no Herman the German; he didn't have any music industry connections, and he didn't have charisma like Herman, but that wasn't a problem for us. It was Petr's radical views that would create big problems for me later. But for now, my team was in place.

Finding a location in Moscow for the showroom became a big headache. It was important to get this right because a Gibson showroom was an exclusive space for artists, not open to the public. I knew Boris appreciated interior design, architecture, and luxury. His showroom was located in a trendy district in East Berlin. He recently opened a new showroom in Paris in a fashionable district. Fashion and design were his things, and he expected the same from me. But those were not the kind of places a rock star would hang out in and jam. I wanted an artist-friendly showroom, not an advertiser-friendly showroom.

I upset Boris by choosing an iconic venue in the city, the stadium built for the 1980 Summer Olympics, as the location for the Gibson showroom. The building was dilapidated; parts were unkept, and a few lower-level floors had been turned into a weekend flea market that sold everything from bathing suits to umbrellas. But the Olympic Stadium was the epicenter of music in Moscow and had been for decades. Concert agencies, music media outlets, and professional audio companies were set up in the enormous stadium. And there was a secret back entrance from our showroom to the main stage. Olympic Stadium was the perfect place for a guitar showroom, so we built it there.

Our first opportunity to publicize Gibson in Russia came after I met a TED Talks organizer named Julia Schukina. She was promoting technology in Russia for an influential Kremlin-connected organization called Digital October. Julia was very eager to do an event featuring Gibson at Digital October's downtown headquarters—across the Moscow River, facing the Kremlin. She called me daily, pressuring me to come up with an idea.

"I told my colleagues that I know the director of Gibson, and they all freaked out. Everyone loves Gibson!" she exclaimed.

But I had no idea what to do. Then, seemingly out of nowhere, a great opportunity came. Boris called and said, "I've got some good news. I'm coming to Moscow."

I thought to myself, "That's not good news. He hasn't seen the showroom in Olympic Stadium yet, and I know he'll hate the location." Then Boris dropped his really big news: "I'm bringing Rudolf Schenker from the Scorpions."

I wanted to say to Boris, "Are you f—king kidding me?"

But I stopped myself.

Then there was *more*: "Best news of all, Rudolf is willing to do any promotion you need."

I knew this was a gigantic opportunity for us. Russians have loved the Scorpions since their hit song "Wind of Change" became a worldwide phenomenon. The Scorpions were coming to Russia for a concert tour, and Rudolf, the lead guitarist, was one of Gibson's signature artists. Gibson made Rudolf Schenker a custom-made Flying V guitar. I called Julia with an idea: "What if we do one of your TED Talks, and we invite Rudolf Schenker from the Scorpions, and we connect live with our factory in Nashville?"

She was in shock. "Oh my God, Rudolf Schenker? He would do that?"

I said, "Yes, he will!"

"What's the technology angle?" she wanted to know.

Then it hit me. "Gibson has invented a robotic tuner for guitars; it's the most technologically advanced guitar in the world. If we connect your Moscow studio to our headquarters in Nashville, the audience can directly ask Gibson experts questions about technology and guitars."

She screamed with delight. "It's a fantastic idea!"

I wanted Henry Juszkiewicz, the CEO of Gibson Brands, to be our spokesperson. It was going to be historic, and it was only right for the owner to speak on behalf of the company. Plus, the robotic tuner on Gibson's guitars was Henry's brainchild; he could talk about this technology. I invited Henry to be the one who would talk to the audience in Moscow. I had yet to meet him, and even though people said he was a scary guy, I thought it was a great idea. My Gibson colleagues from other showrooms thought it was a bad plan. "Why would you involve the CEO? Why would you complicate things?" But Gibson's robotic tuner was his brainchild. There was no one better to speak about technology and guitars.

I invited him, and he got excited about it. "Yes, I will do this. I would love to talk to these Russian kids, and I know a lot about technology."

We sent Henry the equipment for connecting a live feed between Moscow and Nashville. Unfortunately, he couldn't get any of it to work, so he became very angry and said, "I'm not going to do it."

It nearly fell apart, but at the last minute, Henry turned it over to his number two guy in Nashville, the executive vice president, Craig Anderton, who was the right person we needed to talk to anyway; his specialty was technology, and he had written a dozen books and thousands of articles on the topic.

Our evening's host, popular MTV veejay Alexander Anatolievich, posed questions from the audience to Craig on a live video feed to Nashville. Rudolf described the inspiration for the song "Wind of Change" and what it was like meeting Gorbachev in the Kremlin. He was proud of how the song had inspired the Russian leader: "It was really cool to meet him in the Kremlin, right across the river from where we are now."

I also invited a very popular Russian rapper, Noize MC, to participate on the panel. I wanted someone who appealed to Russian youth to talk about technology. He reminded me of Detsl—his lyrics were as provocative—and I wanted to work with him. I gave him a guitar from one of Gibson's legendary brands, Epiphone (the Beatles played on Epiphone guitars). "I use technology all the time in making my music," he told the audience. Noize MC courageously became one of Russia's few leading voices opposing the invasion of Ukraine.

But the highlight of the evening came when Rudolf jumped up, grabbed his Flying V guitar, plugged in, and started jamming. I had placed one of Rudolf's favorite guitars, a Flying V painted by the Brazilian artist Romeo Britto, next to him. The audience went wild while he played a few licks from "Rock You Like a Hurricane." It had to be the coolest thing anyone had ever seen at a TED Talk about technology. It was a triumph for Gibson and a great start for the brand in Russia. We celebrated afterward at dinner, with the Kremlin's lit-up bell tower in the background. I was proud of what we'd done. Music had brought the West and Russia closer together again. It reminded me of how years earlier—very close to where we were dining—rock 'n' roll came to Red Square with the Red Hot Chili Peppers celebrating the launch of MTV in Russia. And on this night in Moscow, music had won again: a German rock star and an American guitar brand were the hottest thing in the city, all in the shadow of the Kremlin.

32

SOCHI

I was certain 2014 was going to be a great year for Russia.

Gibson was running at full speed. The showroom was the talk of the music business; it looked beautiful, stocked with one hundred guitars and walls of amps. Musicians were constantly dropping by. As I'd predicted, they loved it. Some bands even did promotional photo shoots and live performances from the Gibson showroom. Heavy metal rockers, folk music bands, and even teen idol pop artists all loved standing in front of the brick interior with various shiny gold Les Pauls in the background.

A world-famous deejay, Armin Van Buuren, used our showroom to launch his new Philips Boombox M1X-DJ audio system before his sold-out show at the Olympic Stadium. The Russian press was on hand to interview Armin, and then we snuck him through a back entrance to the stage, where he was to perform.

However, the event we were most looking forward to in 2014, our best chance to plant Gibson's flag in Russia, was the country's legendary outdoor rock festival Nashestvie, near Moscow in the summer. We signed on as sponsors; it was the first time an American musical instrument brand had ever done that. It was a massive opportunity that required months of planning and preparation.

It was my job to look for more opportunities to promote the Gibson brand in Russia. Because the Moscow-Nashville bridge event with Rudolf Schenker had been so successful, I wanted to do more live events with Julia

Schukina and Digital October. That inspired me to make a far-out request to the US ambassador, but this time, it was not involving music piracy.

At a social function for American businesses in Moscow that was held at the ambassador's mansion, Spaso House—a place I had been so many times and probably knew as well as the ambassadors that rotate in—I met Michael McFaul, the US ambassador appointed by President Obama in 2012. I introduced myself to him while we were talking on the balcony overlooking the extensive grounds of the residence. He knew about Gibson and was excited to learn that I had opened a showroom in Russia.

I told him, "We just had a successful event linking Moscow to Nashville with Rudolf Schenker, lead guitarist for the Scorpions, discussing guitars and technology."

The ambassador was surprised. "Guitars and technology, I never would have thought about that." He asked, "Where did you do it?"

I explained, "The Digital October complex, across the river from the Kremlin."

He responded, "We are bringing President Obama to Moscow; he wants to meet young, talented Russians. I'm going to have a look at bringing him to Digital October."

Before he walked away, I made a bold move. "Mr. Ambassador, I'd love to host you and President Obama in our showroom when he's in Moscow."

"I'll let you know if the president plays guitar," the ambassador smiled in response.

My fingers were crossed. I wanted us to be the first Gibson showroom to host a sitting US president.

The year 2014 was going to be a big one for Russia on the international stage, as the Winter Olympics were being hosted in Sochi. When my landlady dropped by the apartment to pick up the rent money, I told her I had tickets.

She gleefully told me, "You'll love Sochi. The Black Sea is my favorite place in Russia to vacation."

Fascinated with Americans, she was always eager to converse with me. But then she turned bitter. "I wish I could see Crimea again. That was the most beautiful part of the Soviet Union and had the best beaches. But those *xolols* [a derogatory term for Ukrainians] have stolen it from us!" The anger in her voice kept building.

I didn't understand what she meant. "Why can't you go there now?" I asked.

"Not while the fascists in Ukraine control it," she said. "They hate us there."

I couldn't believe she thought there were Nazis in Ukraine. What she was saying shocked me; I had been there many times and never seen Nazis. I wondered how someone who was so smart and who loved America and the West could be so blinded by this nonsense coming from the Kremlin.

Crimea has long been fought over, dating back to the Russian Empire, when Catherine the Great conquered it. Still, in 1954, when Soviet General Secretary Nikita Khrushchev, wanting to right a wrong, gifted the territory to the Soviet Republic of Ukraine, it didn't cause a fuss. After the breakup of the USSR, Ukraine's borders included Crimea, and Russia and the international community recognized it. But years later, Russia wanted it back despite their agreement to lease the naval base from Ukraine. The deep-sea ports in Crimea gave the Russian Navy a strategic base in the Black Sea and a deterrent to NATO.

Patriotic fervor was boiling in Russia. The Kremlin had engineered it in response to the changes happening in Ukraine next door, which Putin perceived as a direct threat. The Orange Revolution was in full force; Ukrainians were in the streets and in Maidan Nezalezhnosti, protesting the attempts of their autocratic pro-Russian president, Viktor Yanukovych, to thwart the people's will and move closer to Russia rather than the European Union. Most Ukrainians wanted to be closer to Europe. This worried the Kremlin. Their response was to hyperpromote patriotism and a return of all historical lands to the Russian Empire. This love of country had a vile undertone to it: it inherently meant a return of Ukraine to Russia's control.

The Kremlin's propaganda emphasized the historical unity of Ukrainian and Russian people dating back to the ninth century. Kyiv, according to the Kremlin, was the mother of all Russian cities; Ukrainians and Russians spoke a common language and were bound in Slavic brotherhood by the Russian Orthodox Church. The Kremlin blamed Western influence and NATO expansion for tearing these brotherly nations apart. According to Kremlin propaganda, Nazis were in charge of Ukraine now, but, following in the footsteps of his hero, the eighteenth-century Russian tsar Peter the Great, Putin was going to save Ukraine and rebuild the Russian empire, by force if necessary.

At the showroom, my Gibson colleague Petr was tuning guitars and talking nonstop about how great it would be for the Russian Empire to return. "Who is that?" I asked after I'd spotted a photo of a tsar on his phone's home screen.

"That's Nikolai, the last tsar of Russia—a time when Russia was an empire and was truly great."

I was surprised to hear him say that. I had always thought most people were happy to see the Soviet Union dissolve. Indeed, the Ukrainians and Georgians and the rest of the old Soviet Republics were happy there was no longer a USSR.

"What are you talking about?" I asked. "Don't tell me you believe what Putin says, that the breakup of the Soviet Union was the greatest catastrophe of the twentieth century?"

Petr nodded in disagreement. "No, I don't want to see the communists back in power. I want to see the tsar back in the Kremlin," he said. "I'm a monarchist." And then he emphasized, "I want Russia to get back the land that belongs to our empire, from Ukraine to Alaska!"

I laughed. "You want to invade Alaska?"

He realized what he was saying but then finished his point. "Ukraine belongs to Russia, and we will get her back. We are Orthodox people. We are one church under Patriarch Kirill (leader of the Russian Orthodox Church). We belong together, like brothers. Not separated by Nazis in Kyiv."

He made the sign of the cross and turned back to tuning one of the guitars. I was speechless and worried. He was talking about a holy war to save his Orthodox brothers held hostage by a fascist regime in Kyiv. I thought he was losing his mind.

Even my old colleague from Universal Music Russia surprised me with how much he believed the Kremlin's propaganda. I wanted to talk to Alexei about creating a multimedia music project about the golden days at Universal Music Russia, so I invited him to a pizzeria near my apartment on Sretensky Boulevard, directly across from a near-thousand-year-old Orthodox church. As we sat and ate our pizza, I looked out the large glass window at the ancient white church with gold domes across the street. The bells were ringing, and it was a beautiful sound. I was reminded of something disturbing I'd watched on the Russian news the night before: a priest was blessing tanks with holy water as they came rolling off a factory line headed west to the border with Ukraine.

I asked Alexei, "How can a church priest bless a tank? Doesn't that seem ridiculous to you?"

He replied, "Not at all. The church supports protecting Russia from NATO, and if it requires tanks, why not bless them? There may be a war with Ukraine someday because of NATO. We need to be prepared."

I was surprised at his response. I thought with his having worked at an American company like Universal Music, he would be immune to the Kremlin propaganda and too smart to be fooled. But I'd underestimated the power of the Kremlin's propaganda machine. We said goodbye, and I left the pizzeria depressed. Was everyone in Russia going mad?

The only Russian I knew who hadn't lost his or her mind was my other Gibson colleague, Anastasia. She didn't like Petr's speeches and tried to avoid him. She was laser focused on the upcoming event in St. Petersburg and on the art installation we were building to promote Gibson guitars. The installation at the Hermitage Museum, one of the great museums in the world, was taking Gibson into totally unheard-of territory for a guitar company. I was lucky to have persuaded her to take the job, and Gibson had benefited. She was the secret weapon that made us one of the coolest American brands in Russia.

When the 2014 Winter Olympics began, I was eager to visit Sochi. I had never been to an Olympics, and I also wanted to see Russia's massive construction efforts to prepare for them. It was a source of national pride. Walking around the Olympic Village, I was in awe of the massive undertaking. I will never forget seeing the Olympic flame in Sochi for the first time. It reminded me of how I'd felt seeing Red Square for the first time: it took my breath away. The gigantic metallic structure jutting out toward the Black Sea with the flame burning was an awesome sight.

The opening ceremony in the newly built Fisht Stadium began with the parade of athletes from around the world. Then Russia demonstrated its rich cultural heritage by rolling in gigantic, multistory-tall installations on floats. The theme was Russia's greatest composers, ranging from Tchaikovsky to Rimsky-Korsakov. Another installation depicted Tolstoy, Russia's greatest novelist and my favorite author. The ceremony featured more icons from Russian literature, culture, and art. It was about the best things

Russia had to offer the world, and it demonstrated that there was so much more to the country than oil and gas and diamonds. I was proud of Russia, and a tear came to my eye. I'd felt this same way when I'd seen the music video that my marketing team made for our artist Dolphin—a beautiful video about the 1980 Summer Olympics in Moscow that, like the Sochi opening ceremonies, had a message about culture and peace.

Then unexpectedly, t.A.T.u. appeared in the spotlight in the middle of the stadium. Julia and Lena had regrouped for this one-time performance. The opening drumbeat to their hit "Not Gonna Get Us" reverberated through the stadium. It was a proud moment for Russian pop music. I couldn't believe that the band I'd discovered was now in the pantheon of icons of Russian culture together with Tolstoy, Dostoevsky, and Rachmaninoff. Given the anti-homosexuality propaganda laws in place, this all seemed schizophrenic. The Kremlin, at the insistence of the Russian Orthodox Church, was passing anti-homosexuality laws while simultaneously asking t.A.T.u. to represent the nation on the world's largest stage—the opening ceremony for the Sochi Winter Olympics. But t.A.T.u. was undeniably the most well-known music act from Russia. I naïvely thought that perhaps this was the first step to lessening the harsh antihomosexual laws.

Being at the Olympics, believing the message, and seeing the Olympic flame up close, I had an even more naïve idea come to me: What if the Winter Olympics in Sochi marked the beginning of a new era of world peace? If the world leaders—Obama, Merkel, Xi, and Putin—could get together now, in the backdrop of the Olympic message, world peace could happen, starting in Sochi.

Unfortunately, neither of my ideas came to fruition. Life in Russia grew more repressive for the LGBTQ community. The symbolism of t.A.T.u. performing at the Sochi Olympics was soon forgotten by the Kremlin and the Russian Orthodox Church. And in next door Ukraine, an Orange Revolution was catching fire. My hopes for world peace were dashed as soon as the Olympic flame was extinguished. The president of Ukraine, Viktor Yanukovych, fled the country after ordering his secret police, the Berkut, to shoot dozens of protesters in Maidan Nezalezhnosti. Soon after that, Putin ordered his covert army of "little green men" (Russian soldiers without national identity markers) to take over naval facilities in Crimea. The Russian invasion of Ukraine had begun.

33

CRIMEA

On a sunny morning in Moscow, after having breakfast at the Hotel Metropol (where the best brunches in the city could be found), I exited the hotel and instantly noticed a parade of hundreds of Russians chanting and singing as they walked up from the subway and headed quickly toward Red Square. They were waving flags and carrying banners. I thought a rally must be happening and followed the crowd out of curiosity. As the throngs approached the entrance into Red Square, I heard music; now I thought it had to be a concert.

Then I saw a stage set up in front of St. Basil's Cathedral with a large banner that said, "Crimea Is Ours!" A pop star was dancing on stage, belting patriotic tunes and revving up the crowd, with a big military orchestra as his backing band. I asked a young Russian walking into the rally what was going on. He gleefully exclaimed, "Crimea is ours! She's back where she belongs."

They were gathering to celebrate the annexation of Crimea into the Russian Federation.

After Russia's "little green men" invaded Crimea, a vote was held on the peninsula. It was rigged, but it was used to justify the first illegal land grab by an invading country since the end of World War II. The pop star finished singing, and then the new Kremlin-appointed leaders of Crimea came on stage and thanked the Russian people for rescuing them from the "fascists" in Kyiv. It all sounded like nonsense to me.

Then, to my great disappointment, I saw Igor Butman, the jazz saxophonist I had signed to Universal years ago, come onstage to perform. I couldn't believe it. I felt deeply depressed. I couldn't watch anymore and turned away.

No matter where I turned, I couldn't avoid the Russians' new obsessive cry of "Crimea is ours!" The slogan was everywhere in the city: on street posters at bus stops, on billboards, and constantly on TV. Propagandists posing as TV news commentators, like the popular Yevgeny Kiselyov, were justifying the annexation of Crimea as the rightful correction of a mistake made by Khrushchev in 1954.

I watched Kiselyov dehumanize Ukrainians nightly on Russian TV, calling them Nazis and saying they were threatening innocent Russian-speaking people in Ukraine. Kiselyov was lying and he knew it. It was his job to echo the Kremlin's propaganda. I thought only a fool would believe this and certainly that none of my friends would believe this nonsense. But after a night of drinking with some Russian pals, I realized I was mistaken when they revealed their true thoughts.

On Moscow's 867th birthday, the city had a big outdoor party on the Bolotnaya Ploshchad riverbank, and Gibson was a sponsor. We inflated a large branded Gibson tent, with our logos prominently featured on the roof and sides. Inside, we'd filled the tent with guitars. It was a rare occasion when we could showcase the guitars outside of the showroom, directly to the public, and we wanted to do a test run before the big outdoor rock festival in the summer.

Our Gibson tent was very popular at the city event; people were taking photos inside, posing next to the guitars, including a bride who came by in her wedding dress to sit for a photo between two Les Paul guitars. Because Gibson was a sponsor of the city's birthday, I was asked by the event organizers to come up onstage to present a Gibson Explorer guitar to the winner of a battle-of-the-bands contest in front of ten thousand Muscovites. Some old friends from my days at Universal came by the Gibson tent and were impressed.

They invited me to a hard-drinking BBQ party at a friend's dacha in a forest an hour outside Moscow. It was a dude party, with just me, the Russians, copious amounts of vodka, grilled beef and pork kabobs, a Russian *banya* (sauna), and more vodka. In this inebriated state, I asked the guys what the big deal was about Crimea.

"Imagine a map of the world," I told them. "Now visualize Russia on the map—the largest country in the world by territory. Damn, it's nine time zones!" I said, slurring my words.

One of the dudes interrupted, "Eleven time zones, my friend. You forgot Kaliningrad."

He was right. His buddies nodded in agreement, and he raised his vodka glass and said, "Hell, yeah!"

I spread my arms to gesture how big that was. "Much bigger than America," I said.

Then I got dead serious and brought the hammer down. "Why does Russia need to take one more small island in the Black Sea that doesn't belong to you? Why do you need more land? You're the biggest country in the world already, from the Pacific Ocean to the Baltic Sea. Why do you need more? Why do you need Crimea?"

An awkward silence followed. They had no answers. One of the guys mumbled something about Catherine the Great, but another friend quickly shut him down. My inebriated buddies were upset with me because I'd killed the vibe at the BBQ. I went inside the dacha, passed out on a couch, and went home in the morning.

Henry Juszkiewicz, Gibson's Nashville-based CEO, sent out a directive demanding that all showrooms around the world, for wider brand exposure, arrange product placement for Gibson guitars on TV. He made it clear he would hold all of us accountable for how many people could see the Gibson brand on TV. Henry was angry; he had watched the latest Grammy telecast on CBS and noticed more musicians playing Fender guitars than Gibson. He was very competitive and was especially mad at his American team, but he'd sent out the order to all showrooms to increase impressions from TV exposure (impressions is a fancy marketing word for "eyeballs"). Henry wanted many more eyeballs seeing Gibson guitars on TV, as this is how we obtained what was essentially free advertising. Panic ensued among the staff; Henry was genuinely feared by everyone in the company.

We all felt the pressure, but I thought fast and reached out to an old colleague who worked at the central government TV channel on the top-rated late-night TV show *Evening Urgant*, hosted by Ivan Urgant, who was strongly influenced by American late-night hosts David Letterman and Jay Leno. Like American late-night shows, *Evening Urgant* had a house band performing nightly. The house band was called Frukty.

My friend invited me to the government-controlled thirteen-story building known as the Ostankino Television Technical Center. I brought a Gibson Acoustic J-185 from our showroom. After passing through security, including a thorough check of the guitar by nervous guards, I entered the TV studio an hour before that evening's program was to be taped. I was introduced to the Frukty members as they prepared for the show. I could tell they were wondering why I'd brought a guitar case. I pulled the beautiful acoustic out and handed it to their lead guitarist, Alexey.

"How about playing on this tonight?"

He held the instrument like it was a newborn baby. The studio lights reflected on the Gibson logo engraved on the head of the guitar. One of the female vocalists gasped.

Alexey said, "I've always wanted to play a Gibson."

I told him the guitar was his to keep if he would play it every night. He smiled, shook my hand, and started strumming. His band members had never seen anything like this before, and they looked shocked. He played that guitar every night on the show, and when the camera focused on Alexey, millions of viewers saw the instrument, guaranteeing the widest brand exposure possible for Gibson in Russia. I was delighted to deliver for the boss in Nashville.

Meanwhile, Anastasia's goal to introduce Gibson Guitars to the St. Petersburg art community was a big success. At the Hermitage Museum, a place I'd visited many times years ago (when I was a student in what was then Leningrad), Gibson awarded guitars to several musicians who had created incredible art installations with music. It was an odd look—guitars at an art show in the tsar's winter palace, but it received very positive publicity in St. Petersburg.

Working in such a remote location as Russia without direct supervision by Gibson's headquarters in Nashville sometimes gave us autonomy to create cool new projects. One of our favorites was the Girl Guitarist Contest.

I came up with the idea after I met one of the best female guitarists in the world, Orianthi, during her first visit to Moscow. She was supposed to tour with Michael Jackson on his "This Is It" tour, before his untimely death.

She was in Moscow, performing with Alice Cooper's band. The band had a day off before the sold-out show at Crocus Arena, so Orianthi and Alice's musicians agreed to play a private gig sponsored the night before by Gibson at the Hard Rock Cafe on historic Old Arbat Street. She rocked louder than any of the boys in the band and thus inspired Russian girls. To get a famous Russian rocker on board to help promote the contest, I reached out to one of Russia's most famous rock stars, Ilya Lagutenko. His band, Mumiy Troll, from the far-eastern seaport city of Vladivostok, was beloved in Russia. We wanted to widen Gibson's reach to a new and underappreciated audience: female guitarists.

Female guitarists from across Russia were asked to submit a video of themselves jamming to one of Ilya's songs. The winning prize was a new Gibson Futura guitar and a chance to perform live onstage with Ilya and Mumiy Troll in front of a hundred thousand people at their homecoming festival, V-Rox. I wanted to bring a real guitar expert along with me and invited Jansen Press, Gibson's Paris-based virtuoso, to put on a clinic for guitarists in Vladivostok.

After I awarded the guitar to the winner of our contest, the mayor of Vladivostok invited me to his home, together with hometown band Mumiy Troll. He would later be convicted for embezzlement, but that was typical for mayors and governors in Russia. Everyone wanted to be associated with the Gibson brand, and this enthusiasm allowed me to promote our products in other faraway regions of Russia, like Novosibirsk (in the only guitar shop in Siberia), and Volgograd, in the South Caucasus, where the famous Battle of Stalingrad was fought in World War II.

I went to support the Delphic Games, Russia's version of the Olympics for classical musicians. I made Gibson a sponsor of the classical guitar competition; the classical guitar has strings made of nylon instead of steel, and it is more challenging to play than an acoustic. When I awarded the competition winners a Gibson Acoustic, it was the first time they'd seen a Gibson guitar. That was exciting for me. I really enjoyed being a roaming ambassador in Russia for Gibson, giving away guitars to rock stars and to up-and-coming musicians too.

As summer grew closer, the situation in Ukraine worsened. After illegally seizing Crimea, the Kremlin instigated an insurgency in the east of Ukraine in a depleted coal-mining region where many were nostalgic for the old Soviet Union.

The goal was to destabilize the country and return power to Viktor Ya-nukovych, the Kremlin's man who had been chased out of Ukraine. The Donbas region of Eastern Ukraine, bordering Russia, was turned into a war zone. The Ukrainian Army fought to put down the rebellion, but the insur-gents took over entire towns and villages with military support from Russia.

The Kremlin had lied, saying that this invasion actually was a revolt by Russian-speaking Ukrainians who feared for their lives from the new fascist regime in Kyiv, which was so unbelievable that a few Russian artists started speaking out. Sergey Lazarev of Smash!! was one of the first to go public with criticism of the government. He did an interview with a Ukrainian TV crew, which created a scandal in Russia. When the Kremlin threatened to cancel his career, he backtracked and claimed his words had been edited out of context.

The bravest artist was Andrey Makarevich of the classic rock band Mash-ina Vremeni (Time Machine), one of the most famous rock groups in the country. Makarevich is still a living legend, worshipped by generations of Russians. He grew increasingly critical of President Putin and wrote a song titled "My Country Has Gone Insane." Immediately, his concerts in Rus-sia were canceled, and he was banned from TV airwaves. He was labeled a traitor in the State Duma; they wanted to strip him of his many government awards.

What probably surprised him the most was that fellow musicians attacked him. Isoif Kobzon, Russia's Frank Sinatra, was the harshest. But Makarevich called out the Kremlin as the organizer of this campaign and wrote an open letter to Putin, pleading for him to stop destroying his career. The Russian music community was divided between patriots and traitors: few had the courage to speak against the invasion of Crimea, but the Kremlin's favorite artists, including Valery Gergeiv and many others, supported the invasion.

I was waiting for Western leaders to find a way to punish Russia for breaking international law, but it never happened. The diplomatic approach failed to stop the annexation of Crimea. A more forceful posture might have deterred Russia, but Western fear of escalation prevented it. Germany and France were wobbly about standing up to Russia. Western sanctions hurt the Russian economy but weren't severe enough to stop the Kremlin from meddling in Ukraine. The most significant protest made by President Obama was the cancellation of his trip to Moscow. It was disappointing that the US ambassador would not be bringing him by the Gibson showroom. President Obama did the right thing by not coming to Moscow after Russia's illegal seizure of Crimea, but I can't help but think how amazing it would have been if Ambassador McFaul had brought him to the showroom to pick up a Les Paul and jam.

It became impossible to avoid war fever in Moscow. The Kremlin had whipped up a patriotic wave that seized the country, including many Russians in my orbit. On the first of the month, my landlord dropped by for the usual rent money. This time she also asked for tickets for her son to the big outdoor rock concert Gibson was sponsoring in the summer. I asked if she was going to attend as well.

"No, no, we're leaving town," she said. "We're vacationing in Crimea."

I couldn't believe what I was hearing.

"It's peaceful there now. It's Russian soil again," she said. "And the government is offering discounts on flights and hotels, so it's a great deal for us."

The Kremlin was encouraging Russians to travel to Crimea and paying them to do it. I tried to contain my anger. I blurted out, "Do you realize I am out of here in six months because of your Crimea? I'm not renewing my lease."

I was severe, and even though it was spontaneous, it felt right to tell her. She brushed me off, saying, "David, stop worrying. Crimea is ours now."

As she left, she reminded me about the concert tickets. I didn't bother to get them for her.

Throughout this time I had been avoiding my former Universal colleague Alexei. He wanted to meet to finalize plans for our multimedia project. I finally invited him to my apartment; he'd prepared a contract the night before and told me it spelled out the rights. I was skeptical, but before we got into the details, I asked about his position on the invasion of Crimea. I was horrified by his response.

"It's the greatest thing. I can't wait to go on vacation there. It's the most beautiful part of Russia." He could barely contain his excitement.

"You mean Ukraine," I told him. "Russia just took it."

He didn't agree. "You don't understand. It has always been Russia—since Catherine the Great."

I became indignant. "We have friends in Ukraine from Universal Music. Remember them? How can you do this to their country?"

He responded, "The fascists from the western part of Ukraine have taken over the country now. They control Kyiv. We're saving Ukrainians from the fascists. We're not hurting them."

I was devastated by what Alexei was saying. I needed to make a decision. I handed Alexei the contract.

"You need to go."

He was shocked. I walked him to the door. It was the last time we ever spoke.

34

A BRAVE ROCK STAR

By the spring of 2014, I knew I had to get out of Russia. For too long I had witnessed Putin's world firsthand, with his incompetent security forces, corrupt military, and gangster capitalism. Like every other expatriate, I was trying to keep it together despite the madness of living in Russia. But the invasion of Crimea was too much for me. I could no longer live in this country. I felt like I couldn't delay my departure very much longer.

It was tense in the Gibson showroom. Anastasia was growing annoyed at Petr's nonstop dialogue about the return of the great Russian Empire. He was obsessed with tsars and the royal family. On a business trip to Gibson's factory in the Netherlands, he talked to everyone about how great the Russian Empire was and how wrong Ukrainians were to resist it. Workers at the factory were upset by his conversations. I was told to reign him in, but I knew this would end badly. It was exhausting.

I told Anastasia, "I can't escape this Russian patriotism; it's sickening me. I'm ready to leave."

She was disappointed. I told her I would call Boris and ask him to help me find a job in another Gibson showroom or at the Nashville headquarters.

"But you can't leave now. What about the Nashestvie rock festival? At least stay through the end of the summer," she pleaded.

She was right. It was too soon to leave, and I couldn't abandon her now. The Nashestvie rock festival was a massive operation that I was responsible for, and I was the one who'd pushed for Gibson to sponsor the event, not her. I promised Anastasia I would wait until after the festival to leave Russia. Ultimately, it was the best decision I could have made. Staying a little longer gave me one last opportunity to rock the Kremlin: making a politically controversial, LGBTQ-supporting, female rock star Gibson's first officially endorsed guitarist in Russia.

Diana Arbenina was one of Russia's most famous rock stars; her band, Night Snipers, had been together since 1993. Their music was straightforward rock, with many provocative songs about life in Russia featuring lyrics that often reference a corrupt regime. Some of Diana's songs criticize the government's attempts to censor artists. Diana has bravely defended equality for the LGBTQ community and spoken against the Kremlin's harsh new crackdown on gay people. A decade earlier, t.A.T.u. had provided an opening for the LGBTQ community in Russia. But after, the Kremlin grew more intertwined with the Orthodox Church, pushing anti-homosexuality laws. Diana was committed to not letting the LGBTQ community lose their rights.

I met Diana for the first time when she crashed a breakfast meeting I was having with Boris, who had just flown in from Berlin. She had tracked me to Boris's hotel and brought her guitar. I was sitting in a large breakfast hall, eating my omelet and listening to Boris complain about how he was still unhappy that I'd opened the Gibson showroom in the somewhat-dilapidated Olympic Stadium instead of a shiny downtown office tower, like his Berlin showroom. That's when I heard someone shout my name from across the room.

"David Junk! Gibson! Is David Junk here?"

Everyone was paying attention. I slowly stood up, unsure of who was calling my name and why. I saw Diana smile broadly.

"David Junk? Gibson?" she asked me.

I nodded and she quickly approached our table. All eyes in the breakfast hall were focused on us.

Boris looked to me for answers, but I shook my head. "I don't know what's happening," I told him.

Diana reached out to shake my hand and introduced herself. I, in turn, introduced her to Boris. "Oh, I know who he is," she said, charmingly. "He's your big boss from Berlin, right?"

I could see that Boris was really enjoying this.

"My people told me everything," she said. "And that's how I found you here."

I told her it was an honor to meet her and asked her to join us. But Diana didn't have time for niceties. "No, I'm sorry, please forgive me, but I cannot stay. I've got a concert. I have to go to the airport."

She waved her manager, Aset, over to the table, and motioned to her to open her guitar case. Diana lifted out an acoustic Martin guitar, put her foot on the chair next to me, and rested the guitar on her knee.

"I want to be a Gibson guitarist. This guitar is not Gibson, but I love Gibson. If you make me an ambassador for Gibson, I will play only Gibson guitars."

Then Diana riffed spectacularly on the guitar while humming one of her hits. She wanted to demonstrate that she was not just a singer but a great guitar player. I whispered in Boris's ear, "She reminds me of a female rock star we both promoted when we worked for PolyGram."

"Who?" he asked.

"Melissa Etheridge. Diana is also a force of nature."

Boris smiled wide in agreement. Diana finished the song and asked us, "What do you think?"

Boris and I looked at each other, then at Diana, and answered in unison, "Yes!"

We needed Nashville's approval first. Boris presented the case for Diana to Henry, Gibson's CEO, and he agreed. Diana Arbenina was named Gibson's first guitar ambassador for Russia. This was big news. Diana was one of the most famous artists in the country and was the first big Russian rock star to help us promote the Gibson brand. When Diana came to visit us at the Gibson showroom, I told her the news. She was ecstatic and ready to get to work immediately.

We walked through the showroom and checked out our one hundred guitars hanging on the walls and sitting on the floor, then agreed that the best acoustic guitar for her was the J-185. Nashville had asked the showrooms to focus on this new guitar, and with Diana performing on it, it would be great exposure for the Gibson brand. But I wanted to ensure we would care for her needs onstage.

I asked, "What kind of guitar are you missing on the road or in the studio?"

"I need a full-body acoustic guitar that I can plug directly into an amp," she answered. "Sometimes I play loud onstage, but I get feedback from the amp. It's a rare problem. Do you have anything?"

I knew the new J-185 wouldn't work, as it didn't have a plug-in. She needed something rarer. I remembered we'd kept a few old guitars in storage. When we'd first opened the showroom, we didn't have any new guitars to hang on the walls; the shipment was held up by Russian customs officers for months in the St. Petersburg port. But we'd needed guitars to open the showroom, so Anastasia and I flew back and forth to Gibson's showroom in Berlin to bring old guitars that the Germans didn't want back to Russia. When the shipment of one hundred new guitars finally arrived in Moscow, the old guitars ended up in storage. One of those guitars was an ebony-colored Chet Atkins CEC full-body electric acoustic guitar with nylon strings.

"I'm sorry, this is an old guitar, but maybe it will help," I said, a little embarrassed at handing her a relic.

She screamed joyfully, instantly recognizing the guitar. "Chet Atkins is my favorite guitarist!"

She knew more about this guitar than I ever would. She compared it to other acoustics and explained to me the importance of the nylon strings and the full-body sound, as opposed to a hollow-body one. She knew everything about the legendary guitarist Chet Atkins and his Nashville sound. Listening to Diana talk about this guitar was like attending a clinic. Diana educated me, which gave me an idea. Since her band, the Night Snipers, was one of the headlining acts at the Nashestvie rock festival (often referred to as Russia's Woodstock) and we were going to be there with our Gibson tents, we would construct a ministage in the middle of the festival grounds. Diana could give a surprise guitar clinic for festival fans before taking the main stage. We would have to sneak her past her rabid fans to get through to the ministage, but Diana loved the idea.

That year's Nashestvie rock festival was like none other in its fifteen-year history. The festival organizers, including my favorite deejay, Misha Kozyrev, had put together an antiwar lineup featuring some of the few brave Russian artists who were willing to speak against the war in Ukraine, such as Andrey Makarevich and Boris Grebenshchikov. Diana and her band, the Night Snipers, were included in that list. The Russian military, who had always sponsored the festival, responded to the antiwar lineup with an increased presence at the festival of military hardware on a level not seen before.

I was given a lift in a hot air balloon tethered to the festival grounds, and from up in the sky above the festival grounds, I could see dozens of tanks, armored personnel carriers, and antiaircraft systems. It was a military bonanza. Boys took pictures of their girlfriends sitting on top of tanks. A recruitment center was set up and staffed with military officers. Before the first band came onstage, Russian MiG jet fighters conducted a flyover to start the festival, with the Russian tricolor flag smoking out their afterburners above the one hundred thousand festivalgoers gathered there. It was Russia's most militarized outdoor rock festival ever.

Our Gibson presence at the festival was history making. We'd brought two inflatable Gibson-branded tents—one placed in the backstage area to greet the artists going onstage and show them the latest guitars; a second, in the middle of the festival grounds among the festivalgoers, where Diana would conduct our guitar clinic. Anastasia ran it like a military operation, directing a dozen volunteers, mostly her girlfriends, and bouncing back and forth between tents during the three-day festival. Petr was in the tent in the field, managing a green screen that let fans make videos of themselves holding our guitars against fantastic background scenes.

The line of fans waiting to get in was long. Our tent was hugely popular, and we were trying to make it fun. I stayed in the backstage tent and talked to the artists. We invited bands to chill out on a sofa in our tent and have a beer before going onstage. Surrounded by beautiful guitars, our guests reveled in the relaxed backstage atmosphere we'd created for them. The Gibson brand was very well represented at the 2014 Nashestvie rock festival.

When it was time for Diana's surprise guitar clinic, we covered her head with a jacket and snuck her through the crowd to the ministage. Fans were shocked when she jumped onstage and riffed on the Chet Atkins CEC. The crowd quickly grew larger and gathered closer. Diana played different Gibson guitars for thirty minutes and told stories about each one. The fans loved it. When it was time for her to return to the main stage, we quickly ran her back through the crowd to the backstage area. Diana and the Night Snipers rocked the Nashestvie rock festival. Diana and the antiwar rockers onstage that night sent a message of resistance to the Kremlin that spoke louder than the nearby military equipment.

After her performance I congratulated Diana and wished her an early happy birthday. The next day, she boarded a flight to Ukraine for a solo performance in Kyiv's Green Theatre on July 7, one day before her fortieth birthday. It was a trip that would land her in trouble. Her visit to Ukraine was comparable to what Jane Fonda had done in 1969—visiting the enemy and taking photos with the Viet Cong during the height of the Vietnam War protests. This upset the US government, but it could do nothing to Jane Fonda.

However, Russia treats artists differently. The Kremlin has cruel and unlimited means to affect an artist's career. Even knowing that, Diana stood bravely in front of a sold-out crowd of Ukrainians, and before introducing the next song, she announced, "In the face of the Almighty, I apologize for my colleagues, those who play rock and roll, and who for some reason have not yet supported you at this terrible time for Ukraine! I am with your people. Hold on!"

The Kremlin acted swiftly. Diana was labeled a "friend of Junta" (a term the Kremlin used to label internal enemies of Russia who were "friends" with the "Nazi" regime in Kyiv that overthrew Putin's favorite Ukrainian president, Viktor Yanukovych).

Diana's next eight concerts were canceled. The reasons varied from last-minute renovations to urgent repairs of leaky roofs, as well as other lies, but her career was in a free fall engineered by the Kremlin. She was banned from government-owned TV and radio airwaves. Even a poetry reading in Moscow featuring Diana was canceled. I was angry, watching this happen to her. I think I was especially upset because, in my home state of Ohio, where the Kent State massacre is taught in schools as one of the darkest days in our nation's history, we also remember how Neil Young quickly wrote the antiwar song "Ohio," which was released by Crosby, Stills, Nash, and Young. None of those rock stars had their careers canceled by President Nixon.

But in Russia, the repercussions for opposing the Kremlin are severe. I couldn't believe what I was seeing, and I wanted to help her. I had kept my promise to Anastasia and stayed through the end of the Nashestvie rock festival, which had been a big success for the Gibson brand. I could leave Russia now. But Diana's persecution by the Kremlin inspired me to stay in Russia longer and continue supporting her. The Russian music industry cowardly abandoned her, but Gibson kept supporting her. We made our showroom a sanctuary for her.

By supporting Diana, I rocked the Kremlin one more time. I lasted as long as I could, but the war in Ukraine only worsened. In July 2014 Russian fighters in Ukraine shot a Malaysia Airlines passenger jet out of the sky, killing 298 on board. Again, I kept waiting for the international community to punish Russia, and again, I was disappointed that we failed to hold Russia accountable.

I wondered if I was the only person who saw this criminality because I was living in Moscow. It was wearing me down. In the new year, I asked Boris to help me leave Russia. That's when New York City came calling. Henry had promoted me to run the Gibson showrooms on the East Coast; I'd be based out of the legendary Hit Factory recording studio in Midtown Manhattan. It was the crown jewel of Gibson showrooms for Henry. He had turned the Hit Factory into an artist-friendly guitar showroom and space for rock stars in New York City. Before he died in 2009, Les Paul, the inventor of the most famous guitar of all time, would often drop by. I knew when I accepted the job that being geographically closer to Henry would be hell. He was a famously difficult boss, but I was just grateful to him for the opportunity to give away more guitars to rock stars. And I was anxious to leave Russia and return home to my family in America.

Leaving Anastasia and the Gibson showroom we'd built together was sad, but the time had come for me to leave Russia for the second time in my career.

The last time I saw Diana was in 2016, when I was living in Hell's Kitchen and working at the Gibson showroom. Diana's band had come to New York City. She was still blocked from touring in Russia by the Kremlin; to earn a living, she toured abroad, including in America. She tracked me down again and came by the showroom to thank me for supporting her when everyone else had dropped her. It was the most touching thing an artist had ever said to me. I was so proud to know her.

In my career at Gibson, I gave guitars to many rock stars more famous than Diana, from Tom Petty and Elvis Costello to Steve Miller and Cheap Trick. But the most important guitar I'd ever given to a rock star was the old Gibson Chet Atkins CEC, to Diana Arbenina. She is the bravest rock star I have worked with, and I like to think that her continuing to rock on in the face of persecution from the Kremlin is vindication that what I did in Russia had an impact.

EPILOGUE

In May 2023 I took a seventeen-hour train ride from Warsaw to Kyiv on the Kyiv Express, the same train used by visiting diplomats and presidents. It is the only safe way to travel in and out of Ukraine during the time this book is being written; it has been impossible to fly there since Russia invaded its neighbor on February 24, 2022. Fifteen years had passed since I'd been with my Ukrainian friends and colleagues from the music business. I wanted to see with my own eyes how they were holding up after fifteen months of brutal war.

It was also the weekend of the annual Eurovision Song Contest, the biggest television event in Europe that has been a cultural touchstone since 1956. Ukraine won the contest in 2022 (after victories in 2004 and 2016), which gave them the right to host the competition in 2023. And although President Zelenskyy voiced his wish to host the contest, the European Broadcasting Union (EBU) determined it wasn't feasible. The BBC stepped up and hosted Eurovision in Liverpool on behalf of Ukraine.

I felt it necessary to be in Kyiv on the night of the live broadcast, knowing how important Eurovision is to the nation's pride. Ukraine has done better on the show over the past decade than any other Eastern European country. I wanted to be in Ukraine on that momentous evening.

Since the Russian invasion, I have been struggling to make sense of what I had dedicated my life to—namely, bringing America and Russia closer after the fall of the Soviet Union. Thirty years ago, I left Ohio and moved to Russia to raise a family and bring Western know-how to a country on its knees following decades of mismanagement under Communist rule. Growing up in Ronald Reagan's America, I believed the president when he said that the Soviet Union was the evil empire. When it fell, I wanted to help Russians.

I became the first American to run a record label in Russia. I led the modernization of their music industry and fought with gangsters, oligarchs, and pirates for its survival. I discovered Russia's first worldwide pop music act and organized a charity concert during Russia's darkest days after the country had suffered horrific acts of terrorism. But now the country I had dedicated my life's work to was terrorizing its neighbor Ukraine, a country I'd also wanted to help modernize and overcome its Soviet past.

Riding on the train for hours, staring out the window at the Ukrainian countryside from my sleeping compartment, I had time to reflect on my career in Russia: "What was the purpose of my work over the last thirty years? Did anything I'd worked so hard for matter?" I remembered the Russian artists I had worked with and thought, "Where are they now? Some of them are supporters of the Kremlin. Others, like Diana Arbenina and MC Noize, are bravely speaking out against the war, but most have been silent."

Both American companies that I'd opened in Russia, Universal Music and Gibson Guitars, are now closed; most Western companies have moved out. And the Russian government has been more repressive than ever since the fall of the Soviet Union. A new iron curtain is rising. I was distressed reading about a schoolteacher in Penza (a city in Western Russia), who was turned in by her students for speaking against the war; this was a sign that the Kremlin's propaganda was working on Russian youth.

"Why did Putin invade Ukraine?" everyone asks me. After living and working in Russia for fifteen years, including my time as a student in Putin's hometown of Leningrad, I wasn't buying the Kremlin's propaganda that Putin was afraid of NATO expansion and willing to start a war with Ukraine to protect Russian sovereignty. I always knew he invaded Ukraine so his cronies—greedy oligarchs—could steal more resources from the Donbas region in the east of the country. Putin is a former KGB agent, but he also is someone who is very familiar with Russia's criminal underworld. He gained that knowledge by working for Leningrad mayor Anatoly Sobchak, managing relations with the city's mafia gangs. I've watched how Putin often employs the characteristics of a mob boss in his decision making, and since he runs Russia like a mafia state, no one has been able to stop him.

It amazes me how he has ruined Russia's reputation. The war is staining the culture that gave the world Tchaikovsky, Rachmaninoff, and Stravinsky. The bombs dropped on innocent civilians in Ukraine would have scandalized those heroes of Russian classical music, who loved their neighboring country. Even Tolstoy, Russia's greatest writer, who served in the Russian Army and wrote about brutal fighting in the Caucasus, would be ashamed of the brutality of the Russian soldiers terrorizing civilians in Ukraine. His warnings more than a century ago about a warmongering Russian Orthodox Church, which got him excommunicated, seem especially appropriate today.

Vladimir Vysotsky, the most beloved singer in all of the USSR, would be turning in his grave, disgusted with this Slav-on-Slav war. And the biggest rock star of the Soviet era, Viktor Tsoi, who sang about corrupt generals sending young soldiers to the meat grinder in Afghanistan, would be singing about Russian conscripts dying on behalf of Putinism.

While I was in Kyiv with my friends and colleagues, Russia launched a hypersonic missile at the city, just as the live broadcast of Eurovision began at 9:00 p.m. CET on May 12, 2023. Air raid sirens were activated; my colleagues had an app on their phone telling them how many minutes until the expected arrival of the missiles or drones, depending on whether they'd launched cruise missiles or hypersonic ballistic ones. I ran to a bomb shelter and missed the telecast. Later that evening, Russia launched more missiles, hitting the hometown of Ukrainian entrant Tvorchi. It was a not-so-subtle retaliatory move for being banned from the song contest by the EBU one day after the invasion of Ukraine.

Every night I was in Kyiv, I had to run to the bomb shelter. Ukrainian air defenses demonstrated heroic resilience in protecting the city and, with help from American-supplied Patriot missile batteries, countered nightly missile and drone attacks. But I also saw incredible heroism in everyday Ukrainians. I was impressed with how my friends and colleagues were carrying on in the face of war. I also saw unspeakable tragedy when a colleague drove me to the northern suburb of Bucha, where Russian soldiers had committed horrendous war crimes. I met a frail elderly woman working in the church near the site of the mass graves. Fear was in her eyes as she told me about the horror she'd endured: more than four hundred innocent civilians were killed in Bucha, and many were tortured.

When I took the seventeen-hour train ride from Kyiv back to Warsaw, I couldn't stop thinking about Bucha and the death and destruction raged by the Russian Army. It infuriated me. I was leaving Ukraine full of rage and shame. And I was depressed that I had dedicated thirty years to bringing Russia closer to America. Was it all a waste of time?

When we stopped at a train station somewhere in Western Ukraine, I hopped off and headed to the main building to catch a Wi-Fi signal. The train steward informed me this would be the only place to go online until we were closer to the Polish border. I quickly downloaded some news on my phone and saw a clip of a famous Russian filmmaker and propagandist, Karen Shakhnazarov, speaking on a government-controlled TV talk show about the problem the Russian Army was having finding young men willing to sign up.

He was complaining that Russian men as old as sixty were being sent to the war because millions of young men were refusing to go. "They've fled the country or are hiding," he lamented. Then, to my shock, the propagandist said, "The reason this is happening is because of thirty years of Western pop music and culture."

I was amazed that this propagandist had confirmed on state TV that the import of Western pop music into Russia—my life's work—was the main reason a generation of young Russian men were saying no to war. I was overcome with vindication, standing in that train station, latching on to a Wi-Fi signal. At that moment, I realized what I had done for the past thirty years in Russia had mattered. I was so mesmerized by this video that I nearly missed the train's departure. I heard the train whistle and quickly hopped on, just in time.

When the train crossed the Ukrainian border, we stopped at the first station in Poland. Armed border guards entered my compartment and asked for my passport. I noticed them sizing me up. It must have been odd for them to see me, a foreign male, on the train. Ukrainian men under sixty have been barred from leaving the country. I knew they were checking to see if I was a spy or something nefarious. This had happened to me many times during my career; people thought I must have been a spy because I speak Russian and have spent so much time living there. I was always answering questions about that. After a few probing questions about my purpose for visiting Ukraine, the border guards let me continue to the final destination,

Warsaw. However, it reminded me that many of my friends and family are still convinced I'd worked for the CIA. Many Russian colleagues have also thought that. But I never did. I had a far cooler job as the CEO of a record label. And what I did was something a CIA agent could never do.

I'd led an American pop music invasion that had a profound and long-lasting impact on the youth of Russia. What I'd done in Russia could have been a top secret CIA project, but it wasn't. It was too loud and brash, like rock 'n' roll. My hope is that by having brought Western pop culture to the former Soviet Union, I was able to plant the seeds that will lead Russian youth to rise up, stop the war, and take their country back from the Kremlin.

INDEX OF PLACES, ENTERTAINMENT, AND THINGS

INDEX OF PEOPLE, ARTISTS, AND GROUPS

ABOUT THE AUTHORS

For three decades, Ohio native **David Junk** has been a trailblazer in the music industry, leaving an indelible mark through his diverse experiences and unwavering commitment to promoting cultural understanding. Born with a passion for music and a keen sense of entrepreneurship, David's journey has taken him from the heart of the Russian music industry to the epicenter of cultural preservation in Ukraine.

David's foray into the music industry began after the fall of the Berlin Wall and the collapse of the Soviet Union when he answered a "Help Wanted" advertisement in the *Moscow Times*, leading him to join PolyGram, the first multinational record company to establish a presence in Russia. Initially hired as an English-speaking accountant, David's passion for music and business acumen quickly propelled him to more prominent roles. As PolyGram merged with Universal Music Group, David, the first American to work in the Russian music industry, became the inaugural chief executive of Universal Music Russia, overseeing the promotion of international artists, including Elton John, U2, Andrea Bocelli, Bon Jovi, Eminem, Jay-Z, and Shania Twain, introducing hip hop and country to the Russian audience.

His impact extended beyond promoting Western artists; David discovered and signed Russian talent, such as t.A.T.u., the best-selling Russian act in music history. In the face of rampant music piracy threatening the industry's legitimacy, David actively participated in law enforcement raids against pirate factories, testifying in court against criminal gangs and advocating for intellectual property rights in Russia. His efforts drew attention globally, with interviews on television and radio and contributions to esteemed publications like the *Wall Street Journal.*

In 1999, David's career took him to Ukraine, where he became a pivotal figure in establishing Universal Music's first branch office. Facing the challenge of Russian dominance in the Ukrainian music market, he defended the rights of Ukrainian songwriters and fought against music piracy orchestrated by criminal groups. As vice president of Universal Music, David played a crucial role in shaping Eastern Europe's music landscape. David's dedication to bridging cultures continued even after his tenure at Universal Music. David's dedication to social justice led to his involvement in "The Concert for Beslan" in 2004, a charity fund-raising concert featuring Russia's pop stars, aired on MTV. The concert aimed to raise funds for the victims of the tragic siege at a Russian school, showcasing David's commitment to humanitarian causes.

After leaving Russia and returning to the United States in 2006, David took on the role of general manager at Universal's Machete Records in Los Angeles, where he played a big part in transforming it into the no. 1 Reggaeton label in America. His work involved collaborating with renowned artists such as Don Omar and Wisin Y. Yandel, further expanding his experiences in the music industry. David's dedication to bridging cultures continued even after his tenure at Universal Music, and his connection to Ukraine deepened. In 2007, while living in Los Angeles, he conceptualized and pitched the TV reality show *American Chance*, blending Ukrainian and Hollywood elements. The show, a ratings success, showcased Los Angeles on Ukrainian TV and launched the careers of several Ukrainian talents.

In 2013, David embarked on a new career chapter, joining the iconic American musical instruments manufacturer Nashville-based Gibson Guitars. David opened Gibson's first showroom in Russia and signed the very first Russian guitarist to be endorsed by Gibson, rock star Diana Arbenina. After leaving Russia for the second time in 2015, David managed Gibson's East Coast entertainment relations from the guitar showroom at the iconic Hit Factory recording studios in New York City. On behalf of Gibson, David presented honorary guitars to The Steve Miller Band and Cheap Trick to commemorate their induction into the Rock 'n' Roll Hall of Fame and to Elvis Costello, Tom Petty, and Nile Rodgers to commemorate their induction into the Songwriters Hall of Fame. One of David's memorable achievements at Gibson was organizing a national TV performance featuring Andrew Lloyd Webber's *School of Rock* Broadway cast on Gibson's float in the annual Macy's Thanksgiving Day Parade.

Amid his career, David's connection to Ukraine deepened. Witnessing the devastation of war in Bucha during a visit in 2023, he became an advocate for preserving Ukrainian culture. Motivated by the atrocities committed by the Russian Army and determined to raise awareness, David launched a podcast focused on Ukrainian art and culture called *Art during Wartime*.

Drawing from his extensive knowledge and experiences, he aims to illuminate the richness of Ukrainian culture, counteract centuries of overshadowing by Russia, and highlight the importance of cultural preservation in the face of war. As a cultural ambassador, David Junk continues to pursue his career calling by weaving together music, advocacy, and cross-cultural understanding.

Fred Bronson has been called "America's foremost chart journalist" by the editor of *Billboard* magazine and as an expert on music has guest-starred on *American Idol* four times. He is the author of six books: *The Jacksons Legacy* (with the Jacksons), *Dick Clark's American Bandstand* (with Dick Clark), *The Sound of Music Family Scrapbook*, *The Billboard Book of Number One Hits*, *Billboard's Hottest Hot 100 Hits*, and *The Billboard Book of Number One Rhythm & Blues Hits* (with Adam White).

Bronson has written the annual television specials *The American Music Awards* and *Dick Clark's New Year's Rockin' Eve*. His other TV writing credits include *George Strait: The Academy of Country Music's Artist of the Decade All-Star Concert*, *Brooks & Dunn's The Last Rodeo*, *Girls' Night Out: The Superstar Women of Country Music*, *ACM Presents: Lionel Richie & Friends in Concert*, *Tim McGraw's Superstar Summer Night*, *ACM Presents: An All-Star Salute to the Troops*, *ACM Presents: Superstar Duets*, *The 40th Anniversary of the Academy of Country Music Awards*, *ACM Honors*, *Motown 45*, *The Disco Ball*, *Live Aid*, the syndicated TV series *Your Big Break*, two episodes of *Star Trek: The Next Generation*, and an episode of the animated *Star Trek* series. He has written the annual six-hour live holiday special for the PBS station in Los Angeles and the *Spotlight Awards* hosted by John Lithgow. He was head writer on NBC-TV's fund-raising special, *Tsunami Aid*, and co-producer of the Ovation TV music performance series, *Notes from the Road*.

For SiriusXM Radio, he has interviewed Paul McCartney, Smokey Robinson, Benny Andersson, and Bjorn Ulvaeus from ABBA and the cast of the *Mamma Mia!* motion picture.

He has programmed music channels for United Airlines and hosted his own internet radio series, *Fred Bronson's Pop Goes the World*. With Dick Clark, he wrote the weekly comic strip, *Dick Clark's Rock, Roll 'n' Remember*. Bronson also writes for *Billboard, The Hollywood Reporter, Variety*, and *Los Angeles Magazine*. He has reported on the Eurovision Song Contest, Sweden's prestigious Polar Music Prize, and *American Idol*, among many other subjects. He has interviewed dozens of musicians for those publications, including Keith Urban, Lionel Richie, Annie Lennox and Dave Stewart of Eurythmics, Carrie Underwood, Katy Perry, Pat Benatar, Ulf from Ace of Base, Mary Wilson of the Supremes, Lamont Dozier, Peggy March, Luke Bryan, Per Gessle of Roxette, Gretchen Christopher of the Fleetwoods, Mariah Carey, Nile Rodgers, and many, many others.

www.ingramcontent.com/pod-product-compliance
Lightning Source LLC
Chambersburg PA
CBHW030259100426
42812CB00002B/499